SILENT
PARTNER

SILENT PARTNER

A Memoir of My Marriage

DINA MATOS
MCGREEVEY

HYPERION
NEW YORK

Library of Congress Cataloging-in-Publication Data has been applied for.

ISBN: 1-4013-0364-1
ISBN-13: 978-1-4013-0364-8

Hyperion books are available
for special promotions and premiums.
For details contact Michael Rentas, Assistant Director,
Inventory Operations, Hyperion, 77 West 66th Street,
12th floor, New York, New York 10023,
or call 212-456-0133.

Design by Fritz Metsch

FIRST EDITION

10 9 8 7 6 5 4 3 2 1

FOR MY DAUGHTER

JACQUELINE

my constant reminder of the power of love

CONTENTS

ACKNOWLEDGMENTS

SHARING MY STORY HAS been my way of sorting out and coming to terms with my own experience, looking at it calmly by the light of day so I would not be haunted by it in my dreams at night. It has, for me, been a healing venture in allowing me to move on with my life.

I want to thank my collaborator in the fine art of memoir, Elizabeth Stone. In an atmosphere of mutual trust and respect, as we talked, wrote, read, and rewrote, Elizabeth helped me, and sometimes prodded me, much more than you might imagine, to work harder than I ever thought possible as we fueled ourselves on hummus, pea soup, and coffee. Thank you, Elizabeth, for your expertise and boundless energy, and for being there every step of the way.

To my agent, Heather Mitchell, I owe a great debt of gratitude for her empathy, understanding, intellect, and advocacy. Thank you for steering me in the right direction and guiding me through the process. Selecting you as my agent has been one of the best decisions I've made.

For her inspiration, perseverance, and wit, I want to thank Donna Buckingham.

To my friend Carol McKinney, who persuaded me to write this book. Thank you for giving me the push I needed, and for helping me realize my potential.

For her vision, talent, and wisdom in helping bring this project to life, I thank my editor, Brenda Copeland. Her buoyant enthusiasm and astute editing are, to me, apparent on each page.

The confidence and trust that everyone at Hyperion has placed in this book has been truly inspiring. Thank you, Bob Miller, Ellen Archer, and Will Schwalbe for believing with me that my story could be told with grace and dignity. I am proud to be associated with all of you.

To my lawyer, John Post, thank you for your encouragement and your advice.

I also want to thank my friends for their support and understanding. Thank you for being patient with me when I didn't call, didn't visit, and didn't have time to talk.

For all the phone calls, notes, letters, e-mails, and, most important, prayers of friends and strangers alike, I am deeply grateful. They have helped me get through the darkest days of my life.

None of this would have been possible without the constant love and support of my family: my brother Rick and his girlfriend, Cydney; my brother Paul and his wife, Elvie; my nieces, Meagan and Nicole; and of course, my parents, Maria Graciete and Ricardo, who instilled in me values that have carried me through life. None of this would have warranted the effort if not for my daughter, Jacqueline, who has brought me joy every day of her life and given me the strength to go on.

PREFACE

ON AUGUST 12, 2004, Jim McGreevey, then my husband of almost four years and the governor of New Jersey for almost three, stepped before the television cameras in the statehouse in Trenton to make a speech that lasted only five or six minutes. "My truth," he said, "is that I'm a gay American. . . . Shamefully, I engaged in an adult consensual affair with another man which violates my bonds of matrimony. . . . My resignation will be effective on November fifteenth of this year."

I stood numbly at Jim's side as he spoke to the nation. I was devastated. What he said on that Thursday afternoon forever changed his life, my life, and the life of our daughter, Jacqueline, who was then two and a half. Since then, I have been asked repeatedly about my marriage to Jim and the nature of our relationship, about what I knew and when I knew it. Since then, I have remained silent.

Now I am speaking up.

I am tired of having other people concoct my life story, tired of having other people assume they know how I feel. I am tired of all the speculation as to the nature of my relationship with my husband. I am tired of being the silent partner.

Enough is enough. I want to tell my own story. And now that I've begun to heal, I want to reach out to other people like me, people who have been hit with pain so excruciating they're not sure they will survive it. I have survived, and as sure as these stalwart little words march themselves across the page, it is my conviction that others can survive as well. This is my story, about my experience as I lived it at the moment and—not quite the same thing—about my experience as I look back on it. Tell others your story as I am telling you mine. Don't let others tell it for you.

SILENT
PARTNER

I · EVERYWHERE SIGNS

I MISSED THE SIGNS.

People thought I was living the American Dream, and for a while I thought so too. I believed I had married a kind and loving man whom I loved and who loved me. I thought we were building a life based on shared values, a strong spiritual commitment, and a desire to make a difference in the world. Friends and family were important to us, none more so than our beautiful daughter, Jacqueline.

The Jim McGreevey I fell in love with was passionate, direct, and plainspoken, a charismatic man whose warmth and easy manner rapidly took him from the mayor's office to the New Jersey governor's mansion. The Jim McGreevey I married turned out to be passive, evasive, and secretive, a hesitant man whose duplicity and unchecked ambition proved to be his downfall and derailed our lives. And I never saw it coming.

I MIGHT AS WELL start with the engagement, and with a Valentine's-weekend trip to Montreal. It was February 2000, and by this time Jim and I had been together for more than three years. We'd begun dating in 1996 when Jim, then mayor of Woodbridge, New Jersey, was already campaigning unofficially to become the Democratic gubernatorial candidate in the 1997 race. He had gone on to gain the candidacy and had come close to beating the Republican incumbent, Christine Todd Whitman. Jim was a politician on the rise and the overworked mayor of a township with a population of more than a hundred thousand, not to mention a state senator too. I was working as director of public relations and marketing at Columbus Hospital in Newark, a satisfying and demanding job that entailed promoting the hospital and its services to the community. With both of us so busy, we really hadn't had much private time together for a while, and we needed it.

I was looking forward to the weekend. I'd left work early that afternoon—a rare event for me—and I was full of anticipation, attempting to keep my packing down to two bags rather than spilling over to my usual three. I prepared for the cold weather with a few warm sweaters, jeans, boots, and gloves, and for romance with a black velvet ensemble, a pashmina wrap, and a silk nightgown. I also packed an emerald pendant that Jim had just brought back for me from India. I loved jewelry and had tried on the pendant when Jim gave it to me—he'd placed it lovingly on my neck—but I hadn't worn it yet, as I was saving it for a special occasion. An elegant dinner for two in Montreal seemed just that.

The lights were on in Jim's Woodbridge town house as I pulled in to a parking space. That was good news, since it meant he was home. Generally Jim ran late, but as he greeted me at his front door, I could see his already-packed bag on the floor, and I was pleased that he was ready.

"Let's stop at the 7-Eleven for tea," he said as we headed toward my car. He always had a cup of tea with him in the car, generally cold.

"Good, I could use a cup of coffee."

I figured I would be the one doing most of the driving, but as I approached the parking lot, I noticed a familiar car waiting, motor idling.

I turned to Jim. "What's Teddy doing here?" Teddy Pedersen, a handsome college student at Rutgers University, was Jim's campaign driver, one of a crowd of guys in their twenties who always seemed to be around. I came to think of them as the Lost Boys.

"Teddy's going to be driving us to Montreal," Jim said, his tone matter-of-fact.

Was he kidding? When had he planned to tell me this?

"I can drive," I said.

"Well, I'm too tired to do any driving at all, so I thought it would be easier for us both if Teddy drove."

I stopped in my tracks. I really wanted some time alone with Jim. I had never known him when he wasn't campaigning, and I'd really been looking forward to this weekend together. The two of us, not the three of us. Since we'd been dating, I'd seen Jim through one gubernatorial race, then another race for mayor, which had ended only a couple of months earlier. The day after the '97 election, Jim began his campaign for the 'o1 election.

The Jim McGreevey I knew had always been running. As a result our dates often took the form of campaign stops: breakfasts with senior citizens, football games at high-school athletic fields, church picnics, dinners at catering halls. I loved the time we spent together, loved the feeling that Jim and I were working on something important together, but now Valentine's Day was coming up, and I wanted him to take the weekend off so we could spend some personal time together. And that meant no Teddy.

I dug my heels in.

"If Teddy is going, I'm not. It's that simple."

I was usually pretty accommodating, so Jim knew I meant it. "OK, OK," he said with a shrug. "No Teddy."

I don't know exactly what he said when he walked over to Teddy's car, but Teddy nodded and pulled out of the lot, and that was that. Jim tossed his bag into my trunk, and then we were on our way. It was not quite four o'clock. With any luck, we'd be in Montreal by midnight.

I WONDERED IF THIS might be the weekend Jim would ask me to marry him. I loved Jim and was imagining a life together in which we would establish ourselves as a family—I had always wanted children—and work as a team in support of goals we cared about. My only concern was the breakneck pace of politics and campaigning, and how it might interfere with our relationship and our future as a family.

It's not as if the question of marriage hadn't come up. We had just spent New Year's Eve with Jim's best friend, Jimmy Kennedy, a tall, balding bear of a man in his fifties, and his wife, Lori, a petite and bubbly kindergarten teacher. Like Jim, Jimmy was a New Jersey mayor—of a smaller city called Rahway. On that New Year's Eve, Jimmy, who'd had a little too much to drink, turned to Jim and said, "So is this the year you're going to marry Dina?" I was driving when Jimmy asked his unexpected question, but in a quick glance at Jim I saw he was looking at me with an expression that seemed to say that the answer was up to me. Was he hoping that maybe I would answer the question then and there?

"I don't know," he said. "I don't know if Dina wants to get married." Clearly, Jimmy had caught Jim off guard.

I smiled at Jim and said, "Can we discuss this later?"

"Sure," he said.

Jim himself had brought up the subject of marriage a couple of years earlier. We'd been at a conference when he turned to me out of nowhere and said, "I'm going to marry you." I didn't know if he really meant it, and so I tried to think of something noncommittal to say and in the end said nothing. I was attracted to Jim, but I wasn't sure he was really ready for a serious relationship at the time, and I didn't want to find out by getting hurt. I thought he might still be nursing a broken heart following the end of his marriage, a year before we'd met. His wife, Kari Schutz, a Canadian librarian whom he'd met on a cruise, had left him without warning and gone back to British Columbia, taking their young daughter, Morag, with her.

As for me, I was in no hurry to get married. I had a job I enjoyed, a family I was close to—including my two adorable nieces, Meagan and Nicole, whom I loved spoiling—and I had my own rat pack of half a dozen women friends, most of whom I'd known for at least ten years. We hung out together, went on vacations, and generally just had a good time. Jim was not the only person I knew in politics—not by a long shot. I knew quite a few politicians, and many had failed at marriage just as Jim had. Jim hadn't said much about why his marriage ended, though. "Kari couldn't stand politics," was all he would say, and I left it at that.

I'd always loved politics. Being with Jim, I learned I also loved campaigning and was good at it. Still, I hadn't been sure then that I could handle marriage, politics, and public life any better than the others had. And if I was sure of anything, it was that once I got married, I was going to stay married. No one in my family had ever been divorced, and I didn't want to be the first. My parents, who'd met when they were teenagers, had now been married thirty-four years. Different as they were—my mother excitable, my father a man of few words—they were each other's best friend. It wasn't important to me that I get married soon, but it was important that once I got married, I stayed married. I wanted my marriage to be forever, the sort of solid and lasting marriage I'd witnessed growing up. During the course of our relationship, I had come to love Jim deeply, and to trust him. Still, I hadn't mentioned marriage because of the crazy schedule that would be involved in the year and a half left to the campaign. Now Jimmy Kennedy's extra few beers had put the subject back on the table.

We didn't get to have that conversation the next day or the day after that, and right after New Year's, Jim left for India. But a week later Lori called me to ask if I would have lunch with her. "There's something I want to talk to you about," she said. We met at a nearby mall, where we shopped for a while, and then went to a café at Nordstrom's, where we settled in to talk and have lunch.

Since Lori had asked for us to meet, I waited for her to say what was on her mind. She seemed to be a little jittery, and by the time we were up to coffee and dessert, we had darted through quite a few subjects.

Finally the talk turned to Jim. "Have you heard from him since he left?"

"No, not yet," I said.

"Really? You haven't?"

"No," I said. I knew he had a busy schedule, and I didn't expect to hear from him. He didn't have access to e-mail, though I wasn't sure he would have known how to use it even if he did.

But Lori barely listened to my answer as her own words came stumbling out. "Jim wants to know if you'll marry him," she said rather awkwardly.

"What!?" I said, not because I didn't hear what she'd said but because I didn't believe what I was hearing. "So why doesn't he ask me himself?"

"I don't know. Maybe he's afraid you'll say no, and then he'll feel rejected. . . . Oh, Dina, this is so awkward . . . but he doesn't want to feel rejected, so maybe that's why he asked me to ask you if you'll say yes." It was out, and Lori looked relieved.

I was silent, surprised that Jim needed Lori to broker a marriage proposal for him. What was this, high school?

"He *asked* you to ask me?"

Lori nodded.

"Why didn't he ask me himself?" I repeated.

Lori shrugged and shook her head. "I told you what I know—he's not sure you'll say yes. I don't know, Dina. Jim's been really hurt in the past. Maybe he's just nervous and wants to be sure."

I mulled over her response. Was Jim's nervousness born of his doubts about reading my feelings correctly? I'd never known him to be hesitant about anything else before. To the contrary, I thought of him as very decisive, though not exactly an open book. He'd told me about the end of his marriage. I knew that the abrupt ending had to be traumatic, though he didn't quite say so. What I thought as I sat there with Lori was that maybe he was still afraid of rejection or still afraid of misreading his partner and wanted to be positive that I would say yes when he proposed.

She must have been watching me as I processed the conversation, because when I returned to the present moment, her eyes were on me.

"What do you think?" she asked.

"Yes," I said finally. "If he asked me to marry him, I would say yes." I hadn't expected to be proposed to by a surrogate, and so the exuberance I might otherwise have expressed was tempered. But nonetheless, I had already given the matter a lot of thought, so I was excited and happy at the prospect of spending my life with Jim.

If Lori thought there was anything odd about Jim's mode of pursuing a potential wife, she was eager to get beyond it into the safer realm of her own excitement. "I'm so happy he found you!" she said. "It'll be such fun to plan a wedding!"

Driving home, I thought some more about Jim's using Lori as an intermediary. I wasn't sure what to make of it. Politicians often delegate very personal chores to their staff, but this was going too far. They also make decisions strategically, not spontaneously. Was Jim's wish to marry me a decision of the heart or of the head? I knew that he had deliberately left his divorce incomplete until after the election in 1997 because he didn't want his marital status to be an issue in the campaign. He didn't want the media to focus on his divorce, because he felt that it would make the headlines, which in turn would contaminate his campaign. Maybe that was true, maybe not. He also saw his marriage as a failure, and as a candidate for governor he didn't want to be perceived as a failure or a loser; though when I think of it now, I wonder if deep down his chagrin was at having failed not as a husband but as a heterosexual. Then (as well as now, for different reasons), it did cross my mind that possibly he was interested in marriage now because he *did* want his marital status to be part of the campaign.

Later, when I looked closely at Jim's "Gay American" speech, three sentences leaped out at me, all of them about "love." Right at the beginning, he'd said, "I married my first wife, Kari, out of respect and love." Further on came two sentences about me: "I then had the blessing of marrying Dina, whose love and joy for life has been an incredible source of strength for me. . . . She has been extraordinary throughout this ordeal, and I am blessed by virtue of her love and strength." In a speech where every single word was calibrated and calculated, he mentioned his love for Kari and my love for him—twice—but nowhere did he mention his love for me. Feel free to draw your own conclusions.

Jim came back from India a week or so after my conversation with Lori, but he still didn't bring up the subject of marriage. I didn't bring it up either. And now it was two weeks later. Valentine's Day was approaching,

and we were heading off for a romantic weekend. Perhaps Jim really was
planning something.

ON THOSE OCCASIONS WHEN it was just the two of us in the car, I
always drove. Jim was a notoriously bad driver, so much so that it was as
much a part of the lore about him as the fact that he was a good Irish
Catholic boy from Jersey City. He was well known for his speeding, his
multitasking behind the wheel (driving while shaving, for instance), and
his chronic blindness to one-way signs. He also routinely drove with a
cell phone at his ear. He never said as much, but he obviously knew that
his own behavior was dangerous, since after he was elected, he signed a
law making the use of handheld cell phones while driving illegal.

As afternoon turned to dusk, and our trip to Montreal was well under
way, I drove north at a steady pace while Jim rested, his eyes closed.
Occasionally he would crack open an eye, telling me to speed up so we
could get there as soon as possible. I was on an unfamiliar road and it was
now snowing, but I sped up because I wanted to get to Montreal. We
were going more slowly than we'd intended because of the weather, but
with a little luck we could still make it by 1:00 A.M., early enough to get a
decent night's sleep and be ready for sightseeing the following day. I'd
been surfing the Internet and had found a lot I wanted to see. I was eager
to visit the Basilique Notre-Dame (it was in the same style as one of my
favorite cathedrals, Notre Dame in Paris), and some of the smaller art
galleries. I had also hoped to get in some shopping, especially in the
Underground City that Jim had told me about. We were also considering
a side trip to Quebec City, if we could fit it in.

Despite the bad weather, we seemed to be making good time. As we
drove north through New York State, there was nothing but darkness
and a light snow shimmering as it fell from the sky. It was pretty, but the
conditions weren't the best, since the roads were covered with several
inches of snow from a previous storm already on the ground. Suddenly,
not far from the Canadian border, the car went into a treacherous spin. I
had hit black ice. Jim, who'd dozed off, awoke startled, while I tried to

control the spinning car as it careened across three northbound lanes. Finally the car skidded off the road, where it was stopped by, and instantly became stuck in, a mountainous snowbank.

Sitting for a moment in the dark, Jim and I just looked at each other. "We could have been killed," he said.

"Thank God there were no other cars in those lanes."

"Thank God! Are you OK?"

"Yeah, are you?"

"Yeah."

When we caught our breath, we got out of the car to see if we could dislodge it from the snowbank. Rocking it didn't work, and neither did putting it into reverse and pushing. It just wouldn't budge. I hoped there was nothing wrong with it except for a fender stuck in a snowbank. Our cell phones had no signal, so we couldn't call 911, and none of the few passing cars would stop. It was freezing, so we had no choice but to set out on foot in search of help—two stranded, shivering people walking through the dark night with nothing in sight but snow and ice.

We trudged toward the ramp that would take us off the highway, and then we headed left, because that's where the trucks were heading. We were careful to stay to the side of the road and keep out of the way of any passing vehicles. All we saw were trees, snow, and more trees. Then, at last, we came upon signs of life: a truck stop with a small convenience store. Our oasis in the snow was about a hundred feet off the road, so we couldn't even see it till we were right there. That little store was as welcome to us as a four-star restaurant would have been.

Inside, I got coffee and Jim got tea. We didn't so much want to drink as to hold the hot cups in our freezing hands. We were too exhausted to eat, but if we'd wanted to, we could have feasted on Twinkies and Devil Dogs. The friendly clerk helped us find a room at a nearby inn and a driver who would take us there.

Soon we were in our room—a drafty space with cold floors, twin beds, and a dresser—with an adjoining bathroom consisting of a toilet and a sink. No shower, but with our belongings still in the car, we didn't have any fresh clothes to change into anyhow. We didn't even have tooth-brushes. I had pulled back the faintly musty plaid bedcover on one of the beds and crawled in, and now Jim took off his shoes, pulled back the second bedcover, and began to climb into the other bed.

"How about coming in here with me?" I said, patting the mattress. "It's freezing!" He complained good-naturedly that the bed was too small even for one person, but he climbed in anyhow, and we huddled and cuddled together in the chilly room, staying up awhile to watch Bill Clinton on TV. Normally I didn't find a man with his socks on sexy, but hey!—it was so cold I kept my socks on too. At least for that night. How wonderful to be warm in that little bed, curled up next to Jim's lean and muscular body. It was bitterly cold outside, and the room itself was none too warm, but that didn't matter. We generated our own heat. And we spent a beautiful night together—in love, and with love—close as two people could be.

We woke up the next morning and hitched a ride to the Ford dealer-ship in town to see if they could tow my car in. I had had a Toyota for years, but this time when I was in the market for a car, I'd bought a Ford Taurus, because the union workers who supported Jim wouldn't be happy if they saw me driving a vehicle that wasn't made in the U.S.A. by union labor. This was the first of many concessions I would make for the campaign—or "the cause," as I called it.

At the dealer's we learned how dangerous the roads were, especially where we'd had our accident. A few days earlier, a driver had been killed there. That helped keep everything in perspective. I was grateful that neither Jim nor I had been hurt. I made arrangements to have the car towed while we set off in the slushy snow in search of breakfast. We were grungy but hungry. Afterward we walked up and down the main street, where Jim met a couple, formerly from New Jersey, who recog-nized him and wanted to chat. Then we went back to the Ford dealer, only to learn that although my Taurus looked all right on the outside, there was a significant amount of damage. Since the storm had para-lyzed the region, it would take several days for the parts to come. I was resigned to the fact that I would have to go back to New Jersey without the car.

WHAT WOULD MY PARENTS say? They didn't even know where I'd gone. Although I was in my early thirties, I still lived at home with them and would remain there until Jim and I married. This was not unusual for a daughter from a traditional and close-knit Portuguese Catholic family. Guys often left home and moved to their own place, but not the girls. My brother Paul hadn't moved out until he got married to Elvie when he was twenty-four or twenty-five, although my other brother, Rick, had moved out during college when he was twenty-one or twenty-two and single. Still, daughters typically lived at home until they were ready to establish their own home with their husband. My going away with Jim was not something my mother and father would have approved of. But it was not something they forbade either. It wouldn't have worked anyhow. In public I had always been quiet and self-contained—in school, in Girl Scouts, with my neighborhood friends—but in my family I had always been seen as someone who had a mind of her own and would give you a piece of it with very little prompting. I was "determined" if they liked what I was doing and "stubborn" or "headstrong" if they didn't.

By the time I was nineteen and had my first serious boyfriend, my parents and I had tacitly adopted a "don't ask, don't tell" policy. I lived my own life, and I came and went as I pleased, but I was always careful to let them know when to expect me so they wouldn't worry. My parents didn't pry, or at least not too much, and I kept my private life private. I was deeply involved with my family, well mannered and respectful like many first-generation daughters of immigrants, but I was a contemporary American woman as well. So I had told them that I was going to spend the weekend with a friend. Jim and I had gone away before, but I never told my mom and dad that I was going with him, except when we went to Newport with Jimmy and Lori Kennedy.

All the signs on this trip seemed to be pointing me one way—in the direction of home—but in the end Jim and I opted to head for Montreal by train. We got a lift to the Plattsburgh station, which looked like something from an old black-and-white movie, with its worn wooden benches and old-fashioned cash register. There was none of the hustle and bustle of Newark, New York City, or Washington, D.C., just a woman in a corner selling homemade goods—jams, cookies, and crocheted doilies.

At the time of our car accident, we were about an hour's drive from Montreal, but the train ride would take several hours. By now I was really anxious to get there, and by midafternoon we did. Compared to the motel barracks of the night before, our hotel in Montreal was a palace—a room with a hot shower, thick carpeting, and a soft, inviting mattress. No need for socks in this city, or any other article of clothing, for that matter; so in the spirit of the Valentine's weekend, we began our celebration in the most intimate setting. I may have been a Catholic, but I wasn't a nun, and I was happy to share this passionate weekend with Jim.

Now, I'm not the type to kiss and tell, and it goes against my nature to be so blunt, but there is something I need to address if only to get it out of the way. So let me say outright that on this occasion, as on many others, the sex was good. There was nothing in this moment, or in any other—and believe me, I have revisited them—that in any way made me question whether Jim was drawn to me in the way that I was drawn to him. What more can I say, except to add that for the rest of this story, at the onset of any intimate moments, the scene will fade to black.

Once we'd settled in, Jim started to comb the telephone directories to find his friend Christian, a buddy from college.

"Why do you have to call now?" I asked. "I thought we were going to dinner alone."

"We will go to dinner alone, but we already lost a day, and I would really like to see him. It's been years."

I wasn't going to argue with him, but I wasn't happy. Meanwhile, Jim located Christian's phone number, called, and made plans for us to meet him later. Still, we had a fun afternoon exploring and shopping. When evening came, I put on the black velvet skirt and top and the pashmina wrap—a soft salmon color—and I took my emerald pendant out of my handbag and put it on. Before we left for dinner at the hotel's restaurant, Jim gazed at me silently for several seconds. "You look so beautiful," he said. He took the pendant in his hand and said, "It looks great against the black velvet." I could see his pleasure in his eyes, and also tenderness, warmth, and love.

I leaned toward him and kissed him.

At the restaurant I scanned the menu to see what I would order—the steak looked good, or maybe the sea bass. But when I tried to put the menu back on the table, it wouldn't lie flat. I didn't think much of it as I lifted up the menu again . . . and that's when I saw the little white box at my place setting, centered between my knife and fork.

"Go on," said Jim. "Open it. Just open it."

I stared at him. "Isn't there anything you want to ask me?"

Jim looked puzzled. "What do you mean?"

I didn't know how to respond, so I opened the box. Inside was a dazzling diamond ring.

I stared at it speechlessly.

"Well," said Jim with a big smile. "This is a pretty significant ring. Aren't you going to say something? What do you think?"

"Yes!" I said, answering the question he hadn't really asked. We leaned across the table to kiss each other. Call me romantic, call me old-fashioned, but I really wanted Jim to propose to me, to *ask* me to marry him. I didn't expect him to get down on one knee, but I did want him to dot the i's and cross the t's. But still, I was very happy.

Jim took my hand to look at the ring.

"Do you really like it?" he asked.

I did. I thought it was beautiful, just what I would have picked myself. I stretched out my left arm to admire the diamond glittering on my finger. It was a round center stone with a smaller baguette diamond on each side. "It's perfect," I told him.

Jim was exuberant when we met up with Christian and his girlfriend later in the evening. "We just got engaged," he said. I was thrilled that he'd now put it into words. It was the next-best thing to a proposal. Meanwhile the two were delighted to be sharing this moment with us. Christian's girlfriend said to Jim, "Wow, you're getting married for the second time, and Christian hasn't even been married once."

"How do you feel?" Jim asked me on the way back to the hotel.

"Happy and excited," I said.

"And?"

"Maybe a little nervous," I admitted.

The next day, Sunday, Jim again made plans for us to spend time with Christian and his girlfriend. That evening we headed home by train to New Jersey.

Looking back, in light of everything that came to pass, our engagement had a flinch to it, the feel of a pulled punch. It felt like less than a wholehearted impulse on his part. Was it Lori as Jim's messenger? Jim's wish to bring Teddy along? The life-altering question I answered without his quite asking it? Jim's need to bring his college buddy into our circle, not once but twice? All of them, perhaps.

If Jim and I had gone on to have a marriage in which we grew in comfort and intimacy, those moments of feeling something withheld probably wouldn't have stayed with me. But I felt that something wasn't right, even though almost everything I noticed was, on its own, too small to be significant. So I let those moments remain insignificant, not mentioning them at all when I came back to New Jersey, eager to tell my friends and family that Jim and I were now engaged. What was in the forefront was that I was a very happy woman. I was marrying a man I loved and admired, a man whose vision and values I shared.

2 · JERSEY GIRL

IN THE SUMMER OF 2002, Bruce Springsteen released a new album called *The Rising*, and Jim and I were invited to the early-morning launch on the beach at Asbury Park, picked because it was the Boss's hometown. The event was covered by the *Today* show. Standing on the beach with Jim and me, Matt Lauer and Katie Couric interviewed us, and one of the questions they asked each of us was what our favorite Bruce song was.

Jim's answer was immediate. "Born to Run," he said, which didn't surprise me or anyone else there. My answer was immediate too. "Jersey Girl," written by Tom Waits, but also sung by Springsteen and released the summer I was fourteen. I'm very much a Jersey Girl—and proud of it. Yes, I know that New Jersey—like Peoria or Keokuk—has its mockers. I know all the jokes about "the bridge-and-tunnel crowd" and "Joisey" and, thanks to *The Sopranos*, my state being the center of Mafia life. But the bridge-and-tunnel crowd are my people, and, as I always tell my friends from east of the Hudson, no one needs a passport to visit.

If I have all the fervor of the convert, it's because I'm not entirely a product of the Garden State. Not only wasn't I born in New Jersey, I wasn't even born in this country. My birthplace was Coimbra, an ancient city in Portugal famous for its Roman ruins and the country's most elite university. Coimbra is known as the cradle of kings, and its inhabitants are said to have the most admired and prestigious accent. "Oh, excuse me," friends will tease when I offer my unsolicited advice about their Portuguese pronunciation or word choice. "*You* were born in Coimbra."

Actually, I was the only member of my immediate family to be born not only in Coimbra but in a hospital, a result of the fact that my mother went into premature labor with me, her first child, and had to be rushed to the nearest medical center. As far back as anybody can remember, my parents and their families had lived in Pocarica, fifteen miles to the east. With its electricity and indoor plumbing, Pocarica was a town determined to be modern. But it would have been considered undeveloped by American standards. Few residents had cars; almost no one, except the wealthiest, had a TV; and children, including my two brothers, were generally born at home, with a midwife at the bedside.

I was eight by the time we settled in the States. I guess that's why my memories of Portugal are like snapshots: I recall a battery-operated toy—chickens pecking at rice—that I received for my fourth birthday; the cod my mother made on Christmas Eve, which I loved, and the octopus, which I didn't; the presents we got on Epiphany, January 6, from Pai Natal; the brand-new refrigerator we bought to replace our icebox, one of the first in a working-class household in our town; my father and my grandfather playing their instruments in our town's marching band; a dead snake that appeared to come back to life as it slithered off the end of the stick I was carrying, leaving me with an enduring fear of snakes; the parish priest coming to visit our house at Easter; my classroom in Portugal, and the time the teacher slapped *my* hand with a ruler because she said another girl had copied off my paper during a test.

Among my most vivid and pleasurable memories, though, is one of a day at the beach, the sand so hot you had to dance your way to the refreshingly cold water and waves. It was on the Portuguese shore, where we rented a house for the summer with my grandmother, and it was the start of my lifelong love of the ocean, because as Bruce Springsteen sings in "Jersey Girl," ". . . down the shore everything's all right."

But those are memories born of a child's keyhole view of the world, without the benefit of a larger understanding. The truth is, things were tough in Portugal during the sixties and seventies. Good jobs were scarce, and it was not unusual for a man to support his family by doing a stint as a guest worker, living abroad for most of the year, returning home annually for a visit. One of my uncles worked in France, and another (my mother's brother) actually emigrated to the United States. My father considered working in Germany so that he could send home some much-needed money, but my mother put her foot down, and that was the end of that. He ended up working in a German-owned chemical company the next town over, while my mother contributed to the family's income with her own business delivering fish to customers on her bicycle.

The strained economy, I later learned, occurred during the dictatorship of António Salazar, who ruled Portugal for thirty-five years. He had a stroke in 1968 and was succeeded by Marcelo Caetano, who didn't make things any better. I remember a secret political meeting at my parents' house during my early childhood. I didn't understand what was going on, but I somehow knew not to talk about it outside the family. A few years later, in 1974, there was a bloodless revolution, which resulted in greater freedoms for all of us. I don't remember much of that, only that it was known as the Carnation Revolution because the people offered red carnations to the military while urging them—successfully, as it turns out—not to resist the revolutionaries.

My most indelible memory, however, is not of the revolution or even of long, pleasant days at the beach, but of a day that would change my family's life forever. I was about six, and my mother was riding home on her bicycle from visiting someone in town, with my brother Paul, then two, in a seat on the back. Somehow he got his foot caught in the spokes, causing the bike to fall over. In the moment, the spill seemed unremarkable. My mother got herself and Paul back on the bike and headed for home. But that would be the last untroubled day my family would have for many years.

That night Paul was in pain, crying and unable to sleep. Within a few days, his left thigh had become grotesquely swollen and his veins blue and bulging. His leg looked like the leg of an old man. There was no improvement in the days that followed. Our family doctor didn't know what was wrong, though he saw Paul and examined his leg several times over the next couple of weeks. It wasn't a break. It wasn't a sprain. Maybe a torn ligament? No one really knew. But Paul was in constant pain, and he limped as he walked. My mother was distraught because she felt so responsible. She believed that it was cancer and that he would die.

No parents can stand to see their child in pain; thus my mother and father began a journey to find out what was wrong, using all their resources to do so. They took Paul to specialists throughout Portugal, but none of them could diagnose what had gone wrong. Meanwhile, Paul's continuing pain became unbearable, for him as well as for my parents. After nearly three years of doctors not being able to explain, much less correct, his problem, my parents decided to take drastic action. Believing American medicine to be the most sophisticated in the world, they decided to move us all across the ocean. Had that bike never toppled, my family might well be in Pocarica to this day, but circumstances had mobilized us, and we were more than ready to go. So in July 1975, when I was eight and a half, my family left Portugal for the United States, landing at Newark Airport and settling a few miles away, in the Ironbound section of Newark, in my uncle's multifamily house.

Compared to the rest of Newark, my new neighborhood seemed more a small town than a large city, but it was enormous compared to Pocarica. Though the Ironbound was, and is, famous for its Portuguese restaurants, and though almost half of my classmates were Portuguese, the neighborhood was, in fact, ethnically diverse, with most of the rest of the residents being Italian and Irish. For a child it was a manageable neighborhood, largely residential, with even the commercial buildings rarely higher than two or three stories. Anyplace I needed to get to—my school, my church, the shops—was not more than a few blocks away. My school was on Wilson Avenue, right in the heart of the Ironbound section. In the summer we went swimming at the bathhouse right next to the school. Our church, Our Lady of Fatima, named for the famous appearances of the Virgin Mary in Fatima, Portugal, was a short walk from my home as well, and that's where my Girl Scout troop met. My father could walk to his job at Newark's Penn Station, and my mother could walk to hers, at a grocery store and gift shop she owned. Later on, in eighth grade, when I was old enough for a part-time job, I would find one at a nearby gift shop on Ferry Street.

When I arrived in this country, I spoke no English at all, but after a summer with my cousin and friends and neighbors, I had begun to learn a little. Still, my first day of school in the fourth grade here was very frightening, especially after the formality, silence, and order of my school in Portugal. My new classmates seemed rude and unruly and out of control. I felt so out of place. I was more formally dressed—frillier and far more starched and ironed—than my American classmates. I sat quietly and kept to myself, especially in the beginning. I was most comfortable in the few ESL periods I had each week, which sped up my acquisition of English. Thankfully, in a neighborhood with a large Portuguese population, many kids also spoke Portuguese, and some of them translated for me. Within months I could pretty much follow what the teacher was saying. By fifth grade, I'd hit my stride, and by the sixth-grade open house my teacher told my mother (with me acting as interpreter) that I was one of her best students. I was still one of the quieter children and didn't ask questions or raise my hand to answer any unless I was sure I was right, but I was also aware that the teacher called on me whenever she wanted the correct answer, even if I wasn't raising my hand. However quietly, I was proud of myself.

As is the case in immigrant families everywhere, my brothers and I learned the language of our new country more readily than our parents did. In fact, my mother and father didn't want us to speak English at home, so we spoke to them in Portuguese and with each other in English, which meant we could have conversations right in front of them that they couldn't understand. On the other hand, later on, my mother wasn't above seeming in the dark when we spoke English to each other, though eventually we suspected that she understood far more than she let on. I guess she figured she could find out more about us that way.

My parents wanted to be sure we would know about Portugal and were fluent in Portuguese, so three evenings a week they sent my brothers and me to private lessons in Portuguese grammar, history, and culture—which we all hated. It would have been more fun to go to Portuguese school with our friends (our teacher, Mrs. Idalina, was stern), but my mother thought the kids there fooled around too much. She wanted Portuguese school to be a no-nonsense endeavor. The purpose was to learn, not to play.

Our church was only a few blocks from our home and was important to us. The big event was the annual three-day Feast of St. Anthony every June, and two dozen or so parishioners were on the fund-raising committee, raising money to cover the church's contribution to the festival. That committee included my father, who played the trumpet in the church's marching band, putting on his blue uniform with the gold trim that made him look so handsome. A "daddy's girl" right from the beginning, I wanted to go where he went and do what he did, so I accompanied the band during their performances, much later on getting a blue uniform of my own. I also became a member of the fund-raising committee, probably one of the only members who wasn't somebody's father. My dad joined out of a sense of community, and though I initially joined because he did, I stayed on for about ten years because I just loved counting money!

By the second year, I had it down to a science. When we got home from fund-raising in our neighborhood—several blocks on a Saturday or Sunday afternoon—I raced ahead of my father into the kitchen and climbed onto one of the kitchen chairs. My father, amused at my eagerness, walked behind me, carrying the canvas bag in which we stowed the day's collection.

"Give me the bag! Give me the bag!" I said, in Portuguese as always.

"How about 'please'?" he responded with a smile, beginning to clear off whatever was on the table.

"Please can I have the bag?"

My father handed it over and watched as I turned the bag upside down and dumped the contents on the table.

A pile of bills—singles, fives, tens, and twenties—fluttered onto the table, like a pile of dry leaves. There were some coins, too, a few of which, given my hurry, rolled off the table and onto the kitchen floor. I loved counting the bills, but hated counting up the coins, because I hated making those stupid little towers, especially of dimes. I always forgot how many I already had in the pile.

"I'll do the dollars and you do the dimes and quarters," I said to my father.

"Well, first we have to pick all the coins up off the floor," he reminded me.

"OK," I said, leaping off the chair, picking up a few, and, in my eagerness to get to the bills, leaving the rest to him. He didn't protest.

First I put all the bills face-forward and right side up. Then I counted. Then I counted again. Then I was ready to announce my total. "Three hundred and twenty-three dollars!" I said. "Are we going to beat what we did last week?" Last week's take had been $340.

"I don't know. I'm still counting," said my father.

"Hurry!"

He just looked at me.

"OK, sorry!"

A minute or two later, he was ready with his announcement. "All right, I have twenty-three dollars in coins."

Quickly, I did the math. "Three hundred and forty-six dollars!" It made my day—and thus a little fund-raiser was born.

AMID THE ENERGY REQUIRED to get our family settled in a new country, my parents continued their quest to find a medical diagnosis for Paul. They traveled to various specialists across the country and even back to a renowned doctor in Germany, determined to find out what was wrong, to no avail. Not long after we arrived in the United States, Paul's condition deteriorated and his leg became susceptible to fracture. The spring I was ten, Paul broke his leg so badly he had to stay at St. James Hospital for three months with his leg in traction. The hospital was only a few short blocks away from our house on Ferguson, so I could visit him every day.

Six-year-old boys don't generally conduct long conversations with their older sisters, and Paul was no exception, so much of the time I sat at the side of his hospital bed watching TV with him, now and then playing Monopoly or Candyland, or quietly doing jigsaw puzzles together. We were already close, and it just made us closer.

As anyone will tell you, a child with a chronic illness becomes the focus of the family. The impact on the other children in the family is profound, but the way it shows itself will vary from child to child, depending on each one's temperament. I'm quiet by nature, though fierce when crossed, perhaps because I've always been so much smaller than everyone else, the first on line, from first grade to high-school graduation. Given my nature, I could have done a slow, resentful burn or become clingy because Paul required so much of my parents' attention. But I didn't. Instead, perhaps because I was the firstborn, I became someone who could pretty much fend for herself, someone who didn't want, or need, a lot of hand-holding (handy traits if you're contemplating partnership with a politician). Rather than feel resentful of Paul and the attention he was getting, I might have felt a little guilty—why was I OK when my little brother wasn't?

It took another ten years or so before we finally learned what was wrong with Paul. He had an inoperable lymphatic tumor in his leg. He could have been born with it, and if not for the fall, who knows what would have happened? Maybe it would have stayed dormant, maybe not. But when Paul fell off the bike, the impact assaulted the tumor. It was like bashing a beehive with a baseball bat.

When Paul was eighteen, he went to a specialist in Delaware and had his leg amputated almost up to the top of his thigh. It was a difficult period for my family emotionally and practically. In my last year of college by then, I took a leave of absence to make myself available to Paul and to my family. There was rehab in Delaware and then physical therapy as he learned to walk on an artificial leg. Thankfully, Paul's amputation put an end to his physical pain, and the prosthesis gave him back his mobility. But the cost of the leg was exorbitant—almost as much as a new car—and even with medical insurance my family felt it. My parents had many quiet conversations at the kitchen table about this, sometimes including me.

What affects us as children stays with us, often playing a part in what we're drawn to study or what kind of work we want to do, often with no one the wiser. Paul and I were both very outgoing, and our similarities would have made us close regardless of the circumstances. But his medical problems drew us even closer. I felt compelled to help, as I do to this day. Strange to think of it now, but that's one of the first things that attracted me to Jim, his readiness to help people.

I worked in a bank while I was in college at Rutgers, and for a while I considered law school, but when, at twenty-four, I got my first real job at St. James Hospital, I knew I had found not just a job but a calling. I had many responsibilities, but the most rewarding by far was to make sure that people in the community knew what health-care services they were entitled to, and actually help them get those services. I might have remained committed to issues such as these, happy to go home every day at five o'clock—but there was more. My parents needed me to help them navigate their way through an interconnected tangle of bureaucracies—physicians, hospitals, medical insurance, pharmaceuticals, and equipment.

For most children family life is a private matter, and it's a life lived at home. Public life is "out there" somewhere, distinct from private life. But some of our most important and powerful activities as a family took place in the public sphere of hospitals and doctors' offices, as my parents tried to protect and provide for my brother, and I tried to protect and shepherd them all. Once the usual boundaries separating private life from public life had been, for me, removed—or at least redrawn—the political had become the personal (which isn't quite the same thing as saying the personal had become the political, though it's close). Given how I'd been wired and affected by the life I had lived, I became someone for whom a dry position paper on health policy didn't seem dry. If it shed light on the care of a brother I loved, it was personal and it could move me, maybe not quite as much as a love letter could—but almost as much.

The public and private were mingled for me in yet another way, too. Just as my family lived much of our most compelling private life in public arenas, so the public world came into our home through television. Almost as soon as I came to this country, I fell in love with ABC's *World News Tonight*. I watched it every single night, with the same zeal other people reserve for their favorite soap opera. Our family's first anniversary in America coincided with the country's bicentennial, and on the news that night, when we watched the tall ships sail up the Hudson River, we took their journey personally. That year there was a Fourth of July parade on Ferry Street, the only such neighborhood parade I can recall. By then I knew all about the Boston Tea Party, the history of the American Revolution, and the colonists' struggle for freedom.

In Portugal, I had first felt this inchoate hunger for rights and freedoms, but I was so young that it was a hunger I hardly noticed and didn't even think to name. But here, in my new country, that desire for freedom *was* named, and the historic moment—satisfied by revolution—was commemorated and celebrated. In recognizing this American passion, I simultaneously recognized something in myself. So a connection between me and my new country was somehow strengthening.

Gerald Ford was president when I came here, then Jimmy Carter. My brothers said I was a bookworm, and I was. I read biographies and history. I read everything I could find about the Kennedys and about Eleanor Roosevelt. Then there was the Iran hostage crisis, which led to the program *Nightline*, to which I became quickly addicted. But what I was really becoming addicted to—and now, at last, aware of being addicted to—was America and the idea of being an American in a way that's perhaps impossible to understand for someone who is born here. I found it thrilling—that is truly the word—that Americans could effect change in their country and in the whole world just by virtue of whom they voted for.

In high school I joined the Civics Club and the History Club, and I took part in voter-registration drives, even though I wasn't an American citizen myself because I wasn't yet eighteen. So I bided my time until I turned eighteen, and then, as soon as I could, I filed the paperwork to become a citizen. I made sure my parents did too. One spring day in 1985, I received a notice informing me that my citizenship exam was scheduled for the following week at the federal building on Walnut Street in Newark. Even though I'd been helping people to become citizens for years and knew the answers to any of the hundred questions the examiner might ask, I studied the night before.

The following week, at the appointed time, I showed up, accompanied by my father, who was taking his test that day too. We sat in the waiting room until we were called, not speaking much. Out of the corner of my eye, I saw my father wipe his palms on his trouser legs. After about an hour, the examiner, a tired-looking man in his fifties wearing a white short-sleeved shirt, called my name. When I stood up, he waved me into his office.

"You can sit right here," he said, gesturing at a chair near his desk. Then he asked his first question. "What do the stars and stripes on the flag stand for?"

"The fifty states and the thirteen colonies," I said promptly.

"What is the Bill of Rights?"

"The basic rights accorded to all citizens."

"What is a progressive tax?"

I froze. "A *what*!?" I looked at him blankly. "That's not one of the questions. I don't remember seeing that—"

"Only kidding," he said. "You passed. I don't need to ask you any more questions."

My father was called next, and he passed too. Within days we were summoned to the federal courthouse, where we were sworn in. Now that I was a citizen, I could never be thrown out of the country, and I could get an American passport, and I could vote. I could even run for some elected offices if I wanted to.

It was during this period that I became one of the founding members of the Portuguese-American Congress (PAC). I saw that the Portuguese community in Newark got the short end of the stick—a prison in our backyard, an attempt to turn half of our park into a baseball field, an incinerator in our neighborhood—because as a group we didn't vote in large numbers. I understood that the only way we Portuguese could make ourselves felt was through voting, so PAC had as its central mission getting the community registered to vote. Of course you had to be a citizen in order to vote, and so, where necessary, PAC helped people get their citizenship.

In 1984, like many Portuguese families who've been here for a while, we moved out of Newark—to nearby Elizabeth—where I would live with my parents until I married Jim in October 2000.

By this time I had graduated from East Side High School, where I'd done well, finishing in the top 20 in a class of 460. I had applied to several colleges, including New York University, and I was accepted by all of them, but I wanted to go where many of my friends were going, which was to the Newark campus of Rutgers University. Most of my other friends were going to the New Jersey Institute of Technology, nearby.

College was a smorgasbord, and I loved a lot of what I was sampling: architecture, even though I couldn't draw; anything having to do with law; *The Great Gatsby;* psychology; Karl Marx, even though I thought he was a bit far out; Margaret Mead. In the end, I became a political science major with a psychology minor. I also pushed—unsuccessfully, but I pushed—to get a Portuguese Studies major going, so our faces would be represented in the required curriculum along with other ethnic faces. I was active enough that the biweekly Portuguese-American newspaper *Luso Americano* seemed to mention my name regularly. I primarily stayed involved in Newark, although I also became politically active in Elizabeth, where I now lived.

Somehow, by the time I was twenty-two, I came to the attention of Elizabeth's mayor, Tom Dunn, who asked me if I was willing to be appointed to the Elizabeth Planning Board, whose mandate was to approve residential and commercial building projects, landscaping, and so on. I said yes. I was the only board member who wasn't male or over seventy.

The day I walked into city hall to attend my first meeting, there was Ray Lesniak, later Jim's mentor, standing at the door. I knew him by reputation. Everybody did. He was Elizabeth's state senator, but he was also known as the go-to guy. Now he's become a national power broker—a strong fund-raiser for people such as Hillary Clinton and Al Gore, both of whom made pilgrimages to his house to attend his fund-raisers on their behalf and to pay their respects. He was a local lawyer who was then about forty, a man who ate, drank, and slept politics. No other life, so far as anyone knew. No wife, no children, and a succession of much-younger gorgeous blond companions. If you wanted to secure a state or government contract or run for office, he was the one whose blessing you'd have to get. Eventually, he was not only Jim's mentor, but arguably the most important member of his inner circle.

Lesniak and Tom Dunn, who had appointed me, were feuding, and I knew it. That first day, Ray was standing on the front steps of city hall where the meeting would be held. As I walked toward the entrance, he said, "Oh, you must be Dina Matos."

"Yes," I said.

"I'm Senator Lesniak," he said.

I knew who he was. "Nice to meet you," I said. But it wasn't nice to meet him. The manner in which he greeted me was unfriendly. He knew I was Dunn's appointee, and he struck as intimidating a tone as he could. Perhaps he suspected that Dunn had appointed me to the planning board because he had something else in mind for me. And if Lesniak suspected that, he was right. Eight or nine months later, I got a call from the mayor's secretary. "Mayor Dunn wants to see you tomorrow," she said.

I thought maybe I'd done something wrong, but the next day when I went to see the mayor, he sat me down and got to the point right away. "Have you ever thought of running for office?"

"Maybe at some point—"

"How about now?"

He wanted me to run for county surrogate on his slate. I was a woman, I was Portuguese, and there was a growing Portuguese population in Elizabeth. With my last name—Matos—he thought I could get the Hispanic vote as well.

In the end I decided not to run. I was flattered, yes, and I considered it for about twenty-four hours, but in the end I chose not to pursue it. The person I would have been running against in the Democratic primary had been in the position for several years and was quite popular. Second, she had the "official" Democratic organization behind her—Lesniak and company. So I knew she would win the primary no matter whom she ran against, and she would certainly win running against a complete unknown like me. If I was going to run for office, I didn't mind losing, but I at least wanted to lose respectably—by 10 to 20 percent. I didn't want it to be a rout.

BY 1995, I HAD traveled an enormous distance from the city of my birth, and my journey had been determined, as it is in most lives, by both choice and necessity. Though I'd always intended to finish college, my life in the years that ensued had become quite full. I was now very active in local politics, with a powerful urge to help, especially children, and especially children with health problems. I had also discovered by then that state and local politics didn't work at all the way I had learned they did in my political science classes at Rutgers, but I found that I could nudge change along anyhow by joining forces with people who believed as I did.

Political action was a passion, and the public arena was an intimate space. So when Jim McGreevey walked into my life one night, he was the other half of the orange. Some women are drawn to politicians because of their wealth, power, and influence. It wasn't that. When I met Jim, he wasn't wealthy, he wasn't powerful (except as a town mayor), and he wasn't—yet—all that influential. But his values and his passions as he lived them in public were, in light of my experiences, right up there with love potions. We didn't have much of a private life when we met, or later on either. Of course it's clear now that Jim was avoiding a private life, but it wasn't clear then. Still, as a state senator Jim had sponsored legislation to fund centers where kids with special mental or physical needs could get the care they could not possibly get at home. One night later on, when we were out campaigning, some mothers thanked him for what he'd done for their children. As mayor, he had also helped open and fund a medical clinic in a small town called Paraíso in the Dominican Republic. I didn't need much more than that.

3 · FIRST ENCOUNTER

WHEN I THINK OF all that happened during the eight years of my relationship with Jim McGreevey, the beginning—how I met him, how I fell in love with him—is the hardest story to tell, or at least to tell in the right way. When love goes out the door, courtship stories may go into the attic, never to be told again. It's no fun to recount the birth of a love that died a horrible death. My sadness and, yes, my anger, cast long shadows and obscure much that was hopeful and happy. But if I don't tell this story carefully, Jim will look like someone you wouldn't trust to feed your cat over the weekend, much less someone who was the repository of so much trust, public and private. And if that's the man who emerges, what does that say about my judgment in marrying him?

Jim was devastated when his wife left him without any warning, and therefore he came to doubt his ability to read the emotions of someone he loved. Ironically, he put me in the same position, so that now, because I failed to read him, I've come to question my own ability to read anyone I might love. It was my own extreme sense of privacy that kept me from asking questions I would have considered intrusive if anyone had asked them of me. I know that now. And I know that it was my tendency toward privacy (not to mention my steadfast loyalty) that allowed Jim to keep secrets from me and ultimately led to a marriage in so many ways counterfeit. Also ironically, the person I was most suspicious of was Jim's first wife, Kari. That was a tragic red herring. But I'm getting ahead of myself.

Jim and I first met in October 1995 at the Armory, a Perth Amboy restaurant. The dinner was in honor of a Pretender. The irony isn't lost on me. Jim, as both a state senator and the mayor of Woodbridge, was a guest of honor, but the real Pretender, if that's not too much of an oxymoron, was the Duke of Braganza, heir to the Portuguese throne, who was honored annually by a local Portuguese-American organization. This year the dinner was being held in Perth Amboy, a town near Woodbridge.

I noticed Jim when he came in. I didn't know who he was, but I thought he was handsome in a Tom Hanks kind of way, despite his old-fashioned barbershop haircut. He had a wide, easy smile and exuded a kind of warmth that seemed to extend to each person in the small group he was talking to. It was early in the evening, and things were just getting started when Manny Viegas, a friend who took an avuncular interest in me, came over.

"I want you to meet someone," he said. "Come with me."

Manny, like me, was an officer in the Portuguese-American Congress. He and his wife, Grace, lived in Woodbridge and had invited Jim to the event. Manny was a kind man who had been happily married for many years and had two children my age. He knew a lot of people in the community and wasn't shy about putting them together, so I was pretty sure that his "someone" was a guy he was trying to fix me up with.

"Meet someone? I don't think so, Manny," I said. "Not tonight." It was a festive evening, and I was dressed for it, but I really wasn't in the mood to be fixed up.

"Oh, c'mon," he said. "See that good-looking guy with all the women around him?" He gestured in Jim's direction.

"I see him," I said. "Who is he?"

"Jim McGreevey, the mayor of Woodbridge."

I knew Jim McGreevey by name and reputation. I'd heard he was an ambitious politician on the fast track to somewhere interesting. I'd also heard he was charming and good-looking. When I saw him that day, I had to agree. I remembered that a guy I'd dated while at Rutgers—a poli sci major named Frank—had told me about Jim. Frank and I had gone our separate ways years earlier, but because we were both active in local

Portuguese-American political circles, our paths often crossed. Frank was working for Senator Frank Lautenberg at the time. Jim, in pursuit of the Democratic gubernatorial nomination, had consulted with various high-level politicians, including Lautenberg, and Frank had been very impressed with him. "You have to meet this guy," he said. "He's smart. He's going places."

Meanwhile Manny, his hand at my back, was piloting me toward Jim.

"Jim," he said, "there's someone I want you to meet."

He introduced us, and Jim gave me a friendly smile.

"Oh," I said, returning the smile. "I've heard about you through my friend Frank, who works for Senator Lautenberg."

"Oh, yeah, I know Frank," Jim said. Then he eyed Manny, with a grin. "And you know this guy too," he said. "Well, I won't hold it against you."

We chatted a bit more, and then we each moved on to speak with others.

Jim had a seat on the dais that night, and I was seated nearby at Manny's table. After leaving my table for a quick trip to the ladies' room, I came back to find that someone was sitting in my seat.

"There's an empty seat next to Jim McGreevey," Manny said, missing nothing. "C'mon," he said to me, "go sit with him."

Manny, it appeared, was intent on filling a number of roles, and the one that was foremost on his mind this evening was matchmaker.

"Manny . . ." I said, a note of mock exasperation in my voice. In truth, I was not interested in taking Manny up on his matchmaking services, because I'd been dating someone for nearly a year and had recently called it quits. He was a nice guy, but he wasn't comfortable with how independent I was, nor how busy I was with my civic and political involvements, and I wasn't about to change. Still, despite my self-imposed "break" from dating, I *was* interested in sitting down, so I joined Jim on the dais, where soon we were chatting easily in between the evening's interminable speeches.

I hated these dinners and went only because my friends were hosting and would have been upset if I didn't. Thankfully, this event happened only once a year. The previous year's dinner had been unquestionably odd. The duke, a fastidious-looking man with a prominent mustache, had greeted the guests not only in uniform but wearing a rubber snake around his neck. It had always been hard to take him or his speeches seriously, but now it was impossible. And yet here I was again, listening to him ramble on, first in Portuguese and after that in English, feeling more than anything like a kid stuck in high-school detention. In this mood I was quite ready to strike up a conspiratorial conversation with a fellow detainee. That happened to be Jim.

"I don't know what this guy is actually saying, but he sounds like he's certain he's going to save the world," Jim whispered.

"Actually, he's saying the salad was good," I replied.

"He does this every year?"

"Every. Single. Year."

"Any references to the snake?" I had already told Jim about the duke's rubber snake.

"Not yet. Maybe by the time he works his way through the menu and is ready to praise the dessert."

It was more than easy chatting. I felt a kinship with Jim right away. We were bantering as if we'd known each other a long time.

When the duke's speech was over, we continued talking.

"How many people are going to speak?" Jim asked me.

"Too many," I warned him, rolling my eyes. I liked this man. I liked laughing with him and, truth be told, I liked flirting with him too. But there was more to it than that. We connected. We talked about my job doing community outreach, patient relations, and public relations at St. James Hospital and about Jim's work on the Health Committee of the state senate.

"If there's anything I can ever do for you, let me know," he said. If anyone were listening, and I'm not even sure I was, they might have heard the sound of a door opening.

When the evening ended, we went our separate ways—something neither Manny nor his wife was happy with.

"I think Jim's attracted to you," Grace said when we next saw each other.

"Hmmm," I nonanswered.

"The two of you would make such a cute couple."

"Uh-huh," I said, my attempt at a tactful "No comment."

A few weeks later, I heard something similar from another friend, Maria, who had also been at the dinner when Jim and I met. "You know," she said, "my husband and daughter said they think Jim McGreevey is interested in you. Come to think of it, you'd make a great couple."

"C'mon, stop!" I protested, laughing. "There's nothing there. We enjoyed chatting that night, but that's it."

Actually, spark or no spark, for whatever set of reasons on Jim's part, nothing more was forthcoming.

In the months that followed, Manny persisted in telling me more about Jim.

"Did you know Jim's wife left him?"

"Oh, that's a shame." It really was a shame. And, I thought, maybe the reason our conversation that evening hadn't led to a next time.

Taking my response as a sign of encouragement, Manny continued.

"Yeah, in '94." He nodded at me significantly. "She didn't like politics. She couldn't take it."

I'd heard that in Woodbridge, the town where Jim was now mayor, the politics were down and dirty. Another mayoral election had been coming up for Jim in '95, so, said Manny, sometime in 1994 Jim's wife packed a bag for herself and their toddler daughter and headed out the door. She never came back.

"That's the story," Manny said. "Isn't that terrible?"

"It is," I agreed.

"Want to help him mend a broken heart?" That was Manny—subtleties not included.

I retreated back into my noncommittal, monosyllabic mutter. I didn't like being so evasive, especially with Manny, who was so well intentioned, but I just was not ready to be set up. Besides, I had no idea whether this

man I'd so recently met was done with his first marriage, hopelessly pin-
ing, or perhaps trying to repair it. Knowing as little as I did, I wanted to
keep my distance. But on the face of it, I thought it *was* terrible what Jim's
wife had done. What kind of person would take off with her child and
leave her husband behind, depriving him of watching his own daughter
grow up? I could imagine the pain he must have felt, was probably still
feeling. I didn't know what their relationship was like, but to me, if there
was a child involved, it changed everything. The marriage might be so
much dirty bathwater, but you just can't throw the baby out with it. No
parent has the right to destroy or disrupt a child's relationship with the
other parent. And let me say I still feel this way today. At the time Manny
told me about how Jim's marriage had ended, I didn't reply, because I
didn't want to encourage him. But I felt a flood of sympathy for Jim that
might have opened my heart to him a bit more.

Meanwhile Manny and Grace continued to entertain themselves with
their matchmaking plans. I know this because at one of the meetings
Manny and I were at together, he told me.

"Grace and I have been talking to Jim McGreevey about you," he
whispered conspiratorially.

"Oh?"

Manny nodded. "We went to him and said, 'Boy, do we have a girl
for you!'"

"Oh?"

"We asked him what he thought of you, too."

This time I didn't even insert my noncommittal "Oh?" It wasn't that I
didn't want to know. What woman doesn't want to hear how she's
thought of by a man she herself finds both attractive and interesting?
Besides, it was probably a safe question. Since Manny was raising the subject, the news was bound to be positive. But I still wasn't sure I was up for
anything. I was readier than I'd been months earlier, but that didn't necessarily mean ready. Besides, I knew that if I showed any interest in what
Jim thought of me, Manny and Grace would push it with him, and I
didn't want that. The scrutiny would have made my skin crawl. I didn't

want to feel like I was under surveillance and being monitored. I'd never wanted to feel as if my personal life were anyone's favorite soap opera or, worse, sitcom. The beginning of a new relationship was uncertain enough. If something were going to develop between Jim and me, it would happen in its own good time.

I've been reserved my whole life. I grew up in a close-knit community where neighbors were in and out of my mother's kitchen, trading tales about this one or that one, and I vowed to avoid being the subject of anybody's gossip. That seems almost funny now.

I remember an incident my mother often recounts about how one day her next-door neighbor had come in and was telling my mother about another neighbor who had been seen with Somebody Else's Husband.

"And you know what?" the neighbor said.

"What?" said my mother, trying to be polite. She wasn't much of a gossip herself. She was too busy raising three children.

I must have been in my teens by then, and I was brimming over with an adolescent's conviction of her own wisdom. I marched into the kitchen and cut them short. "Don't you have anything better to do? Other people's lives are none of your business." I said it to both of them but really meant it for the neighbor alone. I knew I was being rude, but I guess I didn't care. The neighbor just looked at me and kept talking, while my mother gave me one of those I'll-talk-to-you-later looks.

When the neighbor left, my mother told me what I already knew. "That was bad manners."

"And it's bad manners to talk about others," I huffed.

"What am I going to do with you?" my mother asked, and not for the first time.

Over the years my view about gossip hasn't changed, though I'm less likely to share my unsolicited insights. These days my mother tells me I've missed my calling as a CIA agent, because I never reveal secrets that are told to me.

It wasn't until a year later, in September 1996, that Jim and I were together for more than a few minutes. It was late one evening at a fund-raising dinner in Newark for the Portuguese-American Congress, of which I was then vice president. I knew that Jim had been invited, but when he hadn't arrived by 10:00 P.M., I figured he wasn't coming. But in he walked at 11:30. More oddly still, here he was right in front of me—I was emcee for the evening—asking if he could speak.

"You want to speak." I repeated his request more or less blankly.

"If that's OK . . ."

Well, it wasn't exactly OK. Actually, it wasn't OK at all. The evening had already run far too long, just as it always did. It was invariably the same routine. People came late, so the speeches started late and each speaker spoke for too long. Then there were all the photographs—this one shaking hands with that one, this one holding up his or her plaque with that one, and still another of this one and that one surrounded by all the organization's officers.

Even at this late hour, the coffee, which I desperately needed, wasn't even brewed. Now here was Mr. Senator, wanting me to ask people to pause, mid-chew, to listen to yet another speech. I had recently begun a new job and was pretty tired. All I really wanted to do was get my coffee, get rid of the guests, and then get home and get to bed. There were 150 people in the room, and very few could even vote for Jim, either as mayor or state senator. Not only were we not from his city, we weren't even from his county!

His request to deliver a speech didn't make any sense, but he was an invited guest, so letting him speak was the polite thing to do. I'm stubborn if I feel strongly about something, as my mother would be the first to tell you, but I'm generally not confrontational, and most things aren't worth making a fuss over anyhow. I certainly wasn't about to express my annoyance to someone I hardly knew, nor do so at a microphone in front of a crowd. I let it go but wondered if maybe Jim wasn't quite as charming or quite as astute as I'd thought he was. His talk was brief and warm, though, and my annoyance quickly evaporated.

After Jim spoke, he joined me and some others on the dance floor, where we had gone to revive ourselves. Manny and Grace were dancing, when she grabbed Jim and said, "Here, dance with Dina." We danced a little, and after a few songs he, I, and several others collapsed into seats around an empty table and began the kind of talk that doesn't take heightened concentration—or any concentration. I was twenty-nine, and about to take myself on a Caribbean cruise in early November to celebrate my thirtieth birthday. It wasn't a big deal, maybe because most of my friends were ten or twenty years older than I was. There weren't a lot of people my age in this organization. One of my friends routinely referred to me as "the kid."

Jim, meanwhile, was listening to the conversation.

"When's your birthday?" he asked.

"November fifth," I said. "Election Day, this year."

Jim turned to his assistant. "Get Dina's phone number," he said, "and remind me to take her out for her birthday." His assistant asked for my phone number, and soon after, Jim and his assistant left.

I didn't know what to make of this. If he liked me enough to want to take me out for an event as personal as my birthday, then why would someone have to remind him to do so? Was he trying to come off as Mr. Busy and Important? Or was he just awkward? Or, following his marriage, was he so unused to dating that he was now rusty? I didn't know how to read him, and it made me feel a bit distant.

When Jim's scheduler called a few days later, he told me that Jim wanted to meet with me. Meet with me—what did that mean? By then I had learned that Jim wanted to run for governor the following year, which at least explained his desire to make a speech at eleven thirty at night to people who weren't his constituents. He knew we did a lot of voter registration, so perhaps he wanted to ask for my organization's help in his campaign? But he'd taken my number because my birthday was coming up, or so he said. Didn't that mean it was a personal invitation? I knew that by now Manny and Grace had used up a whole quiver of arrows playing Cupid, and the hints coming my way were that they believed they had at least grazed their target. But wait. If he did want to take me out, why would he plan something that wasn't going to happen for another month and a half? And why wouldn't he call me himself, instead of having his assistant take my number and his scheduler call me?

That's how I thought about it at the time, and even then it threw me a little off balance. Now, after only a mere ten years, I mark this occasion—right at the get-go—as the first of Jim's pulled punches, a suggestion of a not-so-well-concealed ambivalence, or at least uncertainty. It is now clear to me that Jim's invitation was *unclear*. He couldn't even bring himself to ask me a direct question, even one as simple as, "Do you want to have dinner?"

While all my confusion swarmed through my mind like fog on wings, Jim's scheduler on the other end of the phone continued to rattle off dates.

"Thursday?" he asked.

"Sorry, I'm booked."

"The following Tuesday?"

"Um, I have appointments I can't get out of."

"How about the next Wednesday?"

"Afraid that's not good either."

I seemed so busy you would have thought *I* was the one running for governor.

"Well, how about the evening of November third?"

"That's a Sunday," I said.

"Well, that's OK."

The scheduler had caught me off guard.

"Uh. OK."

SUNDAY, NOVEMBER 3, 1996, was a bitterly cold day, and I remember it because I spent most of it in Union, New Jersey, shivering for several hours at an outdoor rally, waiting to see Bill Clinton, then two days away from being elected to his second term. This would be the third presidential election I'd be voting in and the second time I'd vote for Clinton. President Clinton arrived at the rally very late, and by the time I left to get ready for my whatever-it-was with Jim, I was chilled to the bone. All I really wanted to do was take a hot bath and crawl into bed. When I got home, though, there was a message from Jim on my answering machine. He was sorry, but he would have to reschedule. Political gridlock. Jim had been at the Clinton rally too, but since the president was late in arriving, Jim was late in leaving for his next meeting. I was relieved. But how, I wondered, had Jim McGreevey gotten my unlisted phone number? I hadn't given it to him.

The following day Manny called. "How'd your date go?"

Mystery solved.

"It wasn't a date," I said. "And besides, it didn't happen."

Jim's scheduler also called me within a few days to reschedule for Thursday of that week, the day before I was to leave on my cruise. I still thought it was weird that Jim had a scheduler for what I now suspected might be a personal meeting, but—shrug—whatever. We met at seven o'clock, just blocks from where I'd grown up, at Iberia, a well-known Portuguese restaurant in the Ironbound section of Newark. Conversation came easily. We talked about ourselves and our lives.

Many men on a first date seem to think they're required to deliver a monologue—a long monologue, covering everything from their astoundingly high grade-point average to their amazingly low cholesterol count. But Jim wasn't that way. He seemed genuinely interested in me and what I was doing. He wanted to know about my new job at the hospital and why I'd left my old job. He wanted to know about the trip I was set to take.

I was disarmed by his interest, but I wasn't quite sure of my footing. I was interested in him, I now realized, but I didn't want to be if he wasn't going to reciprocate. At the same time, I didn't want to ask him where he stood with his marriage, because then he might *know* I was interested.

The conversation between us, however, never faltered, and I found myself feeling more and more comfortable. Two hours into dinner, I knew that this really was a date after all. After dinner at Iberia, neither of us wanted to end the evening, so we decided to go for a stroll on Ferry Street, even though by then it was 10:30, and I had to leave my house at 7:00 A.M. to get to the airport. We'd been walking about half an hour, when it began to rain. I was wearing a suit, but without a coat over it. Jim was wearing only a suit, but he took off his suit jacket and draped it over my shoulders. If there was a single moment that was a bridge to all the moments to come, this was it.

Still not ready to end the evening, we stopped in at the Riviera Café for coffee. By 11:30, we were among the last customers there. I didn't want to go, but I had to. I hadn't even begun to pack.

Jim gave me a hug and a quick kiss on the lips. "Pack me in your suitcase?" he said.

I THOUGHT ABOUT JIM on the trip. I remained hesitant because, aside from what I'd heard from Manny, I still didn't know where Jim stood in relation to his marriage. Was it over? Was he still trying to get his wife to come back? I wondered what was going to happen when I returned. I didn't have any grand outcome in mind, but I was open to seeing what might develop. The day I returned from the cruise, I began to wonder when I would hear from him, and even if. But I had a fundraiser to go to, and that's what I focused on. When I got there, Manny was already there. "Your boyfriend's coming," he said. "I'm saving him a seat next to you."

Jim walked in soon after. What can I say? We talked. We caught up. We were glad to see each other. That's what I thought then, and that's what I think now. My plan was to leave at 10:00 P.M., because I was tired and was scheduled to work at a voter-registration drive the next morning. As I stood up to put on my coat, preparing somewhat regretfully to go, Jim stood up too.

"Give me a ride home to Woodbridge?" he asked, smiling.

"No driver tonight?"

"No," said Jim. "Once I got here, I told him he could go." He looked pleased and mildly abashed at having revealed his strategy.

"Sure," I said. "I can give you a lift."

When we reached his town house, Jim invited me in. I guessed I wasn't so tired after all. My first impression, as he turned on a table lamp, was that the décor showed a woman's touch. The two couches were upholstered in peach and off-white stripes, with matching peach curtains. The rest was . . . well, eclectic. The pink porcelain lamp he'd just turned on was one of a pair that had come from his grandmother's house, I later learned. In the dining room was a black lacquer table and chairs and a tall, narrow, dark wooden bookcase posing as a china closet, which had also been his grandmother's.

Overall the effect wasn't exactly warm and cozy, but it was comfortable. In the living room was an inviting corner fireplace, which didn't seem to have been used in a while. But all the equipment was there, and from what I could tell, someone might well be able to light a fire in it. I took off my coat.

I don't remember what we talked about, but it felt relaxed, and the conversation came easily. I sensed that something was starting here, a feeling one person can't have alone. We were sitting close together on a couch that could have held three. We kissed—our first real kiss—and soon Jim asked me to stay the night. I'm not someone who leaps. I tend to inch into things. So I didn't stay the night. For the second time that evening, though, I put my coat on with some regret.

From that day on, Jim and I were dating. We were exclusive and intimate, but time for just the two of us was rare, right from the start. That was just the way it was. We might have dinner alone. The Armory was one of our favorite spots, for sentimental reasons, but also because it overlooked the water. Frequently after dinner we'd go for a walk along the Raritan River waterfront. Occasionally we'd go to a movie, but more often we preferred quiet time just hanging out at his house. As often as we could, we'd walk along the shore at Spring Lake. Winter, summer, spring, fall—it didn't matter.

These evenings with me were Jim's only downtime, and I wanted to help him unwind, though it was hard to get him to talk about anything other than politics. It was his passion. People who knew him affectionately called him "the Energizer Bunny." When we began to date, he was a full-time mayor of a township of one hundred thousand people; he was a state senator, which meant a round trip of ninety miles from Woodbridge to Trenton and back once or twice a week; *and* he was a would-be candidate for governor. Where was the time for relaxation?

Jim was a tireless campaigner who did what he had to do. If I thought of it at all, and I rarely did, I figured he might be able to structure his days to make more time for his private life, meaning us, when he won the election. Besides, I'm not so sure I was all that temperamentally different myself. Frankly, his frantic pace and unwavering devotion to his work were what attracted me, beyond our initial chemistry. I didn't want someone who was needy or clingy or who would be put out if I were off doing whatever I needed to do. During the first year we were dating, I was almost as much of a workaholic as he was. I worked full-time at Columbus Hospital in Newark; I traveled with Jim on weekends to local campaign events (where he wouldn't introduce me publicly as his "date," although he often did so privately at meet-and-greets); I was involved in Jim's campaign, behind the scenes, sometimes attending staff meetings, sometimes doing fund-raising; and I continued my own political involvement with issues that affected the Portuguese-American community.

In my view, Jim's candidacy was good for the Portuguese community in New Jersey, a group of seventy thousand or so. New Jersey is among the half-dozen states in the country with the largest immigrant populations, and, as I knew from my own experience, immigrant groups can have great power—but only if they are, first, naturalized and, second, registered voters. Jim understood this as well, and he organized an Ethnic Advisory Board, to which I belonged, along with representatives from such major immigrant groups in New Jersey as the East Indians, Dominicans, Chinese, and Polish.

One good friend who was involved with Portuguese-American politics and whom I'd known for about ten years since my college days also
supported Jim's run for governor. One day, as I was leaving one pro-Jim
event to go to another, she fell into step with me on our way to the
parking lot. "If this guy wins," she said, "I hope he gives you a job in
Trenton."

She didn't suspect we were dating, and I didn't tell her. Nobody knew.
Not Manny, though he did suspect, not my friends, and not even my parents. Part of it was my desire for privacy, and part of it was my cautious
nature. But there was more. As of 1997, Jim was still not divorced from
Kari, and neither one of us thought it was wise for him to be seen dating
someone when he was still legally married.

No one in his family had ever been divorced, nor had anyone in mine.
Worse, my parents would have been disapproving if they'd known I was
dating someone who to them was still a married man.

Jim's divorce, which finally came through at the end of 1997, forced me
to become more accepting of divorce, but our attitudes were both influ-
enced by the fact that we were religious Roman Catholics. Even after his
divorce went through, I didn't tell my parents we were dating until early in
1998, when I invited him to a family christening. He was out campaigning
somewhere and was to meet me at the restaurant where the reception for
my niece's christening was taking place. About an hour before Jim was to
arrive, I said to my mother, "Jim McGreevey is coming, I'm dating him."

My mother, as I'd imagined, was not at all surprised. She told me
she already knew and was just waiting for me to get around to telling
her. (Once, in an attempt to keep *me* from knowing that *she* knew, she
asked me whether "the mayor of Woodbridge" would be coming to an
event that I and the rest of my family were attending. She figured if she
called Jim "the mayor of Woodbridge," then I wouldn't suspect that
she suspected, but of course it was her question that was the dead give-
away.)

During Jim's first campaign for governor, however, there was only one major media occasion when we broke our Vows of Invisibility so that I could appear in public as someone connected to him. It was the day of a big rally at John F. Kennedy High School, in April 1997, which Jim had called in order to officially kick off his first gubernatorial candidacy. I took this invitation to be a sign of our deepening relationship and was pleased when Jim said he wanted me to sit in the first row with his family, whom I had not met more than once or twice.

The press regularly characterizes Jim's father, Jack, as a "marine drill instructor," implying a kind of ramrod severity, but in my experience he was gregarious and warm, just like Jim. As for Jim's mother, Veronica, known as Ronnie, like other members of his family, she worked very hard for him and did everything she could to help her son get elected. But even for Jim, at that time a forty-year-old man, she was more the drill sergeant than Jack—a force to be reckoned with, and often a disapproving force. Ambitious on her son's behalf, she pushed him unceasingly, always thinking he should do more, and criticized his campaign staff, whom she saw not only as lazy but as sloppy dressers. I can't say they were enthusiastic about her either.

When I arrived at the rally, Jim was in the wings somewhere preparing to go onstage, so a member of his staff escorted me down the aisle to where the McGreevey family was already sitting. As I sidled into the row, his father and his sister Sharon gave me a friendly greeting, but all I got from his mother was a quick glance and a chilly hello before she turned her head away. I don't think she said another word to me that day, and I could tell by her expression that she wasn't happy I had turned up. Later I learned that she thought my mere presence would renew speculation about the reasons for the breakup of Jim's marriage, and that in turn would hurt his campaign. But I've always thought that deep down she didn't want him to be with anyone. I guess in a way he wasn't.

When Jim had begun his campaign, he never really imagined he could win, because the incumbent, Christie Whitman, had been so popular. He thought of his candidacy as an effort to gain name recognition and face recognition so he could make a serious run in 2001. But the previous few years had not been good for Governor Whitman, especially because of high property taxes and state budget deficits, and now it looked as if Jim might really have a shot at winning!

Election Day came, and I voted—flipping the switch next to Jim's name—and then I stumbled through a distracted day at work before going to the Sheraton in Woodbridge to wait for the election results. Though Jim and I were both in the same hotel, I was in the ballroom with my friends, including Jimmy Kennedy, who had now become my friend as well, while Jim was elsewhere in the hotel, with his advisers and family. Amazingly, we didn't see each other. We had talked that morning by phone. "It looks like it's really close," he said, excitement in his voice. But in the flurry of events, we didn't make any plans for how we might get together that evening, and we didn't connect.

I experienced a wild range of emotions that night. When Jim was ahead, I was giddy with excitement—a shrieker and a clapper in a way I almost never am. As the count progressed into the early evening, it really did appear that Jim was going to win, and I was jumping for joy. A reporter in the crowd, who didn't recognize me but did recognize exuberance when he saw it, walked over.

"Why are you so excited?"

"He's going to win!" I was so excited that I didn't bother to point out to him how self-evident the answer to that question was.

During the evening Jimmy Kennedy and I spent some time together. "Wow!" said Jimmy at one point. "He can actually win this thing!" He grew silent for a moment. "But you know what? In a strange way, I hope he doesn't win," he confided. Although they'd been friends for nearly twenty years, Jimmy was concerned that if Jim became governor, he would rarely see him—both because of Jim's new responsibilities and the distance between Rahway and Trenton—and that their friendship would be weakened. That was really the first time I realized that if Jim won, it would affect our relationship profoundly, but not in a way I could predict at all. That scared me and made me uncertain. This, like much else, was something Jim and I had never discussed.

But when all the results were in, Jim did not win. In fact, he lost by less than 1 percent.

A news report appearing the next day announced that an officer had later seen me "necking" in the car with Jim, but that when I was observed, I ran away. Just another instance of the fiction that often passes for journalism. But in fact as much as I yearned to see Jim that night, I did not—except from a distance for a few minutes at about twelve thirty that night when he came onstage in the Sheraton ballroom to make his concession speech and thank his supporters. He was perfectly polished in his delivery, but I couldn't tell how he was really feeling from so far away. He left the stage almost immediately.

Jimmy Kennedy had gone looking for him, but he couldn't find him.

Then I tried to reach him by cell phone, but there was no answer. I felt a terrible sense of loss and sadness. We'd been together for a year, and yet on a night such as this, Jim and I had not been together, or seen each other, or even spoken.

I went home, and by the time I got into bed an hour later, I still hadn't heard from him. I cried myself to sleep.

The next day, my thirty-first birthday, I was exhausted and upset. I didn't even want to get out of bed. I finally heard from Jim later in the day. He wished me a happy birthday, and the day after that, when we had dinner, he brought me a bouquet of flowers. He told me he'd been exhausted and upset on Election Night.

That made two of us, though I didn't say so.

The next day, New Jersey's *Star-Ledger* ran an interview that had taken place with Jim the day after the election. I read about Jim calling his estranged wife to tell her about the loss and how "bummed out" she was for him. This troubled me. Why had he called her but not me? I felt worse because this followed another story a few days earlier, describing how well they got along during his visits to British Columbia to see his daughter. The report depicted them holding hands while taking walks with their daughter. I began to have doubts. Was he playing games with me? Was he still in love with Kari? That apprehension stayed with me.

But Jim McGreevey gay? It never crossed my mind.

4 · LIMITED ENGAGEMENT

❦

BEFORE THE SELF-DESTRUCTIVE AND feverish eruption of his admitted relationship with Golan Cipel, Jim had years of low-grade symptoms, a mild rash of sexual secrets, though I only found out later, after he had resigned. Jim was known to have a taste for strippers, women who worked at New Jersey clubs much like the fictional Bada Bing! where Tony Soprano and his buddies liked to hang out. This yen for strip joints, whether real or meant to create the impression that he was straight, was part of Jim's life long before he knew me, even long before he knew his first wife, Kari. When the story about these visits broke (and again, this was after Jim's resignation), it was reported that Kevin McCabe—mayoral aide to Jim, later his labor commissioner and best man at our wedding—often accompanied him. The press also reported that Jimmy Kennedy, Jim's good friend, sometimes went with him on these outings, which could take place any time of the day or night, supposedly as a way for Jim to blow off steam that built up on the campaign. Much later, when a reporter asked about these side trips with Jim, Jimmy said, "As far as I'm concerned, he was like every other guy that I knew. Sometimes when people are in politics, they want to give the impression to everybody that they are a regular guy." This is a regular guy?

In addition to favoring strip joints, Jim was also said to patronize prostitutes. One in particular, a woman named Myra Rosa from Perth Amboy, announced to anyone who would listen that Jim McGreevey had been her client for a couple of years, maybe as early as 1995. She told the police as much in a tape-recorded statement. On October 21, 1997, just two weeks before the election, a reporter from the *Star-Ledger* asked Jim directly about the prostitute's claims. Jim is reported to have burst into tears, and the story was quashed, only to surface again in 2004.

Apparently, Jim's sleazy encounters with women were only a cover for his sleazy encounters with men. As I later learned, his past was littered with casual sexual encounters, visits to gay clubs, public parks, and truck stops, although how he concluded that one set of adulterous, career-destroying secrets could protect him from another remains beyond my grasp.

I knew none of this. I was looking in the wrong place, insofar as I was looking at all. The only person I considered any sort of threat was Jim's first wife, Kari, though she was thousands of miles away in British Columbia. What I saw as Jim's connection to Kari—not what he might do with her, but what he might feel for her—blinded me to the possibility of other, more perilous connections. But, frankly, I didn't think Jim had either the time or the opportunity for dalliances. Politics was his mistress. Also, I knew he never went anywhere without a driver, a ready-made chaperone.

I traveled in political circles, and I'm pretty sure that I must have had at least a dozen acquaintances who knew, or suspected, what Jim was up to. But there's an old saying that explains why none of them told me, and it's the one about killing the messenger. Can't you just see it? "Hey, Dina! I heard your boyfriend carries five-dollar bills in his back pocket to give to the strippers."

With one exception, my closest friends didn't know these rumors, and the friend who did know dismissed it. She'd heard other rumors she knew to be false—one that Kari had left Jim because he was "abusive," which was obviously ridiculous, since they maintained a cordial relationship—so it was just as easy for her to dismiss the stripper rumor. Plus, the rumor about Jim and the strippers just didn't fit with how we seemed as a couple, and not just to her.

Beyond our acquaintances there was a small crowd of dedicated onlookers who must have known a lot more than I did. One was Ray

Lesniak, Jim's longtime mentor, whom I'd first met a dozen years earlier in Elizabeth's city hall. As a member of Jim's inner circle when he was both the mayor of Woodbridge and a gubernatorial candidate, Ray was in a position to know everything there was to know about Jim, which was far more than I knew. I don't know if Ray thought I was aware of the rumors of Jim's affinity for strip clubs and prostitutes, but he certainly never told me anything, or warned me even obliquely. I wondered if he'd even made the connection that I was the woman he'd met years earlier as the Planning Board commissioner his opponent had appointed. If he did remember me from that day in the Elizabeth city hall, he never acknowledged it. Our relationship, such as it was, was polite and existed only because of our mutual connection to Jim. What Jim's circle of advisers—later characterized by the press as his "cleanup squad"—knew with certainty, the press knew as rumor. But in each case, especially because I was involved in local politics myself, some of Jim's advisers must certainly have thought that if *they* knew what they knew, then *I* must know what they knew. But I didn't. I would have to be out of my mind to have had an intimate relationship with a man who engaged in such behavior. And since I didn't seem to be out of my mind, there had to be some other explanation. Many people knew that Jim wasn't what he appeared to be, so I guess that made it easy for them to take the next step and conclude that *I* couldn't possibly be what I seemed to be either. Their conclusion? Collusion. I must have struck some sort of bargain with him. There must have been something I wanted from him politically, in exchange for my appearance of partnership. That's the only way I can make sense of the charge that I was just a "political wife."

Of course, the local press was also on watch, especially reporters for the *Star-Ledger*, the *Bergen Record*, and the New Jersey Bureau of the *New York Times*. They didn't have as much information as Ray and Jim's inner circle did about Jim's sexual risk-taking, but they did know the rumors. And so they reached more or less the same conclusion as those who knew more: Every woman has her price.

I rarely read the newspapers. As a working mother, First Lady, and wife, I read mostly letters, e-mails, and speeches I was to deliver. I had little time for the papers. That's not to say that I didn't follow the news or keep up with what was happening. I remained as interested as ever, but I got my information from television and radio, which I could do while riding in a car. So, while some of these rumors may actually have appeared in print (and many of them didn't), they never made it to TV or radio, and they never made it to me. But what if someone from the press had presented me with the rumors? It wouldn't have made any difference. The better I got to know Jim, the more I saw how often the press got things wrong. There was the tidbit about my necking with Jim on Election Night outside the hotel, when I wasn't. Then there was another report that said we got engaged at an Italian restaurant in Middlesex County on Valentine's Day, when we hadn't. There were many errors and much speculation. I decided early on just to ignore them all.

All politicians are subject to scrutiny and rumor, not to mention a fair amount of mudslinging. But a politician with a secret such as Jim's is a politician who can be blackmailed, and a politician who can be blackmailed can leave his constituency vulnerable. The incompatible rumors—about both strippers and gay men—actually afforded him a certain amount of protection, each set undermining the other, but Jim's sexual secrets did make him a target for blackmail. As the election approached, questions about Jim's fidelity and sexual orientation were again newsworthy, because Jim was again newsworthy. He was setting his sights on the most powerful elected office in the state.

After Jim lost the election in 1997, he caught his breath and began campaigning to win in 2001. Our courtship continued pretty much as it had been—public community breakfasts, public fund-raising luncheons—but the character of our relationship was changing. I was with Jim more, for one thing, sometimes working the crowds with him, sometimes watching from the sidelines when he gave a talk. Helping Jim campaign was exhilarating, and it was during this time that my respect for him grew. Here was a man who advocated educational reform and state-sponsored health programs to help care for uninsured children, a man who wanted to reduce New Jerseyans' exorbitant property taxes and auto insurance rates, both the highest in the nation. And he was tireless. Yes, I knew that Jim had his critics, that many who followed politics called him a "perpetual campaigner," but what other people saw as ambition, I saw as passion. I believed in Jim and in the integrity of his message. I found his politics attractive, just as I found him attractive.

I'd always looked forward to our private dinners as a chance for Jim and me to unwind and get to know each other better. Now, with the campaign in full force, a new element was added. We still found time to relax here and there, but we became a team sharing invigorating postgame analyses. Jim knew that he could appear too scripted—no friendly, off-the-cuff asides—and too rehearsed, as if he'd given his speech hundreds of times before, which of course he had. He was trying to change that. *We* were trying to change that. Running through the events of the day to see where improvements could be made, we were partners, sharing the same ideals, working toward the same goal.

"How'd I do today?" he asked as we settled into our booth at a diner outside Hamilton in Mercer County. It was 1:00 A.M., and we were eating for the first time since breakfast, sharing a toasted bagel with cream cheese. Even at this hour, it was black coffee for me, tea with milk and no sugar for Jim. It had been a ridiculously busy day, with a stop at a senior-citizen center and three or four fund-raising dinners, at the last of which we were so hungry that even the rubber chicken looked good—not that we had the chance to eat it.

"It went well," I told Jim. He was great at engaging in one-to-one conversations, an opportunity he always had with seniors and at picnics.

"Yeah, but how'd I do with the speeches?"

I thought Jim was hitting his stride and sounding more relaxed in his speeches, and I told him so. "Even someone hearing both of those speeches today wouldn't have the feeling that they were hearing the same words," I said. "You were on message, but you found different ways to say it each time."

"Well, I'm glad I don't have to give another speech until tomorrow night," he said with a smile.

Then the talk turned to when we might get some time for ourselves.

"I know you have something next weekend, but how does it look for two weeks from now?" I asked.

I'd been wanting to spend a weekend in New York City, where we could take a hansom-cab ride through Central Park, go to a museum or two, and have dinner in SoHo. We'd had a few romantic evenings in New York, and I was eager to repeat them.

"Sounds good," Jim said. "Let me check the schedule, and I'll call you." Romantic or not—and Jim could be romantic—we needed to tend to our various responsibilities. Still, we were always in touch by cell phone. Jim might be upstate or downstate, but we'd always find time to speak.

My trust in him continued to grow during this period, as did my admiration. Yes, he was charming, but I'd met a lot of charming guys, enough to know that charm is just the wrapping paper. What touched me about Jim was that he was caring and kind, consistently so. One snowy winter night, for example, as he was entering Woodbridge after driving back from a visit to his sister Caroline and her family in Delaware, Jim saw an elderly woman stepping off the curb. She was tugging her loaded grocery cart across the street as if it were a balky mule. It seemed bigger than she was, and getting to the other side of the road appeared to be an exhausting undertaking. Jim was overcome with sympathy for the woman and wanted to help. He stopped his car, leaving his motor idling as he helped the woman across the street.

He didn't announce who he was, but this was Woodbridge, and she obviously recognized him.

"Oh, thank you, Mayor," she said, continuing to make her way up the block.

"How far do you still have to go?" Jim asked.

"Oh, a few blocks. It's not a problem," she said.

"Don't be silly. I'll give you a lift."

It was typical of Jim to look for a way to help people. He'd go out of his way for kids, too, especially high-school kids. Jim had earned spending money working part-time in the admissions office at Columbia when he was an undergraduate, and he'd often strike up a conversation with kids he met at a football game or picnic, inviting them to come to his office because he knew he could guide them through the application process. He seemed to me to be an idealist, a man who thought that just by virtue of his position in public life he could change the world.

I knew that Jim saw me as a political asset, and I appreciated it because it meant he saw something in me that wasn't immediately apparent to other people. Jim recognized that my being reserved didn't mean I wasn't something of a people person. I was never as gregarious as he was—Jim would talk with anyone who was still breathing—but if I sat down with a group of strangers at a table, I could move a conversation along and then some. I also knew that to Jim I was both beautiful and stylish. Any woman who knows that a man sees her that way is bound to credit him with astounding perceptiveness, and I was no exception.

I liked taking Jim 101, getting to know him, getting to know all about him: He had a pet snake as a kid, drank coffee (but only at breakfast), showered in the morning rather than at night, and had very sensitive skin. He worried that he was too short and prided himself on his warmth and friendliness. If Jim had placed a personal ad at that time, it might have read "Single white mayor, with ideals to spare, looking for like-minded Democrat. Must be interested in and knowledgeable about politics (esp. cult figures like Abraham Lincoln and Robert F. Kennedy), a C-Span junkie. Also desirable: interest in beachcombing, St. Patrick's Day parades, Springsteen, and Italian cuisine."

I felt increasingly drawn to Jim; nevertheless, I remained somewhat cautious. Even in my close relationships, which also include my friendships, I'm never the first to declare my feelings, never one to express anger. I don't usually voice criticisms, and I never ask questions that might seem intrusive. I wait for people to show themselves, if they care to. Jim told me that he loved me, and then he built on that with thoughtfulness. He often sent flowers, not only for my birthday or Valentine's

Day but when I had an important meeting or function I was hosting. When my grandmother died, though he'd never met her, he bought me a Tiffany-style lamp. He knew I liked the style, and he thought it would cheer me up.

But what I appreciated most of all were the quiet times we had together, just walking and talking. And as much as this sounds like a cliché, we really did take long walks on the beach. One walk always stood out for me. We were strolling along the water's edge, hand in hand, both in our windbreakers, with the wind blowing at our backs.

"You know," said Jim, "there's one positive to having lost the election."

"What do you mean?"

"We'll have more time to get to know each other better and to develop our relationship," he said.

"I guess that is the silver lining," I agreed happily. I hadn't always been sure he wanted me in his future.

"And maybe I can spend a little bit more time with Morag, too." His transition momentarily sobered me. Always in the back of my mind were questions about his feelings for Kari. He was hesitant about letting me meet Morag, and that seemed to me a measure of his continued involvement with Kari. Morag, who was five and a half, had started doing Irish step dancing and had already won a few local competitions. I didn't want to spoil this special afternoon with a possibly complicated conversation, so instead I asked about her progress in step dancing.

"How's Morag doing, getting ready for her competition?"

"She's been practicing a lot. And she's growing so quickly she needs another new costume already." I'd seen a photograph of the costume—a beautifully embroidered green skirt and top.

Morag was thriving, and that made Jim happy, but the fact that so much happened for her in between each of his visits made him sad. He had seen her the previous New Year's, but now he wouldn't be visiting her again until Easter.

"It's hard having her so far away," he said, as he'd said many times before.

"Why don't you have her come and visit you here?"

"It's not that easy," was all he'd say.

BY FEBRUARY 2000, JIM and I were engaged, and my role in his campaign now became fully visible. I didn't have a lot of time in which to plan the wedding—the campaign took precedence—but in the time I did have, I began to look at bridal magazines to get an idea of what I might like to wear. My friend Ana, who would be my maid of honor, had once owned a bridal shop in Newark and was willing to discuss gowns with me endlessly. I knew I wanted simple and elegant, with not too much lace. And my height required that I stay away from puffy. It didn't take me long to decide that I wanted a Vera Wang design, and once I'd made that decision, with my mother along I began looking at and trying on Vera Wang gowns in varying shades of white.

"What do you think?" I said, the first time I tried on a gown, the most elaborate one I would ever try on.

"I like it," my mom said.

"Well, I don't. I think I look like a Christmas ornament."

And that set the tone. Elaborate? She loved it. Simple? Not so much. In the end, when she first saw—on a hanger—the gown I eventually selected, she said, "I don't like that. Why are you even trying it on?"

"Because *I* like it."

To her credit, once she saw it on me, she liked it too.

A multitasker like most brides-to-be, I soon started looking around at wedding bands—in magazines, at jewelry stores, and online.

As for a wedding shower—my mother should've known better than to bring it up. She knew how much I disliked showers. I complained about the ones I'd had to go to and sent my regrets to the rest. I'd told her, "When I get married, whenever that happens to happen, *no shower.*" After I got engaged, she'd tried hard to bite her lip. But she couldn't help herself, and eventually she broached the subject. "So how about a bridal shower?" she said to me one day while we were looking at wedding gowns.

"Absolutely not," I said. But I said it with a smile.

MEANWHILE, MY GREAT JOY in our upcoming marriage floated merrily along on a tainted sea. In March 2000, just weeks after our engagement, while I was eyeing my first Vera Wang wedding gown, Jim took a trip to Israel, meeting Golan Cipel, then spokesperson for the mayor of an Israeli town Jim visited. There, apparently on impulse, he invited Golan to come work for his campaign, thereby setting the stage for all that came later.

But what is the most disturbing to me, and perhaps the most damaging to my capacity to trust even my own judgment, is that Jim's deepest feelings were absolutely invisible to me. His conflicts over his sexual orientation, and the risks he took with his health and possibly mine, must have tormented him. And yet his torment was as imperceptible in our relationship as carbon monoxide would have been in our home. If there was ever a time when Jim seemed happy, loving, and connected to me, it was in the months leading up to our marriage.

I never heard him have a moment's doubt about getting married, and wherever we went, he was quick to announce our upcoming marriage. He was even eager to go shopping with me for china and crystal for our new life. As you might imagine, these days I don't often peruse our wedding album, but I happened to do so recently. That book, and the accompanying videotape—me in my gown and Jim in his tux—brought back a rush of memories. I tried very hard, Monday-morning-quarterback style, to see in the photos or in the videotape or in my recollections clues to the duplicity, a crack in the armor. But it just wasn't there.

On the morning of July 4, I picked Jim up early, and we headed to the train. We were going to Washington, D.C., to look for sites for our wedding and reception. Although Jim and I both grew up in New Jersey, we'd ruled out getting married in our home state. Since I had already shared so much of Jim with the public and the media, I wanted this day to be private, our day, with only our family and our friends present. Jim agreed to keep the wedding private—not even an announcement in the *New York Times* or the *Star-Ledger*—and I was grateful, although I have wondered again and again at the readiness of his agreement.

If Jim's persona as solid heterosexual citizen was then so precarious, wouldn't he have wanted a visible marriage to anchor that identity? Wouldn't stabilizing that identity further advance his appeal as a gubernatorial candidate? Wouldn't a man as astute as Jim in the management of appearances want his wedding to be a page-one story? Perhaps. But then again, news stories need a hook, a reason to tell them *now* rather than at some other time, if at all. Maybe a news story about our wedding might have sent reporters in pursuit of riskier stories. Maybe Jim feared that a high-profile wedding story might renew an open investigation into the rumors about his sexual orientation or renew interest in his first marriage and the real reason it had died.

So New Jersey was out. New York was briefly in the running. Since Jim had been an undergraduate at Columbia University, the thought of getting married in the campus chapel had briefly crossed his mind. But New York was too close to New Jersey, so that was that. Portugal was another possibility. This was Jim's idea, and it touched me deeply. We gave it serious consideration, and my mother even checked out reception halls—including one on the outskirts of Coimbra, the town of my birth—on one of her visits, but when the U.S. ambassador to Portugal told us that for our vows to be legal we would have to get married at the U.S. embassy in Lisbon, we decided against it. Too secular.

Whatever else we were, we were a Roman Catholic couple. Perhaps we were a couple each engaged in a lover's quarrel with our church, especially in regard to our views on birth control, a woman's right to choose, and stem-cell research, but we were both at the time—and I still am—observant Roman Catholics. That was central to who we were. One day, driving between campaign stops, we talked about setting our wedding date. "Let's pick a date that will have some significance," said

Jim. "Maybe a feast day." The following day, I scanned a Roman Catholic calendar, the kind the church hands out at Christmastime, and I looked for dates in the fall that had some significance. I picked October 7, the feast day of Our Lady of the Rosary, the name by which Mary was known in her appearances at Fatima, in Portugal. During our conversation that evening, I suggested the date to Jim, and he said, "Great, then let's do it that day."

Once we had a date in mind, we started looking for chapels, which is why we were on a train heading to Washington, D.C., on the Fourth of July. Jim had gone to Georgetown University's law school and knew there were several chapels on campus. We encountered a pale, elderly Jesuit priest almost the moment we set foot on the campus. He showed us around, and we left thinking that one of the chapels, Copley Crypt, would be perfect, though we knew that Jim's status as a divorcé might be a problem. For our reception, we chose the Hay-Adams Hotel, because we were both charmed by its terrace overlooking both the White House and the Washington Monument.

And that was it. No angst, no uncertainty, no hesitation, no retreat. Not on his part and not on mine.

5 · TWELVE DAYS OF TORRICELLI

BACK FROM WASHINGTON, I was now in a position to start planning our wedding. But the next few weeks would turn out to be full of more than tulle and white roses. Just days after our return, Jim found himself in the middle of the biggest political battle of his life, one that threatened to undo five years of hard work and eliminate him as a contender for the governorship.

The week before our train trip back from D.C., Robert Torricelli, a Democrat and then the junior senator from New Jersey, had made the same journey, during which he discussed his political future with his chief of staff, Jamie Fox, later to be Jim's chief of staff. Torricelli had always wanted to run for governor but thought of the statehouse as something he would, or could, pursue later in his career. And now it was later. For one thing, Torricelli knew that with the possibility of George W. Bush in the White House and a Republican majority in both houses of Congress, life wasn't going to be much fun for a Democratic senator, who would find it difficult to accomplish anything. But there was more to it. A gubernatorial campaign costs money, and Torricelli had always prided himself on being a powerful and charismatic fund-raiser—rightly so, since he set a record by taking in $2.15 million in campaign contributions in March 1999. However, when Torricelli learned that Jim had beaten his record by nearly a million dollars, he concluded that knocking Jim out of the running was a now-or-never proposition. Jim might not be beatable if Torricelli waited too long.

Meanwhile, two days after our return from D.C., on Thursday, July 6,

Jim asked former governor Jim Florio for his backing. But Florio, a South Jersey Democrat, wouldn't support Jim due to a rift between the North Jersey and South Jersey Democrats. Jim's home county, Middlesex, was in the north, and though he knew Jersey politics as well as anyone and realized that Florio's endorsement might be unlikely, he thought it wasn't out of the question either. And it would've been nice.

Over the weekend, Torricelli apparently resolved that he would run for governor, though he didn't make the decision public for a few days. Meanwhile Jim had begun to hear the rumors about Torricelli eyeing the gubernatorial race, but he just didn't believe that Torricelli would stoop so low as to challenge him for the nomination when he'd earlier assured Jim he had no interest in the governorship.

By July 9, the press had caught wind of Torricelli's interest and an article ran announcing that he was seeking advice on whether to run. Two days later, on the eleventh, the headlines announced that Jim's supporters might be deserting him because they were either remaining neutral or backing Torricelli. One Democrat who watched the battle between Torricelli and Jim heating up said that it was like watching Mark McGwire versus "the home-run king of the Pee Wee League."

Publicly Jim maintained his civility toward Torricelli, telling the press in a story that ran on July 11, "For the past seven years I've been working very hard towards seeking the governor's office, and I'll continue to pursue that aspiration." Privately he was furious and disgusted. "The guy has no honor," he told me. He'd thought that he and Torricelli had a good working relationship, but now he saw what Torricelli was doing as a betrayal of his earlier assurances.

For the next week or two, Torricelli tested the waters, seeing what kind of support he might be able to muster while also watching to see if Jim's support remained firm. But support for Jim had softened, and on July 19 the headlines proclaimed, CORZINE LEADS A RETREAT IN SUPPORT FOR MCGREEVEY. WITH TORRICELLI IN RACE, DEMOCRATS TURN NEUTRAL. (Jon Corzine was then running for the U.S. Senate.) That day Torricelli announced his interest in becoming New Jersey's next governor. His rationale was that he felt he, more than Jim, could best heal the divisions between the counties of North Jersey and the counties of South Jersey and, in so doing, could deliver the state to Al Gore, the Democratic presidential nominee.

"So what's the plan for this weekend?" I said to Jim when I spoke with him on the night of the nineteenth. We'd already been fighting Torricelli for a week, and we were determined to win. Jim had enlisted his entire family—his parents, Ronnie and Jack; his Aunt Kathleen; his Uncle Herb; his sister Sharon—and they were phoning voters practically round-the-clock. In just a few days, they made over two thousand calls to Democratic committee members. The majority were to members in my home county, Essex County, which had the largest number of voters and hence was the jewel in the crown for anyone seeking statewide office. Without the support of a county as large as Essex, you don't even have a shot at the kingdom. Therefore Jim's strategy was to try to hold his support there to demonstrate his power. If other counties saw that Essex was supporting him, they might postpone realigning themselves with Torricelli or even making a decision about it. As Michael Murphy, a prosecutor from Morris County who had once himself been interested in the governorship, put it to a reporter, "If Torricelli gets Essex, it'll be tough for McGreevey to overcome it [but] if McGreevey gets Essex, then it's a horse race." Regardless of where Murphy's sympathies lay—and I always thought they lay with Jim—his own bets were on Torricelli.

There was another part to Jim's strategy that I interpret differently now from how I did then. It was the received wisdom at the time that the governor of New Jersey needed to be a married man. (Still, it's worth noting that this "wisdom" is at odds with Jon Corzine's recent success in getting elected, despite the fact that just days before the election his opponent got Corzine's angry ex-wife to ventilate publicly.) Nevertheless, Jim's idea was that while New Jerseyans were perfectly willing to elect state and federal legislators who were merely faceless names on a ballot, a governor had to be different. He believed that a governor needed to have a face—a family and an identity voters could relate to. Torricelli was childless and divorced.

His mother was still alive, but his father was long gone, and he never had any other relatives appear at a podium with him. All his advocates were on his payroll.

Jim felt he already had at least three advantages over Torricelli. First, he believed he was willing to work much harder than Torricelli. Second, his extended family was heavily involved in his campaign. And third, he now had me.

Usually Jim's weekend schedule involved about five events, but now he and I were driving upstate and downstate, going to maybe eight events a day. He was fighting for his political life, but it was exciting. He liked the battle, and so did I. We'd go into a sea of people, and he'd hold my hand, pulling me through the crowd as if I were a water-skier and he were the motorboat. People would shout out, "Could you be in a picture with me?" or "Come meet my sister . . . my brother . . . my grandmother." It was thrilling, and it turned out I was good with crowds after all.

Jim wouldn't say anything as explicit as, "OK, you take the left side of the crowd and I'll take the right." He didn't have to. We were in sync. Like good dancers, we just knew how to read each other spontaneously and go from there. And that kind of attunement is exciting. During those events, I could see Jim's admiration for me and a kind of gratitude in how he looked at me. It was fun, and it felt good to have a connection that didn't need words.

Also, in my new role as visible fiancée I could take on the additional role of wardrobe mistress, picking up a well-made suit or two for him here or there. Jim once joked that he had 180 white shirts. Whatever the number, he wasn't about to make the cover of any men's fashion magazine. Every other guy I knew would go to a picnic wearing khakis and a polo shirt, but Jim would happily show up in dark suit, white shirt, and tie. He'd wear the same undertaker's outfit to the football game that afternoon and to the church dinner that night. Jim used to laugh at me because once I knew the day's itinerary, I'd pack for it, sometimes bringing along two to three outfits. I'd always liked dress-up anyhow, and so it was fun to think of the events of the day and what to wear to them—a tailored suit with a leather bag for a church service, a blue linen sundress for an afternoon picnic (no bag needed, but earrings to match the dress), and a black beaded evening gown with coordinating accessories for the black-tie dinner.

As Jim and Torricelli pursued their battle for the nomination, they both engaged in public "county counting," an old political game where the candidates assess not just what counties were "theirs" but what those counties could offer in votes, money, and influence. It would take an advantage in all three realms to assure a potential leader's likely efficacy. Even though the central county was Essex, the most populous of New Jersey's twenty-one counties, an advantage in any one area wasn't going to be enough to assure that Jim would prevail. Before Torricelli came on the scene, Essex County, and indeed all the counties, were perceived to be Jim's because of his success in the '97 election and the absence, prior to Torricelli showing interest, of any other viable candidate in the field. But as time went on, Torricelli claimed to be loosening Jim's grip, finger by finger, on the county. Jim felt that Sharpe James, the powerful mayor of Newark, in Essex County, was in his corner. But now Torricelli was claiming that *he* had Sharpe James's support. Torricelli's claims had Jim worried, but Jim's strategy was to assert, with practiced complacency, that Essex was his, while working tirelessly behind the scenes to try to keep Sharpe James in his corner. He hoped that other counties would then hold off before aligning themselves with any other candidate. There was some risk for county leaders in remaining neutral, even temporarily. Torricelli was widely perceived as a bully. If he had prevailed, those who hadn't rushed to support him would have reason to fear payback. Jim, on the other hand, didn't have the reputation of being vengeful, and besides, in this particular contest he was the underdog.

On Tuesday, July 25, Jim held a rally in Newark. He knew there wasn't going to be a big turnout, so the night before, he asked me if I could get some of my friends to show up. I knew I could get at least a handful to go, and they spent that night making signs saying JIM MCGREEVEY FOR GOVERNOR and PORTUGUESE-AMERICANS FOR JIM MCGREEVEY. Meanwhile I tried to conduct my own barometric readings. If I saw a political leader, no matter how small his or her constituency, I would say, "You're supporting, Jim, right?" Some would say, "Of course I am!" while others would just sort of smile and walk away. In the end, even the walkaways supported Jim. Beyond that, I can't claim to have rallied Newark behind Jim. Sharpe James was not a mayor who paid a great deal of attention to the Portuguese-American community, so my organization didn't have much leverage there.

During that time, Jim was more energized and more in-your-face than I'd ever seen him before. Jon Corzine had stepped back into neutrality. Nevertheless, one night when Corzine was holding a postprimary event to thank African-American clergy who had supported him, Jim walked unannounced into the restaurant where they were having dinner, shook hands with everyone, and left. A week later, on Friday the twenty-eighth, Jim stuck out his stubborn jaw and filed his application to run for governor—a full eighteen months prior to the election. Just what I would have done in his position.

On July 27, Jim got the support of local labor unions at a rally, and by Sunday the thirtieth, it was all over for Torricelli. That day, Jim and two members of his inner circle, including Ray Lesniak, met at a Newark Airport hotel with leaders from Essex and Hudson counties. That's when it became clear to Jim that Sharpe James, who attended the meeting, was supporting Jim after all.

Once James announced publicly that he was backing Jim, the contest was over, though Jim and his staff were astounded at how quickly Torricelli had crumpled. Watching this all close up, I was riveted—but surprised. I remembered what I'd learned in my political science classes at Rutgers University, and this had been nothing like that. The books I read on the electoral process, and dutifully underlined in yellow highlighter at the Rutgers library, talked as if elections took place in an ideal universe where the best candidate would invariably win. It's not like that anywhere, except maybe in the movies. In real life, the best candidate may not even be able to afford to run. What I learned about politics during this battle is that it's a down-and-dirty business.

What I learned about Jim was that he was willing to work harder than almost anybody to get what he wanted, that he had guts and passion—all qualities you'd want in a candidate, not to mention a husband.

6 · FROM THIS MOMENT ON

❧

THERE WERE GLITCHES, OF course. A wedding just isn't a wedding without glitches. In the beginning, we had planned to get married at one of the chapels on the Georgetown campus. When the paperwork from Georgetown arrived, confirming our reservation for Saturday, October 7, I presumed that they were giving us permission to marry in Copley Crypt, the chapel we had requested. I went ahead and prepared the wedding invitations—after all, as a fund-raiser, I'd also had a lot of experience as an event planner—and when they came back from the printer, I went online to get directions to include in the invitations. This was about four weeks before our wedding date, so when I realized that the online photograph didn't remotely resemble the chapel we'd chosen, I called Jim in a panic. He happened to be in D.C. that day. As soon as he could, Jim went to Georgetown and discovered that, sure enough, there was an error in the paperwork. Instead of being given permission to marry in Copley Crypt, a cozy little cave of a chapel, we'd been given permission to marry in St. William's Chapel—a large, drafty barn.

"It's awful," Jim said when he called me a couple of hours later. "It's much too big, not intimate at all. The rugs are frayed, the seats are old and uncomfortable. We can't get married in this place."

"OK," I said. My panic had subsided now, and I switched back to event-planner mode. "I'll take care of it." I remembered that the catering director at Hay-Adams had said we could also marry there if we wanted. I called him right away. Luckily, the ballroom was available all day, which meant we could have our ceremony there, as well as our reception.

We had known all along that, because Jim was divorced, the ceremony wouldn't be performed by a Catholic priest, so we'd asked Robert Counselman, an Episcopal priest and Jim's friend, if he could come to Washington and officiate.

"Sure," Father Counselman said. "I'd be honored."

That's when we encountered our next glitch. Father Counselman had spoken too soon. As it turned out, he didn't have the authority to marry us in Washington, D.C., because it was outside his jurisdiction. Luckily, he figured out an alternative pretty quickly. We'd have to come to his church, Trinity Episcopal in Woodbridge, sometime before we left for D.C., where he'd take care of the legally binding technicalities—a set of no-frills "I do's." Then, on what we continued to think of as our "real" wedding day, he would come to the Hay-Adams and perform a more elaborate ceremony. With those issues resolved, we went forward with our plans.

On October 4, Jim and I were scheduled to meet Father Counselman at 7:00 P.M. at his church. Jim was coming from a fund-raiser for Al Gore at Jon Bon Jovi's house but had promised to leave early and get to the church on time to meet me and Kevin McCabe, his best man, and Celia, my matron of honor. Beyond the five of us, no one knew about the Thursday-night vows. Why should we have told anyone? To us, it wasn't the "real" wedding. No wedding rings, no music. Just technicalities and paperwork.

It rained torrentially that day, and Jim called to say he was running late.

"The rain is so bad, and there's so much mud here that our wheels just keep spinning," he said. "We are really stuck in the mud. We'll get out, but it'll take a couple of guys to give us a push."

In a movie, with appropriate music, the image of a car spinning its wheels in the muck might correctly augur the future that awaited us. But this was real life, and so, at least for that day, the mud was just mud and the rain was just rain.

I was wearing an off-white suit for the occasion, which luckily was protected by my raincoat. Nevertheless, after arriving at the church, I had spent the first few minutes getting mud off my stockings and fixing my makeup, which was threatening to wash out. The four of us stood around in Father Counselman's office, a plain room with a desk and some book-shelves. No altar, and if there was a cross, I don't remember it.

Suddenly Jim burst in. "Sorry I'm late, folks," he said, turning to me and giving me a wet hug. He kissed me and held my hand, then took his place in the little semicircle where we'd all been standing.

"Well, is everyone ready?" Father Counselman asked, after a few more minutes of chat.

Jim squeezed my hand. "I'm excited," he said to me. "Are you ready?"

"Ready as I'll ever be."

I didn't have a single doubt or a moment's hesitation, but it all felt a little unreal. I had never thought that I would get married in someone's office, much less an Episcopalian's.

Then Father Counselman took us through our vows.

It was over in just a few minutes. Still standing in Father Counsel-man's office, we signed all the paperwork, and then he told us we were now legally husband and wife. Jim seemed ebullient. I was happy, but it all felt faintly surreal to me. Jim and I kissed, and Celia turned to me and said, "Congratulations, Mrs. McGreevey!" If there was any moment that made it real for me, this was it.

By now, it was 8:30 P.M. and still pouring. Jim and I had planned to go out to dinner somewhere in Woodbridge, just the two of us, follow-ing the ceremony.

"Do you still want to go out to dinner?" said Jim.

"Not really," I replied. "Let's wait till we really feel married."

We had finished later than expected, and the weather was still awful. That would probably be another sign in a movie, but in our lives it just meant we didn't have to get even wetter than we already were. Jim walked me to my car, where we kissed good night. After that, he went to

his home, which soon would be my home, and I went back to my parents'
in Elizabeth, knowing that this would be the last night I slept there. I realize that might seem strange to some people, but I didn't even think of
going to Jim's house. For one thing, the evening's formalities didn't seem
like our "real" wedding. For another, I hadn't told my parents about this
little matrimonial detour. I wanted the formality and excitement of our
wedding ceremony to be shared by everyone, at the same time and in the
same place. As far as I was concerned we didn't exchange vows that night,
we just signed a contract. Besides, we were leaving the next morning for
Washington, and I still hadn't packed for our wedding and honeymoon—
ten days in Italy.

Soon after I got home, my phone rang. "So, Mrs. McGreevey, how
does it feel to be married?" Jim asked.

"I'm not sure," I said. "I don't think I feel married yet."

"Are you happy?" he asked. "I am."

"Yes," I said. "I really am happy."

The next morning, as Jim and I sat together on the train to Washington, D.C., I wondered what married life would really be like. I knew that
ours would not be a typical marriage, though I was certainly not prepared for just how atypical it would be. I was marrying someone who I
believed would be governor, maybe even president. But what did it mean
to be the wife of the governor? I wouldn't be able to compare my marriage to any of my friends' marriages or to the marriages of any of my
relatives. The only political wife I knew well was Lori Kennedy. I did
know that many political marriages ended in divorce, and that made me
wary. I was going to make my marriage work.

I WASN'T ONE OF those little girls who played bride, so I hadn't really
imagined a fantasy wedding for myself, but our wedding ceremony two
days later was close to perfect, a lovely mix of happiness and hope. There
wasn't a Catholic priest or a church (that would have made it perfect),
but I did wear my beautiful Vera Wang dress—a strapless gown in antique

white—and my dad did walk me down the aisle. All the people I loved were there to share in the day.

During the ceremony, we had not two but three wedding rings. My mother had a plain gold ring that I had asked for, since I knew that it no longer fit her. I wanted my marriage to be strong and happy like my parents', and bringing my mother's ring into our ceremony was a concrete way of expressing my deepest hopes of what the future would bring to Jim and me. When we said our vows, my voice was soft, while Jim's carried throughout the room. He was accustomed to making speeches, and I was moved by how much strength and conviction he expressed in his vows to me. In the background throughout was the sound of young children—my nieces—chattering, and that also seemed somehow appropriate in terms of what I was hoping my marriage with Jim would bring.

The banquet was beautiful—ivory damask tablecloths, with a white-rose centerpiece framed by lit candles. We had a five-person orchestra for the occasion, an elegant group all dressed in tuxedos, which played "From This Moment On" for our first dance as husband and wife. Throughout the evening, we talked, laughed, and danced with each other and with our guests. Altogether we filled the room with about eighty people—family and close friends who had traveled down to Washington to be with us. About half a dozen of our guests were union and political leaders who had come forward to support Jim when his run for governor was threatened by Torricelli. Including them in our wedding was our way of saying thank you. In his toast, best man Kevin McCabe recalled a visit the three of us had made to D.C. for a conference, which was followed by a long, long evening at the Irish Pub. In a comment that didn't mean half as much at the time as it did later, Kevin said if I could endure that, I could endure anything.

Soon after dinner began, Jim was up and walking from table to table, as I'd seen him do at dozens of fund-raisers. I was sitting near Jimmy Kennedy, and our eyes met as we watched Jim circulate. "Look at him," I said with amusement. "He just can't help himself. He thinks he's campaigning."

Jimmy smiled as well. "I guess it's automatic." It was a telling moment in this very new marriage. I knew what I was getting into as I watched my husband work the room. It was fine with me, I decided. This is who he was.

The day's celebration ended around midnight and would have gone longer if we'd let it. The band had packed up, our families had left, the waiters were looking at their watches. It was just us and the stragglers. We were hanging around to be polite, but it was time for the guests to go. Finally, I stood up and said, "We have to let these guys clean up. Party's over, folks." Actually, I had a wedding night to get to.

We made our way to the bridal suite, Jim still in his tux, me still in my wedding gown. We were tired and happy. When we were at last in our room, Jim turned to me. "Didn't we have a great day?" he asked.

"Yes," I said. "It was beautiful."

"You looked spectacular. You made a gorgeous bride," he said as he helped me out of my wedding gown. Finally we were together as husband and wife, alone at last.

I GUESS I SHOULDN'T have been surprised, but even on our honeymoon in Rome, Jim worked. One evening before dinner, he said he had to call his campaign manager, Gary Taffet. Since there was no phone in our room capable of a transatlantic call, Jim had to call from the hotel lobby. After fifteen minutes, I wondered where he was. After half an hour, I was a little edgy. After an hour, I began to wonder if he'd been abducted. But no, when I went down to the lobby, there he was, phone glued to his ear. Not only did I have a lot to learn about marriage, I had a lot to learn about this marriage, to this man in particular.

Despite Jim's umbilical attachment to the telephone, we enjoyed our honeymoon in Rome immensely. One day, our guide, a fine-arts curator based at the American embassy in the Vatican, showed us the Caravaggios, the Michelangelos, and the Raphaels. But the high point of the entire wedding experience, and what we had hoped for most, was a private audience with Pope John Paul II. A morning or two after we arrived, we went to St. Peter's Square to meet Sister Roberta, the aunt of a friend. Sister Roberta lived in New Jersey, and I'd met her before; happily, she was there on vacation and had been able to help arrange this papal audience for us.

"What do you think I should wear?" I asked Jim—probably the only time I'd ever asked him for fashion advice.

I wound up wearing a black sheath dress and a long black wool cardigan. Around my neck, I wore a necklace with a gold pendant designed by a Catholic priest in order to raise money for orphans. Jim, on this of all occasions, wore khakis, a long-sleeved button-down shirt, and a tie. He hadn't brought a suit with him, but he did have a sports coat, and that would have to do. We met Sister Roberta, who took us to the entrance of the papal apartment—in a seventeenth-century palace, adjacent to St. Peter's Basilica. When the Pope greets the faithful in St. Peter's Square, it's the balcony of this apartment from which he waves. In the papal apartment, we were met by a monsignor who took us through a series of hallways to the Pope's personal chapel. I was surprised at how modest it was—a rectangular white room with bare walls, in all maybe the size of a large dining room. Not more than twenty people were in there, and most were from John Paul's home country of Poland. Among them were a bride and groom in wedding attire who had come to be blessed by the Holy Father.

The room was silent with anticipation. Within minutes, the Pope would enter from a side door and we would be in his presence, a historic moment for two devout Catholics who'd never imagined anything remotely like this. At last the Pope came into the room, escorted by another priest. He looked frailer and paler than I had expected, and he walked quite slowly. I'd seen him once before, though at a distance, when he came to the Meadowlands, a sports complex in New Jersey holding thousands. He had aged since then, and yet he exuded dignity and serenity. As he entered, all of us, as if we had rehearsed, fell to our knees. The Pope was dressed entirely in white, and his presence was overpowering. I felt as if I were before God himself. At that moment, I experienced a complete sense of joy and comfort inseparable from his presence.

Once at the altar, the Pope celebrated mass in Polish. Although we didn't grasp much, other than recognizing that some of his words were in Latin, this was the most meaningful mass either one of us had ever attended. It was an exquisite occasion full of joy and promise. Here we were, married for less than a week, and the first mass we went to together as husband and wife was celebrated by the Pope. We received communion from one of the attending priests, and then, following the mass, another papal aide escorted us to a separate area of the Pope's residence for our private audience with him. We were joined by those who had been in the chapel. Again, the room was in almost total silence. While we waited, Jim said to me, "You should say something to him in Portuguese." We knew that it was one of the many languages the Pope spoke.

One by one, or as couples, we were escorted to Pope John Paul II as he sat on a massive dark wood chair. We trembled. Jim was momentarily speechless, something I'd never encountered in him before. Then we were presented to the Pope by his aide, who announced our names and where we were from. Jim, having regained speech, told the Pope that we were newly married. I asked the Pope to bless our marriage and bless our family. Then, in Portuguese I said, "I'm originally from Portugal." He nodded with a smile and answered me in Portuguese, "Home of Our Lady of Fatima," as Mary is known in relation to her appearance to the three shepherd children at Fatima. The Pope was well known to be devoted to Mary and credited her with saving him during the assassination attempt on his life on May 13, 1981. That was the feast day of Our Lady of Fatima.

"Yes," I said.

He handed us each a rosary in a small pouch imprinted with his coat of arms and motto—*Totus Tuus*, meaning "All yours," signifying his devotion to Mary. Then we were escorted from the room. At that moment, I thought his blessing would guarantee that Jim and I would have a great marriage. How could we not? We had just been blessed by the holiest man on earth.

Soon we headed for Florence, where we admired the architecture as well as the incredible works of art, including Michelangelo's *David*. And we explored a different restaurant every day, reveling in the marvelous pastas, meats, breads, and wines. It just didn't seem possible to have a bad meal in Italy—not that we tried. One day back in Rome, we met some doctors from my hospital and joined them for dinner. It was nice seeing familiar faces, but strange, too, since I was used to seeing them wearing white coats and walking purposefully through the corridors, not wearing sports clothes and ambling leisurely through the streets. It was fun to see them, though, and fun to introduce Jim as "my husband," a phrase that felt very new to me.

We went wherever our impulses and inclinations took us—to museums and churches, to the Forum and the Colosseum. Somehow we always managed to begin our days at one of the cafés near the Spanish Steps. And since it was a mild autumn, mild enough for us eat outside, we always managed to end our days with romantic dinners al fresco. We were both avid walkers, so we spent the daylight hours walking the streets. On one occasion, Jim said teasingly, "What's the matter? Can't you keep up with me? That's not a good indication."

"I can keep up with you anytime," I replied.

"You told me you walked the streets of Paris for hours. Now you can't keep up?"

"Why don't we switch shoes," I challenged, "and let's see who can't keep up with whom."

In the four years that I had known Jim, I had yearned for this kind of extended time alone with him. And it turned out to be everything I'd hoped for. We returned home after a spectacular ten days. I took it as a good start to an excellent marriage, a positive sign of our happy future together. In truth, I'd never been happier. I had just married a man I loved dearly, a man I believed would love and respect me, a man I would build a life with, could grow old with. Who knew that the honeymoon would be over so soon?

7 · NEW LIFE

EVERYONE SAYS THAT THE first year of marriage is particularly hard—a period of adjustment—but it just didn't feel that way to me. I came back from my honeymoon feeling closer to Jim than I ever had, and I quickly grew comfortable living with him. We enjoyed having each other to discuss the news with in the morning and the day's events, good or bad, at night. If either one of us had had a hard day, we could see it on the other's face rather than having to sense a tone of voice on the phone. Also, because most of Jim's premarital meals had consisted of tepid soup eaten on the go, I wanted him to come back in the evenings to a home-cooked dinner. Sometimes it was just the two of us, other times he arrived with two or three staffers, and on the nights he worked late—which were many—I had a dinner ready to heat up for him.

I began to know him in the small, intimate ways you can only know someone you live with: Jim talked in his sleep; he always wore a T-shirt under his shirt; he never wore the same shirt twice but he might wear the same tie three days in a row. He left the cap off the toothpaste and the milk out of the refrigerator. Jim didn't really care what the house looked like—the carpet had stains; his walls were in need of a paint job; and his television was twenty years old, which was good enough for his favorite program—*The West Wing*—and for watching tapes and the news.

But we were too busy for home improvements. Jim was campaigning more than ever, and now that I was his wife, I was not only more visible in his campaign but often his surrogate, representing him on the campaign trail. I felt that the people I met campaigning welcomed me warmly, almost as if they were members of a new and vast extended family I'd married into. In fact, the campaign really *was* a large family—Jim's parents worked hard on his behalf, and I even brought my nieces into it. At one meet-and-greet, my niece Meagan parked herself on a chair near the door, where she proceeded to distribute flyers. "Everybody vote!" she told passersby. "Vote for my Uncle Jimmy!"

One night, Jim came in and told me that he'd been offered $50,000 by a law firm. They would put his name on their letterhead, which would add to their prestige, and in return all he'd have to do was show up once or twice a month.

"What do you think?" he asked me. "Should I accept it?"

"I don't think it's worth it," I said. "People will criticize you, and the press will be down your throat."

"Are you sure?" he asked. "It would sure buy lots of trips to Greece," referring to a vacation we'd recently discussed.

In the end, he turned the job down, as I knew he would. Jim was almost completely indifferent to money. As mayor of Woodbridge, he hadn't taken a raise in salary for five or six years, and when he became governor, he wouldn't claim the entire salary he was entitled to either. He was permitted $175,000 but took only $156,000 because the state's finances were precarious and he wanted to do his part in cutting costs. I thought it was admirable.

Meanwhile Jim and I were in full campaign mode, and it wasn't going to let up until the day after the election. That meant two or three evenings a week and most of the weekend. Weekends we were out of the house by 7:00 A.M., going up and down the state, often driving a couple of hundred miles. Often we weren't home until 10:00 or midnight.

When we were first back from our honeymoon, everyone, friends and strangers alike, asked to see my wedding ring. Not long after that, another question emerged. Everywhere we went, people wanted to know, "When are you going to have a baby?"

"It's a little too soon," I'd respond.

"Oh, but it would be so nice to have a baby around."

"Are you going to baby-sit?" I asked more than once.

Jim and I had taken the approach that a child would come whenever it came. He was forty-three, and I had turned thirty-four a month after our marriage. Given the demands of the campaign, and given my age, I didn't think I would get pregnant all that quickly. However, one morning early in April 2001, I opened the refrigerator in our kitchen and was blasted by the overpowering smell of eggs and broccoli. I'd never even noticed that either one *had* a smell. I knew a change in the sense of smell was a sign of pregnancy. Could I be pregnant? My period wasn't even late.

I wanted to be a mom. I just wasn't sure that I wanted to be on the way to motherhood right this minute. I knew women who had severe morning sickness, and I certainly wasn't looking forward to that. Morning sickness, especially if it extended into the afternoon, wouldn't go over well at a church picnic. By the end of the campaign, I'd be waddling, with thousands of strangers patting my stomach as if I were a character at Disney World.

But I wanted a baby, and Jim did too. I knew that on a very deep level he was still anguished about the fact that his daughter, Morag, had been ripped from his life. More than once, in the middle of the night, Jim had bolted out of bed, still asleep. "Where's the baby?! Where's the baby!?" he'd yell in a voice flooded with panic, as he rushed into the bedroom that had been Morag's. It was a recurring nightmare, a night terror. The anxiety in his voice broke my heart. I'd have to guide him gently back to bed, and in the morning he'd have no recollection that it had happened.

He didn't have that panic in his voice during his waking life, but I'd seen his reaction when the subject of his daughter came up. One time, we'd been at an event in Woodbridge when one of his constituents approached him.

"Hi there, Jim, how are you doing, and how's Morag? She must be getting big."

"Yes, she *is* getting big," Jim said, attempting to exude a cheer that, to me, barely concealed his sadness. You could *see* the sadness. The subject of Morag wasn't one he wanted to talk about.

Nevertheless, Jim was also looking forward to our having our own family. Now and then, when we fantasized about what life would be like if Jim won the election, we thought about how wonderful it would be to someday have a toddler of our own running around the governor's mansion in Princeton.

These thoughts and others milled around in my mind as later that day I went to do our weekly shopping on my way back from work—and added a home pregnancy test to the list. I did the test the minute I arrived home, even before I faced opening the refrigerator to put the groceries away. The result was unmistakable. Sky blue! We were going to have a baby! I was thrilled. But the campaign. Back and forth, my feelings ping-ponged. In the end—no doubt about it—my happiness won out.

I debated whether to tell Jim, who would be arriving home very late after a full day of campaigning, and chose not to say anything that day. By now it was April 4, and in three days—the Saturday ahead—we would be married for six months. I bit my tongue and decided that I would wait those three days because it would be a terrific "semi-anniversary" present.

April 7 was a full day on the campaign trail. We didn't have a single moment alone until we were back home. Jim was already in bed by the time I climbed in with a greeting card in my hand that made note of our six months of marriage and how happy I'd been during these months. At the bottom of the card, as a way of easing into the news, I'd written some words about "new beginnings and a new life." Jim read the card, kissed me, and said, "Thank you."

"So what do you think of what I wrote?" I asked.

He looked a bit puzzled. "It's very nice and thoughtful."

"Anything else?" I said.

"Am I supposed to say something else?"

"Well, does it make you want to ask any questions?" I said. This wasn't going quite the way I'd imagined.

"What kind of questions?" I didn't expect him to guess that I was pregnant, but I thought he might ask what my words meant.

"Well, I guess I'm going to have to tell you straight out."

Jim had had a long, exhausting day. "Tell me what?" He sounded a little frustrated.

"I'm pregnant!"

"Now?" he said weakly. "This isn't exactly great timing."

I felt something in me sink, and my excitement evaporated. "I thought you would be happy!" I said. I wasn't prepared for this response. I thought he'd be even more excited than I was at the prospect of having a child in the house again. I was deeply stung.

He must have seen the look on my face, because he immediately reached over to touch me. "I am happy, Dina. It's just that it's going to be tough during the campaign."

"I know it is, but what can we do?"

He was silent a few seconds. "Are you sure you're pregnant?"

"Yes, I'm sure," I said, telling him about my newly acute sense of smell, as well as the results of the pregnancy test.

"I'll call Cliff Lacy tomorrow to ask who he thinks is the best ob-gyn." Clifton Lacy was the medical director at Robert Wood Johnson University Hospital in New Brunswick, New Jersey, and would become the commissioner of the Department of Health in Jim's administration. Jim knew him well and trusted him to give him a good recommendation. That was fine by me. Having moved from Elizabeth to Woodbridge, I was in the market for a new physician anyhow.

"How are you feeling?" Jim asked when we got up the next morning.

"I feel fine," I said.

"You have to make sure you take care of yourself," he said.

"I am," I said, pleased at his interest.

"You have to make sure you're eating right and getting enough sleep and taking the right vitamins. . . ."

This was Jim through and through. When presented with any new piece of information, he invariably framed it as a problem (even if it wasn't) and went in search of a solution. Once he had the solution, he'd faithfully follow it, never looking back. Jim frequently quoted his father on this approach to life: "Have a plan to follow and then follow the plan."

But racing from Problem to Solution, Jim rarely took the time to Proceed Through Feeling. Oh, how I wish he had.

I reflected on this a few years later when, not more than a week or two after Jim's national confession and long before the dust had settled, I found some sheets of paper on the kitchen table that looked to me like evidence that Jim was planning to write a book. In them, he'd written that he'd married me not for love but for "political reasons." Even now, I'm not sure that's true, but I've had plenty of time to reflect on this and to wish that he'd just once taken into account his deepest feelings—all of them, no matter how contrary and contradictory they were—before settling on his plan for his life. It would have spared me great pain, and it would have spared him pain too.

But if Jim and I agree on anything, it's that the best part of our marriage, our best gift to one another and to ourselves, was our daughter, Jacqueline, and so when it came to managing my pregnancy, our "plan" was the same: to do everything in our power to ensure a healthy baby. As someone who worked in a hospital setting and wrote newsletters for pregnant women in English, Portuguese, and Spanish, I already had a trilingual understanding of how a pregnant woman should take care of herself. I was eating healthily, exercising as frequently as my schedule allowed, and, in the biggest concession of all, had given up my half dozen cups of coffee a day.

Meanwhile, with the help of Cliff Lacy, I soon had an appointment with Dr. Charletta Ayers, an ob-gyn practicing in New Brunswick. I liked her right away. She was a woman in her forties, with two young children, one of whom had been premature. I found her to be no-nonsense and direct, traits I've always been comfortable with. I knew that many ob-gyns got out of obstetrics as soon as they could, because the hours are grueling, but Dr. Ayers was passionate about her work, day and night. Before I saw Dr. Ayers, the nurse took my history—date of last menstruation and so on. At this point, I hadn't yet missed a period, so the nurse asked why I thought I was pregnant. When I told her about my home pregnancy test, she was dismissive. "Oh, it's too early for you to test positive on that." She looked at me sympathetically, sure that in front of her sat a woman in her mid-thirties so desperate to be pregnant that small delusions might be possible. She came back within a few minutes to tell me that I'd been right after all. Unscientific though this theory is, it has occurred to me that my unusually early awareness that I was pregnant with Jacqueline suggests that her forcefulness was there in her DNA all the way back to her early days as a blastocyte. She has turned out to be a powerful personality, to say the least.

Now that my pregnancy was duly noted in a medical chart, it was official, and that's what I told Jim. By now, he had grown more comfortable with the idea of our having a child, and he was happy. And now that he was happy, I knew he would want to tell everyone. I didn't want him to say anything to anybody, at least until the end of the first trimester, but Jim couldn't keep a secret—at least not *that* secret.

I had another reason for trying to keep it between the two of us, and it was that I wanted my mother and father to be the next to know. They were on vacation in Portugal, and I didn't want to tell them over the phone. I wanted to see the reaction on their faces when I told them. Besides, whenever my mother calls me from Portugal, which she does daily when she's there, it's as if she thinks her voice has to carry across the Atlantic by the sheer force of her lung power. And so she shouts. I didn't think I could manage a full-volume conversation about gestation.

I had some morning sickness, but not anything a few crackers couldn't combat. Before long, I also stopped having the olfactory sensitivity of a basset hound and once again resumed diplomatic relations with raw eggs and broccoli. But while I felt fine, there was a complication early on, predicting what was to come. When I went to Dr. Ayers for my appointment at the end of the second month, my blood-test numbers were awry. She asked that I come back to the medical center in New Brunswick within forty-eight hours to have blood drawn again—Mother's Day, as it turned out. Afterward Jim and I went to mass at a local Roman Catholic church, where the priest blessed all mothers. For the first time, I felt included in their ranks, ready to face the awesome responsibility of raising a child, desperately hoping I would have the opportunity. I also prayed for normal test results, an uneventful pregnancy, and, more than anything, a healthy baby. After the priest blessed the mothers present, Jim turned to me and said, "Happy Mother's Day." It was a special and powerful moment, not only because the father of our child was the first person ever to acknowledge me as a mother but because I realized that he really was delighted we'd be having a baby. The fact that he was now so happy made *me* happy—and suggested that he would be as devoted to our child as he always tried to be to Morag. I couldn't throw my arms around him in church, but I smiled and squeezed his hand tightly. He squeezed back.

For the next day or two, my heart jumped every time the phone rang, but usually it was Jim calling to find out if I'd heard anything. Finally the test results did come in, and they were fine. But Jim remained worried at what we might not yet know and suggested that we should go for genetic testing, amniocentesis, and counseling. I agreed. I would be thirty-five by the time the baby was born, and I knew that after age thirty-five a woman runs a greater risk of pregnancy complications, as well as of having a child with birth defects. Jim accompanied me the day I was having amniocentesis.

Jim and I were both practicing Catholics, but, as I've said, we both also believed that it's up to a woman to decide whether she wants to proceed with her pregnancy. We never talked about termination, because our overall feeling was that we weren't going to end this pregnancy, but if there were a problem in our child, at least we would have time to prepare ourselves. If I'd been told that the child would suffer enormously or die very prematurely . . . well, who knows what we might have considered? But that was one of those what-if questions I prayed we would never have to face.

Once we were in the doctor's office for my amniocentesis, everything went without incident. The same day as the amnio, I also had an ultrasound, and the doctor asked us if we wanted to know what the sex was. We each reacted in character: I hesitated, while Jim, without a moment's pause, said, "Yes, we do want to know."

"Wait," I said, "let me think about it a bit."

"What's there to think about? This way we can plan."

What could I say? I really couldn't fight city hall. "OK," I said, "tell us."

"You're having a girl!" said the doctor. "Congratulations!"

Jim's face lit up. He was beaming with excitement. He kissed me. "Isn't this exciting?" Jim said. "A little girl!" I said, "Yes, it is exciting." But I was a step or two behind him. For whatever reason, I had been convinced that the child I was carrying was a boy. The doctor told me to go home and take it easy, and at least that day I followed those instructions. Later, when the results of the amniocentesis came in, we learned that the fetus was healthy and developing normally, so we relaxed a bit.

After that, despite the fact that I was on the brink of my third trimester, I became even more engaged in the campaign. I attended as many events as possible, both with Jim and on my own. In addition to campaigning for him, I was also asked to, and did, campaign on behalf of other Democratic candidates who were on the slate with Jim. Jim was at the top of the ticket, but the more recognizable its other members were, the more they too could bring in votes.

IT WAS LATE JUNE when we learned that Bret Schundler, the mayor of Jersey City, had won the Republican primary (defeating the party's handpicked candidate) and would therefore be Jim's opponent. He was brash and outspoken, a pit bull of a man with an appetite for personal attack that he seemed unable to muzzle. Jim thought of himself as pretty thick-skinned, so he wasn't worried about Schundler in that regard. Besides, there was every possibility Schundler would shoot himself in the foot before Election Day.

Jim was also happy that he was running against someone further to the right than most New Jerseyans on key issues such as gun control, school vouchers, and a woman's right to choose. True, a Republican, Christie Whitman, had won the last two gubernatorial elections, the last against Jim in 1997, but most residents of the state, when they're not in a state of revolt, have historically been moderate and likely to vote

Democrat. The voters' repudiation of Jim Florio in 1993 had been seen as a statement of indignation by citizens about New Jersey's out-of-control property and sales taxes more than a broader repudiation.

All along, the polls had shown that Jim was ahead of Schundler, though as we moved past Labor Day into the last stretch of the campaign, Jim, who'd acquired the nickname "Robocandidate" in his first bid for governor, wasn't slowing down a bit. Plus, there were several live debates with Schundler to prepare for. Jim was being prepped for them by the wife of a politician who had once run against Jim and knew Schundler's record, as well as how he was likely to handle himself during a debate. And that's where we were when the sun went down at the end of the day on September 10, 2001.

8 · THE FALL

※

WHATEVER SEPTEMBER 11, 2001, became or will become in our national story, it was an astoundingly beautiful day—a day so crisp and clear it allowed you to make peace with the coming fall. Kids were back at school and their parents back at work. I remember it as if it were yesterday. Don't we all? Jim had gone off that morning for a full day of campaigning, and I was still at home. Though I was well along in my pregnancy, I was feeling fine, not yet like the beached whale I was shortly to become.

That morning, I was watching *Good Morning America*—as usual—while I prepared to leave. Suddenly the station broke for a special report: A plane had crashed into the World Trade Center. The reporter's voice was grave. The screen showed smoke billowing out of the tower. I stood there, frozen by the image, aghast at what I imagined to be the carelessness of a private pilot who had somehow made a wrong turn.

I watched for several minutes before shutting off the TV and heading to work. I was unaware that the world had changed, unaware that, driving north to my job in Newark, I was heading closer to what would shortly be known as Ground Zero. I had the radio on and was listening to WCBS Newsradio 880 when a caller reported that he had just seen a plane hit one of the towers. The newscaster thought he was getting an account of the crash that had already happened, but almost immediately he understood that a second plane had struck the towers. And then, for the first time, I heard the phrase "terrorist attack."

Once I arrived at work, I and many of my co-workers gathered in

front of the television in the doctors' lounge, riveted to what was happening onscreen. Nobody could believe it when the South Tower came
down in a monumental swoon, followed by the North Tower twenty-
nine minutes later. Meanwhile I had called Jim on his cell phone—several
times, in fact—but had reached only his voice mail. I knew he hadn't
planned on going into Manhattan, but still . . .

It was unbearable feeling so helpless. I tried Jim again, and again no
answer. My fear was mounting. Maybe he'd gone into New York after all,
for a meeting with a supporter, or maybe he'd gone to a fund-raiser? I
contacted my parents and brothers, and they were OK, thank God, but I
was worried about Jim. As I wondered what to do next, the hospital's
loudspeaker broadcast an announcement: "Code One, Code One." It was
official. We were now in disaster mode. Four or five department directors
hurried past my door to the Command Center, which was just two doors
down from my office. Walkie-talkies in hand, they were preparing for
communications with emergency personnel. Columbus Hospital was
only a dozen miles from the World Trade Center, and we were expecting
a huge influx of victims. But first we waited. The focused quiet of anticipation was palpable as medical personnel readied themselves for the grueling hours they thought awaited them. As time passed, however, the quiet
grew flat and deflated. Not a single ambulance had approached the entrance of our ER. Slowly we began to face the grim realization that just a
few miles away, thousands of people were likely dead.

A little after 11:00 A.M., Jim called me back, safe in South Jersey, where
he'd been at a breakfast meeting. Like many, he had first imagined that a
small plane had accidentally hit one of the towers, and he'd then gone
ahead with his plans for the morning. But once he knew the extent of the
attack, he presumed that there were probably Woodbridge citizens who
wouldn't be coming home, and he went into mayor mode. "I'm headed
back to my office," he told me.

At the hospital, hours passed, and we grew more certain—and devastated—that thousands were dead. There was nothing to be done, but
the helplessness of doing nothing was intolerable, so my assistant and I

decided to buy white ribbons to give out to the staff as we had done during the Gulf War. Incongruous as it seemed, we headed to a party store in a neighboring town. There had been no visible signs of the tragedy at the hospital—there were too many tall buildings in a region that was more or less a valley—but the party store was located in a shopping center on a hill, fifteen miles or so northwest of where the towers had stood. From the top of that hill, before someone driving east would head downhill again, the towers—the whole New York skyline, in fact—had always been visible. Now as we approached the mall, all we could see was a dark cloud of smoke coming from where the towers had been. That smoke claimed the sky and darkened that beautiful day. Seeing it on TV was one thing. This was quite another. It was sobering and unimaginable.

Late in the afternoon, I returned home and waited for Jim. He was home at about dinnertime that day, unusually early for him.

He'd been at the mayor's office as well as at his campaign headquarters, where he too could see the smoke-filled Manhattan skyline. "We're lucky to be home safe and know that our families are all safe and sound," he said. He told me he'd decided to suspend his campaign for a few days.

"That's the right thing to do," I said.

Meanwhile the facts of death were everywhere. Everyone knew, or knew of, someone who had died. Each day when I came into my office, I pulled out faxes with photographs and descriptions of people who were missing. These were their families' desperate attempts to find their loved ones alive—hoping against hope that they were lying in a hospital bed rather than incinerated under tons of rubble.

All told, 2,973 people had died that day.

And 674 of them were from New Jersey.

I ATTENDED ONE OF the first funerals of a 9/11 victim at the Cathedral Basilica of the Sacred Heart in Newark. His name was Tony Rocha, and he was a friend of Celia's, my matron of honor. Tony was thirty-four, the father of two small children, one an infant. He had also been a bond trader at Cantor Fitzgerald, a job to which he had commuted a mere two dozen miles from his home in East Hanover. Tony's body was one of the first to be recovered, and so his was one of the first funerals. But at the cathedral, as the throngs of mourners entered, news vans and crews swirled around the family, not always at a respectful distance. I wondered how the family tolerated it. I was appalled at the disruptive swarm during such a painful and private moment and relieved that the crews were not permitted to enter the cathedral. And yet I also realized that it was a very public moment, as if the whole country were part of the congregation. The media had a responsibility to be there, to help ensure that this was a shared national moment, that those who died did not die in obscurity.

As the weeks passed, I thought about what might await Jim if he were to become governor. I had never thought political leadership was something to be assumed casually, but 9/11 made me think gravely about the position Jim was so avidly pursuing. We were all more vulnerable now, and therefore we would need real leaders, people of vision and stature. I felt that Jim was capable of such leadership, but as his wife, and the mother of the child we would soon have, I was fearful of what the costs of that leadership might mean for our family.

During this period, the phrase "homeland security" entered the public parlance, and the structure of government—federal, state, and local—would soon be altered to accommodate this new and crucial priority. Becoming the governor of a state had to be about more than personal ambition, more than just the next step after being the mayor of Woodbridge.

Jim went to visit Ground Zero a few days after the attack, somehow getting there and back without the press knowing. At that point, the fires were still burning, and the smoke still hung acrid in the air. There was not a single square inch untouched by the devastation. There were photographs of missing loved ones, swarms of weary firefighters, piles of bent and twisted girders. Jim came home that day sobered and sooty.

"It was like nothing I've ever seen before, not even in the movies," he said.

When I asked him to tell me more, he just shook his head.

"I don't even want to talk about it. But the smell was unbearable," he said. "You can't imagine the smell."

I *could* imagine the smell; but I didn't even really need to. He'd brought it all the way back with him on the blackened soles of his boots.

SINCE I'D COME TO New Jersey some thirty years earlier, I'd listened to joke after joke about New Jerseyites being "the bridge-and-tunnel crowd." But in this not-so-brave new world that was just coming into being, the many millions of us who used our bridges and tunnels (not to mention ports, railroad lines, and airports) were now terribly vulnerable. Safety could no longer be assumed.

The hijackers who left that morning from Newark Airport were a mere four of the 31 million people who came through the airport that year. New Jersey would need a governor whose first priority would have to be to take their safety seriously. If Jim won the election and became governor of New Jersey, it would fall to him to make sure the people of the state remained safe, by the standards he set and by the competence of the people he appointed.

How unconscionable, then, that once he was elected, he would violate that public trust by appointing his lover, Golan Cipel, to a homeland security position for which he was completely unqualified.

9 · ELECTION EVE

~·~

AFTER A FEW DAYS of no campaigning, we returned to our regular schedule, or tried to. But nothing really felt regular anymore. I was in my sixth month of pregnancy by then, and I thought at least a dozen times a day about the safety of my unborn child. Up until then, I had considered myself her fortress, but after September 11 I felt no more substantial than a pup tent. I was frightened whenever I was in a tunnel or on a bridge. I tensed whenever I heard a descending plane—how could I possibly keep this child safe? She would be coming into a far more dangerous world than the one I'd grown up in, a far more dangerous world than it had been only last week.

As a candidate for governor, Jim was now acutely aware of the added responsibility he'd have for keeping the citizens safe, a view undoubtedly intensified by the fact that soon one of those citizens would be his own child.

With that newer, darker mind-set, we resumed campaigning. In addition to the fund-raising and other functions, the debate preparation continued. I had attended all the debates thus far between Schundler and Jim and thought that Jim did very well. He expressed his views clearly and with compassion, and he held his ground when threatened. The hard work was paying off. Jim had clearly come a long way.

And then it was time for our first anniversary. There was much to celebrate. Jim and I would soon become parents, and everything we had worked so hard for was on the horizon. All the signs suggested that Jim would be New Jersey's next governor. Not only was he doing well in the polls, but many people were already calling him "Governor." During that time my sense of Jim as a principled and compassionate human being had grown. He was still mayor of Woodbridge, and though Woodbridge had not been under siege in the same way New York City was, it too had lost some of its citizens in 9/11. As mayor, Jim had a role as leader and comforter. I admired him for that. I trusted him.

It was about a week after our anniversary that I happened to visit Drumthwacket, the governor's mansion in Princeton. Jim and I were attending a fund-raiser for D.A.R.E. (Drug Abuse Resistance Education), a school program urging kids to resist drugs and violence. The dinner, attended by hundreds, was held outside under a huge tent on the thirteen-acre estate. Before we left, a staffer gave Jim and me a tour of the public rooms on the first floor of what would within months become our home. A firsthand look at the private residence—eighteen rooms on the second and third floors—would have to wait.

My first impression was that it was a magnificent structure. From the outside, it was beautiful—white siding, an elegant six-columned portico in the front. The dining room and the library impressed me too. But when I had the chance to look further, I was dismayed. The first floor had had some ceremonial uses during Christie Whitman's governorship, beginning in 1993, but Whitman had never lived at Drumthwacket, and with no governor in residence all the rooms on the first floor needed attention—not only the dining room and the library but the music room, the parlor, the governor's study, the sunroom, and all the private offstage offices and kitchen. In the public rooms, the rugs were frayed, the paint looked dingy and chipped, the window treatments were old and faded, and the furniture needed to be either replaced or reupholstered. It looked more like a down-at-the-heels museum than a mansion meant to signify New Jersey's wealth and prominence. As for the private residence on the upper floors, God only knew what condition that might be in.

During our visit, the staffer gave us a brief history of the house and told us that there was an organization—the Drumthwacket Foundation—charged with its maintenance. Before this day, I had not given any thought to living there. Unlike many other New Jerseyans, however, I had actually heard of Drumthwacket. During Christie Whitman's first term as governor—long before I knew Jim—I'd received a solicitation for a donation to the newly formed foundation. I made a twenty-five-dollar donation, simply because of my interest in politics, never imagining I would even visit, let alone live there. (Had I known that it would one day be my home, I might have been more generous!) If this were to be our residence and if I were to have any say in its upkeep or maintenance, I knew I would have to make many changes.

"So what did you think of the place?" Jim asked as we drove off.

"Well," I said, "it's an imposing structure, but the inside needs some sprucing up."

"Well, it sure beats 323," the address of our town-house complex on Gill Lane where Jim had lived for many years. "Here we certainly won't hear the neighbors."

I laughed. "And they won't be able to look in the windows the way they do now."

"Can't you just see our little munchkin running around here?"

"Yes." I smiled. I could.

JIM'S FINAL DEBATE WITH Bret Schundler, which would be telecast live, was scheduled for Sunday, October 28, at the NBC Studios at Rockefeller Center, with Gabe Pressman moderating. Jim and I drove in together—taking time out to pull over to the side of the road, thanks to my daily siege of morning sickness. Then Jim, Schundler, I, and several other people stood around exchanging pleasantries. During airtime, I sat on the side and watched. When Pressman asked both Jim and Schundler about their views on the issues, the sparks flew. Schundler, who was anti-choice, took a shot at Jim for his pro-choice stance. He pointed to where I was sitting, beyond the range of the cameras, and said, "His wife is pregnant right now. His baby is kicking. He can feel it. That is a human being."

Jim was so shocked at what he considered to be an unprovoked personal attack that all he could say was, "Please . . . !"

I was furious. I clamped my hand over my mouth to keep myself from blurting out something that would make headlines the following day. Instead I just clenched my teeth and shook my head. I wanted to rush onto the set and slap Schundler. Too bad I couldn't have put my morning sickness to better use. And too bad my kicking baby couldn't have kicked him.

During the same interview, a second interviewer, Larry Mendte from WCAU-TV in Philadelphia, knowing that both Jim and Schundler had daughters, asked whether they would be trick-or-treating. To Mendte, this was an inconsequential question, a pleasantry. But immediately Schundler lunged for the jugular. "Do they celebrate Halloween in Canada?" he asked acidly, meaning to draw attention to Jim's divorce. "My nine-year-old will be out for Halloween in Jersey City." I grew even angrier. This was a painful topic for Jim. How could Schundler be so vicious? There was no principle or policy at stake—merely an ad hominem attack. It was Schundler's way of saying, "You're divorced. And you never see your child." Jim was again stunned—I could see it in his eyes—but he recovered, feigning equanimity in the way that seasoned politicians have to if they're to survive. When Schundler said good-bye to us at the end of the taping, I just gave him a dirty look. Jim bade him a polite, even cordial, farewell.

"How could you even be civil to that man?" I said to Jim as we headed to the car, where the driver awaited us.

He was angry and disgusted, especially at the trick-or-treat remark. "It was a pointless personal attack," he said. "Absolutely uncalled for." But then he shrugged. "That's politics." Though in almost any circumstance, I was less likely than Jim to speak my mind, temperamentally he was less fiery than I was. I always thought that he was able to mask his feelings better than I could, though I didn't know then how much practice he'd had.

I had always wanted Jim to win, and to win big, but now, after this personal experience with Schundler, I badly wanted Schundler to lose. And in just a few more days, he would—at least if I had anything to do with it.

That was the twenty-eighth, a Sunday. During the week, I was up at seven, at work from nine to five, and out campaigning—now truly with a vengeance—until ten, eleven, midnight, whenever. On Friday, November 2, I arrived home after Jim, probably around midnight. Jim was already asleep. I was keyed up from the day and about what awaited us tomorrow—the last big rally before the election, to be held at a hotel in New Brunswick. Hundreds were expected, and Jim wanted me to give the speech introducing him. I'd been practicing my speech over the last few days, and a little after midnight I went through it one last time while looking at myself in my bathroom mirror before collapsing into bed next to Jim.

In the morning, I got up, excited and ready for the day. Then I noticed that I was spotting. Maybe I'd strained myself somehow? I felt terrific. Bulky, yes, and therefore a little tired, but not more tired than usual. Jim was showering, so I went downstairs into the kitchen to make toast and coffee—decaffeinated, because of my pregnancy. Jim came down and asked me for a glass of juice. That's all he was having, because he was rushing out to his first event. We would meet up later at the New Brunswick Hyatt for the rally.

"I'll see you later," I told him, "but first I have to call Dr. Ayers. I think maybe there's a little problem."

"A problem? What's the matter?" he asked, stopping in his tracks.

"I'm spotting. I don't know what it means."

"Do you want me to go to the doctor with you?" he asked, obviously concerned.

"No," I said. "I'll call her and see what she says. I might not even have to see her." Wishful thinking. I wanted to minimize what was going on, although on some level I knew better. Jim did too, but he knew me well enough to realize that if he expressed concern or looked worried, it would alarm me further.

"But you will call her?"

"Yes, I promise."

"So I have your word?"

"Yes," I insisted, with just a hint of exasperation. Besides, he knew by now from the medical concerns earlier in my pregnancy that whenever something came up, I really wanted to take care of it myself. That's just the way I was. I really didn't want anyone, not even Jim, with me. If I was concerned about something, I might be willing to accept help, sometimes even graciously. But if deep down I was really scared? Forget it. I was going to whistle a happy tune and insist on being on my own. Besides, this weekend there was so much for Jim to be doing.

"Call me after you talk to the doctor and tell me what she says."

"OK," I said.

He kissed me and headed for the door. "Don't forget to call me."

"OK, OK, I won't." But the truth is, I stalled a few minutes longer before calling the doctor. I knew that she would want to see me, but I didn't want to miss the rally. I was energized and ready to campaign almost nonstop until Election Day. But my sense of reality was stalking me, dogging my heels. I needed to do what was best for my baby. I paged the doctor.

In minutes, my phone rang.

"I'm spotting," I told her.

"I'll head to the hospital now," Dr. Ayers said without a moment's hesitation, "and I'll meet you there in a half hour." It was about 9:00 A.M. now.

"I'm introducing Jim at a rally at noon," I said. "Can't this wait till after that? Say, three P.M.?"

"You're unbelievable! You're not going to any rally," she said firmly, "and you're meeting me in half an hour."

"I haven't even showered yet," I said. "I can be there in an hour."

"I'll see you in an hour," she said. "And my office is closed today, so meet me in Labor and Delivery."

Labor and Delivery? Me, in labor? Couldn't be! Nevertheless, I decided against driving myself since I now had the clear feeling that, warranted or not, I was going to be hospitalized at least overnight. I didn't want to call my parents to let them know what was happening, because I knew that my mother would panic. She'd be calling me every five minutes, saying, "Did you go yet? Did you go yet? Are you at the hospital yet?" My father delegated worrying to my mother. Or, if he didn't, he was at least less vocal, hoping to exert a calming effect on my mother, to the extent that that was possible.

Though Paul and his wife, Elvie, lived just up the street, I didn't want to call them, because I knew they would tell my mother. Jim was at an event, and I wanted him to be able to make contact with as many people as possible, so I wasn't going to call him either. I wound up calling my friend Freddie Da Silva, who would later be director of protocol in Jim's administration, to ask if she would drive me to the hospital.

"I'll be there in half an hour," she said.

I went to shower and get dressed, knowing I was doing the right thing, knowing that my baby's health trumped everything else, but all the same I was really upset. There was a momentum and an excitement that had been building and building over the last week or two, as the election approached with all the signs so positive. To leave now was like suddenly going cold turkey.

When we arrived at the nurses' station of the Labor and Delivery area, Dr. Ayers was already there.

"Come with me," she said, walking me to a vacant room.

For the first time, I felt how nervous I was.

"Here," said the doctor, handing me the regulation blue-print hospital gown after the nurse had left. "I need you to put this on. Then I'll be back to help you into the bed."

When she returned, she drew the curtain around us and lowered the bed as far down as it could go. I sat down on it and started to swing my legs up.

"Wait, wait, wait!" she protested. "No sudden movements. Let me help you get your legs up here." She lifted my legs gingerly onto the mattress.

"OK. Slooowly, move yourself back."

I watched her face as she examined me, trying to gauge the seriousness of my condition from her expression. She asked if I'd been feeling contractions, and I told her, truthfully and with a slight bit of relief, that I hadn't. "Not a one," I said.

"Well, I have some news for you," she said. "You're in labor."

I was stunned. I was in the twenty-ninth week of my pregnancy, and I knew that my child was nowhere near ready to be born. It was November 3 and I wasn't due until January 10.

"Does this mean I'll be here for a while?"

"You're more than a centimeter dilated, and the baby's head is putting pressure on your cervix. If we can't stop these contractions, you're at risk of having this baby today. So you're not going anywhere. I think it's time for you to call your husband and tell him what's going on."

Contractions? Really, I *hadn't* felt any. Maybe I didn't know what a contraction was? I lay there blankly as the nurse, now in the room again, inserted a needle in the back of my hand and set up the IV drip.

"Let's hope your little girl understands that she doesn't have to make an appearance anytime soon," said my doctor. "She's still not more than a pound and a half. Meanwhile these steroids will help her lungs develop."

I was in a state of shock, terrified that our child would not survive this crisis.

"You need to call your husband," the doctor repeated, handing me the receiver. "What's the number? I'll dial it for you."

I held the receiver to my ear as Dr. Ayers punched in Jim's number. It was 11:30 A.M., and I knew that right now he would probably be arriving at the rally. At the first ring, however, he picked up, and I gave him the news.

"In labor? You're being admitted?" He was alarmed. He hadn't expected this. Well, neither had I.

"You OK? Just hang in there. I'm telling the driver to turn around this second, and I'll be there right away."

While I waited for him, my mind raced with every imaginable worry. Would our child live? We didn't have a bassinet. Would her organs be compromised? I didn't even know how to do breathing during labor. I hadn't had my Lamaze classes yet. The baby's room wasn't ready. Would the steroids work? I'd better make sure to breathe calmly, right this very minute. If I cried, would that trigger full-blown labor? If Jim lost the election, I would feel guilty. It would be my fault. Who would she look like? If she was born now, would she have medical complications for the rest of her life? All these thoughts and more were racing through my mind.

As soon as Jim arrived in my hospital room, our doctor filled him in.

"Yes, chances are good your child will survive," she said, "though I can't make any promises, and no, your wife's life is not in any danger." No, she couldn't say there would be no complications. No, she couldn't say exactly what the complications would be if they did occur, aside from the lungs probably being too undeveloped for our child to breathe on her own.

Meanwhile, outside the hospital, a caravan of reporters was milling around. They'd been following Jim from his previous event to the rally and stayed on his tail all the way to the hospital. Now they knew that something was happening, although they hadn't been given any details and weren't being allowed into the hospital. But by the evening, throughout the tristate area of New Jersey, New York, and Pennsylvania, the newscasts were reporting that Jim had suspended his campaign to be by my side at the hospital. Just before Jim arrived, I had called my mother to tell her what was going on. She did panic, though I can't say she didn't have her reasons, and, as I expected, she rushed to the hospital. She would have pitched a tent in my room, but once she saw that I was comfortable and being attended to, she was willing to go back home.

My sense of being comfortable was really only skin deep. Actually, I was in a state of terror, deeply concerned about the well-being of our child. For more than a dozen hours, I'd been on meds that were supposed to stop my labor, but they weren't working. My labor was progressing. And if the contractions caused my water to break, then the baby would have to be delivered. No other choice was possible. The only prudent course was to prepare for my delivery, a delivery Dr. Ayers and my medical team believed would take place within hours. "We haven't been able to halt the labor as yet," Dr. Ayers explained to Jim and me. "You need to be in a place equipped with the staff and technology to deal with a premature birth."

Late that night, perhaps at 1:00 or 2:00 A.M., I was transported by ambulance to St. Peter's University Hospital, less than a mile away, with Jim riding along in the ambulance with me. St. Peter's had a neonatal intensive care unit (NICU) and, at the time, the medical center I'd been admitted to did not.

In the meantime, I had now become conscious of feeling what must have been contractions, though they felt less like pain than like pressure—as if my whole abdomen were a fist, clenching every few minutes and then unclenching again. But this was still nothing like what I understood labor contractions to be. As the ambulance drove between one hospital and another, I gripped Jim's hand, registering every bump in the road as if it were a ten on the Richter scale, each one enough to explode me into labor. I was petrified.

Once at St. Peter's, I was admitted to Labor and Delivery. I spent the entire night awake. Every few minutes, someone was coming into the room. A doctor, a nurse. An aide. Jim stayed with me all night, sitting on the chair beside my bed. He was exhausted from the campaign and slipped in and out of sleep. His jacket was flung over the back of his chair; the top buttons of his shirt were unbuttoned; his belt, which he'd taken off to give himself more breathing room, was at his feet; and his feet were resting on his shoes.

My vision was blurred from the medications, but still I could see how sapped he was. I was too anxious to get any sleep myself. Besides, with all the traffic continuing to stream in and out, I couldn't really settle down. Instead, throughout the night, I would ask each of them what was happening to me. Was I still in labor? Had the labor stopped? Was the baby all right? Would she stay in there where she belonged?

"We're doing everything we can," said my doctor. She didn't go home that night at all. Just before dawn, she stopped in yet again. "How am I doing?" I asked, probably for the twentieth time.

This time, she smiled. "I've been monitoring your contractions from the nurses' station, and I think we're finally making some progress here. The meds have slowed your labor down. With any luck, we'll be able to stop it. At least, it's looking that way."

Sometime during the night, Jim's press secretary had prepared a statement for the media, and in the morning the state of my unpredictable uterus and the child I was carrying were fodder for all the local morning news programs. Had this happened to me six months earlier, I would have told only my parents and maybe half a dozen very close friends. Jim wasn't even governor yet, but the most private details of my life and body were now being broadcast to everyone in the state of New Jersey and beyond.

Throughout the morning, the hospital handled a flurry of media inquiries. Reporters were camped outside the hospital, and nurses told us they were trying to get through by phone. No one did. My vision was so blurred that I couldn't even watch television. My second day at St. Peter's was Monday, November 5, the day before the election, but also my thirty-fifth birthday. The hospital staff made me a beautiful chocolate cake. It was a very special touch. Jim and my parents, as well as the staff, helped me celebrate the day. In effect, he'd ended his campaign on

Saturday, the moment he'd headed for the hospital rather than the rally. Except for going home to shower and change his clothing, he'd stayed with me since then.

By now, I had accepted that I was not going to be standing by Jim's side when he won the election (neither I nor anyone else had any doubt that he would win), but at least I wanted to be able to vote for him. Happily, the campaign staff arranged for me to get an absentee ballot so I could do just that.

10 · ELECTION DAY

A LANDSLIDE! JIM HAD won by a landslide! This was the first moment of the rest of our lives, and I was ecstatic. And yet while I was grateful to be in a safe place, relieved to be in the care of the tribe of doctors and nurses who were getting my baby and me through this crisis, I was saddened to be flat on my back in a hospital bed. With all my heart, I wanted to be standing on my own two feet, in a hotel ballroom next to Jim, as confetti and balloons rained down on us. But it wasn't to be. And so, for the second time, I wasn't by Jim's side as the election results were called.

Chalk it up to pregnancy, stress, relief, and joy, but soon I was unable to control my emotions at all. I burst into tears. In moments, my friend Mona, who was keeping me company, was crying along with me. She turned to me, clutching her damp tissue: "Congratulations, First Lady!" I was glued to the television as Jim gave his victory speech from the ballroom podium of the Hilton in New Brunswick. My vision was blurred, but these were such familiar faces that I could still tell who was who. Up there on the stage with Jim were my mom and dad; Ronnie and Jack; Jim's sisters, Sharon and Caroline; Caroline's husband, Mark; and Jim's Aunt Kathleen and Uncle Herb.

I was thrilled that my parents were onstage with him to celebrate the culmination of many years of hard work and perseverance. My mother had wanted to stay with me in the hospital so I wouldn't be alone, but I really wanted her to enjoy Jim's victory party. She insisted that she stay. I insisted that she not. I was happy that I had won that battle and very happy to see her enjoying the limelight.

Jim thanked everyone—and me especially. "Dina, I love you," he said, his voice trembling, blowing a kiss into the television camera. Jim thanked me for my support, for my love, and for working so hard along with him on the campaign. That launched a new flow of tears. I knew I was doing the right thing being in the hospital, but I really wanted to be on that stage.

Mona stayed with me for the next hour or two as we watched additional news coverage. Jim had coattails, it turned out, and his victory was credited with helping elect other Democrats on the ticket. It was the first time in at least a dozen years that the Democrats had controlled the governor's office and the legislature.

"I'll just stick around until Jim comes in," Mona said. "I don't want to leave you alone."

I didn't protest. After midnight, Jim swept into the room, the sudden energy he brought with him palpable. He leaned down to kiss me and gave me as much of a hug as he could without dislodging or getting tangled in either my IV or my fetal monitor.

"You did it!" I exclaimed.

"*We* did it," he corrected. Then I dissolved again in tears. I knew it was true. We had done it as a team.

"Why are you crying?" he said. He understood, but he was hoping to ease me into a calmer frame of mind.

"How was it?" I asked.

"Great, but I wish you'd been there."

"Well, that makes two of us. Or three."

"Dina's had quite a day," said my friend, congratulating him—calling him "Governor"—and saying good-bye to me.

As she left, I noticed that she had to make her way past two rather large men in suits who were standing in the doorway.

"Who are they?" I asked, though I thought I already knew.

"State troopers." They'd been at the hotel all day in anticipation of

Jim's victory, and they took on their new assignment as his bodyguards at the moment he finished his victory speech. The troopers were members of the Executive Protection Unit (EPU) and by law were assigned not only to the governor but to his immediate family, including me, as well as to each member of the cabinet. Jim and I talked for a while—he was especially pleased by how happy his father was—and then I told him it was time to call it a night. He was exhausted, and so was I.

"I'll be back early tomorrow morning," he said. "I have to start working on a transition team, and I'm going to have a couple of staffers meet me here."

Even from my hospital bed, I could feel Jim's ascension to power. The next morning, I received dozens of floral arrangements, and the hospital staff set aside a room adjacent to mine to house them. The staff also had another cake for me, this time celebrating Jim's victory. It was shaped like the state of New Jersey, and it said, "Congratulations to New Jersey's First Lady." Someone cut me a slice of Essex County, where I'd grown up and worked. I enjoyed it down to the last crumb.

In addition to the celebrity treatment, there was now heightened security. The moment Schundler conceded the election and Jim claimed victory, the hospital posted one of its own security guards outside my door. From that moment on, my room was guarded twenty-four hours a day.

When Jim arrived at the hospital the next morning, we found that they had made not one but two adjoining rooms available. At least, I was told they were adjoining. I wasn't allowed up out of bed to see for myself. One was the room for the flowers. The nurses brought me each of the cards, and if they thought the floral arrangement was particularly spectacular, they would carry it to the doorway for a three-second appearance before whisking it into what we now referred to as "the flower room." There were so many that I encouraged doctors and nurses to take what they wanted for themselves and to disperse the rest among the other patients.

As for the third room, Jim held his meetings there, while the troopers hung out in the hallway. When he was with me, the troopers hung out in the meeting room. It was hard for me to get used to Jim's perpetual retinue of troopers.

THE DAY AFTER THE election, I was taken on a tour (in a wheelchair, since I wasn't allowed to walk) of the NICU. If my daughter arrived too early, this is where she would be. The NICU was one large room with several bassinets and incubators, many of them filled with the tiniest babies I'd ever seen. Some were no larger than an eggplant. Others were even smaller than that. It broke my heart to see these helpless babies with tubes and wires coming out of their mouths, noses, and every other bodily opening. One little boy, now three months old, had battled his way, ounce by ounce, from less than a pound to three and a half pounds. The nurses called him "Our Little Fighter." The stronger infants cried, while the others lay there silent and almost motionless.

Just as heartbreaking were the fear and anxiety on the faces of the parents and grandparents as they sat by, watching their tiny kin, talking to them through the incubator holes, because for the most part they couldn't hold them. The NICU staff was dedicated, taking care of the babies as if they were their own, often getting their own hearts broken with setbacks or worse. I was terrified that Jim and I might soon be among the parents watching a child lying in an incubator amid a tangle of tubes and needles, but it encouraged me to know that the hospital had both the equipment and the remarkably compassionate humans ready to care for her.

Once I'd spent a few days in Labor and Delivery, my condition stabilized, and I was moved to another section at the hospital, again commandeering three rooms—one for me, one for flowers, and one for the troopers or Jim's meetings. The security guard was still stationed outside my door, and I was still confined to bed.

After a couple of days, I begged the doctor to let me go home, and—to my joy—she agreed, though only if I agreed to a set of conditions: I would have to learn how to read the strips recording my contractions and how to inject myself with steroids, and I would have to agree not only to having a visiting nurse but to having a nurse monitor my contractions independently from a remote location, Big Sister–fashion. Being at home would make it easier for Jim and my family to spend time with me, although I was to be on bed rest 24/7. I admit that I harbored fantasies of jailbreak—visiting Drumthwacket was high on my list—but I never even got to enact a single act of insurrection, because my home stay was short-lived. I began having contractions, perhaps because I made one or two trips down the stairs to the kitchen. By the second week of November, after being sprung for a mere twenty-one hours, I was back in the hospital, the doctor turning a deaf ear to my pleas, my bargaining, and my tears. And here I would stay for the next five weeks.

The doctors and nurses tried to make me as comfortable as possible; nevertheless I became more restless with each passing day. The hospital staff had installed cable television and Internet service, had provided a laptop for my use, and had given me a room large enough to accommodate my visitors. They even cooked a full Thanksgiving meal for me and Jim, setting up a table with a real tablecloth, real dishes, and a beautiful centerpiece with real flowers. (Well, I guess there was no shortage of real flowers!) It was a turkey dinner with all the trimmings, served up by someone from the hospital's dietary department. There was so much food that we could have fed our entire family and then some.

Because it was a special occasion, Dr. Ayers gave me permission to get out of bed for the first time, and Jim and I sat together at the table and had Thanksgiving dinner. After that, however, it was back to bed, and it was from there that I hosted the rest of our visitors—my parents, Jim's parents, his sister Sharon, and his sister Caroline and her family. I wished that Jim and I could have had our traditional Thanksgiving with Caroline in Delaware, and I missed that, but I was grateful that we could improvise as satisfyingly as we did.

DURING THIS FIVE-WEEK period, Jim visited me most days. Some days he visited me twice. And some days he didn't visit me at all. It was during this time that Jim is said to have begun his adulterous affair with Golan Cipel. I knew Golan. Not well, but I knew him. And here's what I knew: Golan was an attractive Israeli in his early thirties, with a pleasant, boyish face and thick, dark hair. Jim had met him in Israel in March 2000, just several weeks after he and I got engaged. The two men had hit it off, and Jim had invited Golan to come and work on his campaign. Taking Jim at his word, Golan arrived in the United States in April 2001 to work, not for Jim but for a public relations firm associated with Charles Kushner, the wealthy real estate magnate who had contributed well over a million dollars to Jim's campaigns. In fact, Kushner was Golan's sponsor for a work visa. By September 2001, Golan had begun to work directly for Jim's campaign as his liaison to the Jewish community. It seemed odd to many that Jim had picked an Israeli with no connection to New Jersey or to New Jersey's Jewish community for this position, but Golan did have a definite connection to Charles Kushner, who was very active in the New Jersey Jewish community and, given his donations to Jim, very influential in Jim's campaign choices. In politics everywhere, he who pays the piper calls the tune, so I just always assumed that Jim was accommodating Kushner.

A report published in the *Bergen Record* places Golan at the Democratic headquarters at Woodbridge on 9/11. "He was one of many campaign officials who gathered at Democratic Party offices on the top floor of a Woodbridge skyscraper that had a clear view of the World Trade Center towers," wrote a reporter in an article published after Jim announced his decision to resign. "With arms crossed and his brow furrowed, Cipel paced the floor propounding on the effect the terror attacks would have on U.S.-Mideast relations." If that report is accurate, Jim probably crossed paths with Golan that day, since Jim likely stopped at the Woodbridge headquarters on his way home.

I didn't find anything particularly unusual in Jim's relationship with Golan that fall. Jim often had three or four young men on his staff who were in the throes of "finding themselves," and he had a solicitous attitude toward them. The other Lost Boys—there were six or seven of them—were sort of mellow or laid back. One of them, for instance, was Teddy Pedersen, Jim's driver, who had stayed behind that Valentine's Day weekend. He was a slim and boyish college student, maybe five-seven, fair, with a baby face. He was in his early twenties, going to Rutgers part-time. Another, quiet but slightly more mature, was Jason Kirin, also in his early twenties, and newly graduated from a local college, Fairleigh Dickinson. He was Jim's traveling assistant, which meant that he traveled with Jim Monday to Friday, making his phone calls and appointments, keeping track of his schedule, and taking notes at meetings. Teddy, Jason, and the others were all willing to fade into near invisibility, never overshadowing Jim or making demands of their own on him.

And then there was Golan.

He was older than the others, and also intense and demanding. During that time, I was at a few of the Jewish community-related events he was involved in at Jim's behest—fund-raisers, usually. Regardless of what Jim was in the middle of, if Golan had something he wanted Jim to do, it was always something he wanted done *now*. It might be that Golan wanted Jim to be photographed with a potential donor or that he wanted to schedule an appointment between Jim and a guest, but whatever it was, in Golan's mind it had to take priority over anything else Jim might be doing. Jim didn't seem to mind Golan's insistent self-importance, nor did he mind, as I did, when staffers, Golan included, simply dropped in during the rare hours Jim and I were home alone. Golan came by a few times that fall. He was courteous enough to me, but he obviously had something urgent to discuss on those occasions, something he'd wanted to lobby Jim about.

But now, looking back, I wonder at the timing of Jim's affair with Golan. I wonder at its coming so soon after his election, his marriage to me, and so close to the birth of our daughter. Did family life, or marriage to me, a woman, fill Jim with such despair and such a sense of incarceration that it catapulted him into a relationship with Golan? Was it that the closer he came to realizing his dream, the more he had to punish himself, good Catholic boy that he was, by threatening to destroy what he must have guiltily felt he didn't deserve? Was it arro-gance—not simple arrogance but a rather complicated arrogance—whereby Jim felt he could have whatever he wanted, whenever he wanted? Or maybe some part of him was objecting to the loneliness he felt, finding it too high a price for an achievement that hadn't left him feeling as gratified as he expected to feel.

JUSTIFIED OR NOT, JIM had had coattails. With his election, the Democrats had again become the majority in the state assembly, and in the state senate at least there were an equal number of Democrats and Republicans. Though Jim had billed himself as a consensus builder, almost immediately he found himself embroiled in an intraparty dispute over who would be the new assembly Speaker. He had backed a particu-lar candidate and as a result had to spend a great deal of time defending his choice and persuading others to support it. I witnessed many scream-ing matches early on and assumed that there would be more to come.

Meantime, as November moved glacially toward December, I tried to keep busy while baby-waiting. Since my doctor had refused my numerous requests to leave the hospital for only a few hours to visit Drumthwacket, I requested that the residence manager there come to the hospital to meet with me. She showed me a layout of the house and told me that there was really no bedroom that could serve as the nursery. Our only two options were to take either a dressing room or an exercise room and turn it into a nursery. Either option would necessitate significant renovation. With me stuck in the hospital, it was all going to have to wait.

There was only so much television I could watch, so much reading I could do, and so much surfing on the Internet I could stand. My family and a few friends visited me almost daily, and my mother and Ronnie never skipped a day, even though I'd tell them they didn't really need to stay. They thought that I was asking them to leave because I didn't want them inconvenienced, but the truth was that I really wanted to be alone. The only person I wanted to see daily was Jim, but right after Thanksgiving, during a visit, he informed me he was going to Las Vegas to attend a labor convention.

"Las Vegas? Why do you have to go?"

"The unions were crucial to my victory. I have to show my appreciation."

"I'm sure they'd understand if you didn't go. Especially now! They know I've been hospitalized and that we're expecting a child any day!"

"It'll be fine," he said. "I'll be back before the baby is born."

"What will happen if I go into labor tomorrow? It's not like you're across the river in New York. You'll be five hours away by plane."

"If you go into labor, I'll get on the first available flight," he said.

I couldn't change his mind. It was absurd that he was going away at such a critical time, with a baby due any moment. How could he have taken his public responsibilities so seriously and not have invested equally in his family responsibilities? How could he be leaving at a time like this?

The answer was Golan. I didn't know it at the time, but Golan Cipel would be going to Las Vegas with Jim, or so the papers eventually reported. Lust, it seemed, trumped everything else.

11 · WELCOME TO THE WORLD, BABY GIRL

❧

SOMETIME ON THE EVENING of December 6, as I lay in my hospital bed, my abdomen suddenly tightened, and then it slowly relaxed. A few minutes later, it happened again. I was in labor. I felt it, and the fetal monitor, my constant companion, confirmed it.

The fact that I was in labor wasn't a shock, despite my due date still being five weeks off. The doctors had told me that once I had reached the thirty-fifth week I would be home free, and that they might be willing to discontinue the medications that had halted my labor. I couldn't stand much more time flat on my back, or in bed, or in the hospital. So as soon as Jim returned from Las Vegas, I lobbied Dr. Ayers to get me off the meds. I wanted to have my baby *now*, I told her. After some deliberating, she and the rest of the team agreed that I could stop the meds. "But be patient," she cautioned me. "It could take a day or so for labor to begin."

Just hours later, though, I had what I was sure was a real contraction. Jim was in the room at the time.

"I think I'm in labor," I told him.

He practically bolted out of his chair in his eagerness to tell the nurse. It wasn't just new-father jitters. Both of us knew there might be another problem ahead: The baby had her umbilical cord wrapped around her neck. My medical team didn't think this was necessarily worrisome, since about 30 percent of babies are born with the cords wrapped around their necks, and in most cases the cords can easily be slipped over the baby's head at birth with no problem. But in some cases, if the cord is squeezed or stretched, blood flow is reduced, and that can cause a slowing down of the fetal heart rate, with brain damage as a result. There was no way of knowing in advance whether the cord would be a problem or not. The uncertainty itself was yet another worry, and I wanted to have it resolved.

Jim was now keyed up, but the staff doctor told him that it might be many hours or even the next day before I was ready to deliver. I told him to go home because I knew he was exhausted. But it wasn't just altruism. I was also reacting in character. Now that the going had gotten a little bit tougher, I wanted to be on my own.

Close to midnight, the staff doctor came back. "Well," he said, "we're not there yet, but we're getting there. Time to transfer you to Labor and Delivery."

At 2:00 A.M., the staff called my doctor, who arrived within the hour. I asked her if it was time to call Jim.

"Yes, I think that's a good idea," she said. "I think we'll have a baby soon."

I called Jim and told him to come to the hospital right away.

Meanwhile Dr. Ayers was nervously eyeing the data from the fetal monitor about the baby's heart rate. The heart rate *had* dropped down a couple of times, and she was concerned, but so far each time the rate had climbed back up to normal again. "We're just going to watch it for now," she said.

When Jim came in, I told him I was nervous and scared.

"It's going to be fine," he said. "Soon we'll have a beautiful little girl."

The doctor wasn't up for uninformed optimism. "If the heart rate drops again," she explained, "we're going to have to do a C-section."

I was praying that it wouldn't happen. I wanted to have a natural birth. "What's the point of being in labor for hours if I'm only going to end up having a C-section?"

She said, "I know how you feel, but let's just wait and see," then added firmly, "I'm not going to compromise this baby's health."

So we waited. Jim took off his trousers, tossed them over the back of a chair, and curled up in his boxer shorts on the window seat a few feet from my bed. Soon he was dozing. All my concentration was focused on managing labor, so I wasn't really paying attention to what Jim was doing, but in hindsight, while I attribute some of Jim's apparent complacency to the fact that he didn't readily panic, I found his behavior oddly detached, and I've since wondered why. Both his public life—as governor-elect and father-to-be—and his secret love affair with Golan Cipel were at the boiling point, and I imagine he was exhausted and in need of sleep. I do know he wasn't sleeping deeply, though. Every few minutes, he'd wake and ask me how I was doing.

I told him I was doing OK, which was the truth. Labor was painful but bearable. It wasn't severe. At about 5:30 A.M., the doctor walked into the room. She had been at the nurses' station watching the fetal monitor, and she didn't like what she saw. There were just too many decelerations. "This is it," she said. "We're taking you into the operating room. We have to do a C-section."

She went up to Jim, who was half asleep, and said, "Come on, Governor, time to put on your pants. We're going to do a C-section."

I was close to tears.

"I know," said Jim. "It's a bummer."

"Are you sure we have to do this?" I asked the doctor.

"Yes," she said without hesitation. "There's no other alternative. Many babies have the cord around their necks in utero, but it doesn't always interfere with the heart rate during birth. In her case, with the way the cord is around her neck, she might not survive a vaginal birth."

Jim held my hand and said, "It's going to be fine. I'll be in there with you." I felt calmed by his confidence.

Within minutes, I'd been wheeled into the operating room and was surrounded by nurses, the doctor, and a resident. They administered an epidural injection and waited a brief time. Jim sat next to my head and held my hand.

"I'm scared," I told him. "And I'm having difficulty breathing."

"Just take deep breaths," he assured me. "It'll be over soon, and we'll have our beautiful daughter." I could hear everything in the room. I knew they were cutting me open, and it was a strange sensation.

And then our daughter announced her presence in the world with a cry.

It was 6:13 A.M., December 7, 2001. "Here she is," the doctor said. They held her up for us to see right away. Then they weighed and measured her. "Four pounds, five ounces, sixteen and a half inches."

I wanted to hold her, but I knew I wouldn't be able to. The doctor had prepared me for the fact that since she was five weeks early, they would immediately transport her to the NICU in an incubator as a precaution.

Jim rushed to the incubator as they were putting our baby in, then came back and said, "She's beautiful. And she has all her fingers and toes!" He'd counted them. "Are you OK?" he asked.

"I am," I said.

"I'm going along with them to take the baby," he said. He wasn't going to let her out of his sight, and I was glad.

Back in the recovery room it was time to settle on a name. While Jim had been given his uncle's name, my mother had selected "Dina" for me simply because she had liked it. Since the only Dina she had known was a girl she had beaten up in grammar school, the choice wasn't sentimental! I wanted something fresh for my daughter, a name that would really belong to her, so I had been browsing baby-name books for months for something suitable. We had whittled our selection down to two—Caitlin or Jacqueline. I've since been asked whether I chose "Jacqueline" with Jacqueline Kennedy in mind, and the answer is that I didn't. I just liked the name.

On the way back from NICU, Jim had been polling the hospital staff. He even polled our families when they came in soon after. "Jacqueline or Caitlin?" he asked. "Which one sounds better?" My niece Meagan, then four, said we ought to wait and let the baby pick her own name when she got older. Luckily, naming a child isn't a democratic process, and I don't think Jim ever bothered to tally the responses, including those from underage voters. Eventually we settled on Jacqueline Matos McGreevey. It had a classic ring to it.

After Jacqueline was whisked away, I was kept in the recovery room—imprisoned—for hours, which felt like months. I longed to hold her. I hadn't felt so much as a finger or a lock of her hair, and I hadn't yet smelled her new-baby smell. I had heard her cry, but I hadn't looked into her eyes.

Jim came back into the recovery room, elated. He was exhausted, but there was lilt enough in his step for both of us. "She's beautiful," he said. "Just beautiful and just perfect." He gazed at me tenderly, smoothing my hair back from my brow.

"You must be exhausted," he said, "but you really did a great job. She's beautiful," he repeated. "Just beautiful and perfect."

I begged him for more details, urgently interested despite my fatigue. "Who does she look like? How many inches is she? Can she cry? Can she cry really loud? Is she moving? Is she kicking?"

"I'm not sure who she looks like," he said, "but she has your big eyes, and I think they're going to be brown. She's sixteen and a half inches, but she's bigger than just about every other baby in that room. And louder."

"I have to know. . . . Does she have big feet?" The ultrasound had revealed a child with rather sizable feet, not quite Bigfoot, but the doctor had asked, carefully, whether anyone in our family had particularly big feet.

"Big feet? Well, they're tiny, tiny feet," he said, chuckling. "But I guess you'd have to say they're big in relation to her body."

I couldn't wait anymore. I desperately wanted to see those feet and kiss each toe. "Get me out of here, please! I need to see her. Can you talk to the nurse?"

"I'll see what I can do." A few minutes later, after checking my vital signs, two nurses, with Jim's help, got me out of the bed and into a wheelchair for my journey to Jacqueline. My anesthesia was beginning to wear off, and I could have used another shot, but I kept it to myself. I couldn't stand any further delays.

There she was, and, thank God, she *was* perfect. I reached into the incubator. Her hand was palm down, and I placed my hand, palm up, under hers. It was soft and pink and almost weightless.

"I want to hold her," I said. "When can I hold her?"

Our tiny baby had wires connected to small patches on the backs of her hands, on her arms, on her chest, on her belly and legs—enough for a small marionette. But I wasn't alarmed. I had worked in a hospital for a dozen years and knew all the heavy equipment they could have brought in. Its relative absence told me that Jacqueline was breathing on her own, which meant that her lungs were sufficiently developed despite her prematurity. There was no feeding tube either, which meant that her sucking reflex was developed, also a good sign. Still, all in all, it seemed an awfully brutal welcome to the world.

Once the nurse had checked Jacqueline's vital signs, she swaddled the baby in a blanket and gently lifted her out. The nurse's palm alone, not large as palms go, was big enough to amply cradle Jacqueline's head, while her other palm could support the rest of her body. The nurse handed my baby to me. "She's so light," I said to Jim, in awe. He murmured yes and nodded, as he had first held her moments after her birth. And so the three of us sat there, enjoying our first moments as a family. It had been quite a journey.

WITHIN HOURS OF JACQUELINE's birth, every television network and local radio and cable television station had reported her arrival. Congratulatory notes, phone calls, and even more floral arrangements poured in from all over—from the newly elected New York City mayor, Michael Bloomberg, and from Governors Gray Davis of California, George Pataki of New York, and Ruth Ann Minner of Delaware, as well as Acting Governor Donald DiFrancesco of New Jersey (Christie Whitman had resigned to head the EPA in George W. Bush's administration), who now welcomed Jim as one of their own. New Jersey's senators, Jon Corzine and Robert Torricelli, also sent their congratulations, as did a dozen New Jersey state legislators. All told, there were about one hundred greetings from politicians, both Democratic and Republican, welcoming our child.

When I'd first visited the NICU after being hospitalized in early November, I had noticed a little girl named Stacy who was so tiny I could have held her in one hand. Now, more than a month later, Stacy was still there—right next to Jacqueline. When I came in, her mother, a tall, tired woman of about forty, with short blond hair and dark circles under her eyes, was softly humming "Rock-a-Bye Baby" to her little girl, through one of the incubator's openings. I learned later from Stacy's grandmother that Stacy had suffered cardiac arrest more than once, and each time she'd been jolted and pounded back to life. "Your baby's huge," Stacy's mother told me. I could hear the longing in her voice. She knew she and Stacy's father were facing months, and perhaps a lifetime, of caring for their very vulnerable child. That's if they were lucky.

The health of children had been important to me ever since *I* was a child trying to help my family figure out what was wrong with my brother's leg, but now my own experience—a preemie myself and the mother of a preemie—gave me a special interest in premature babies. As First Lady, I got involved with the March of Dimes, which had been founded by President Franklin Delano Roosevelt in 1938 to combat polio. Following the development of the polio vaccine, the March of Dimes had to change its focus, and in 1958, the organization announced that it would begin to devote itself to a mission of preventing premature birth, birth defects, and infant mortality. In 2003, the March of Dimes launched a National Prematurity Awareness Campaign, and invited me to become a spokesperson, a role I gladly took on and continue to play.

Holding Jacqueline for the very first time, joyful and grateful to have her safe here in my arms, I tried to imagine what life might have in store for her. As a child who would take her first steps in a governor's mansion she called home, she would, in all likelihood, be exposed to a remarkable array of interesting people, have an orchestra seat to the workings of government and the media, come of age with a heightened sense of service, and eventually attend the college of her choice. But grateful as I was for the opportunities that might await her, I was delighted to welcome her into our new family, as well as into our extended families. I hoped and believed we would be parents who loved her and one another deeply, who would offer her a solid foundation based on love, faith, and social values on which she could build a gratifying and meaningful life. Of all the pain that Jim has caused our family, the pain he's brought to Jacqueline is the most difficult for me to live with or forgive. Before her third birthday, this little girl, so precocious and yet so vulnerable, would have to contend with an utter upheaval that permeated every area of her life. In a touch of excruciating irony, just as her father suffered recurring nightmares because someone else had made the choice to remove his daughter from his daily life, so too has his daughter suffered recurring nightmares because her father made the choice to remove himself from her daily life and forced her to leave nearly all the faces and places that were familiar to her in her short existence.

Looking back on it, I wanted Jacqueline's arrival to bring about some changes in Jim. Now that he had finally been elected governor, and with the heady days of campaigning behind us, I hoped he would not only make more time for us but also pay more attention to us. I was hoping that we could draw him away from the spotlight and all its seductions. But on the day after Jacqueline's birth, Jim was already lobbying for me to hold a press conference—the first of many orchestrated public displays of his "perfect family."

I didn't want to do it. I'd just had a C-section. My stitches were so raw that even a hiccup was painful, and I was so weak after six weeks in bed that my arms and legs felt like they had weights attached to them. I couldn't even shower.

"Let's hold off a few days," I said to Jim. "I can barely move."

"I promise it won't be a long press conference, and you won't have to exert yourself," Jim said. "It's just that people are really concerned about you and the baby."

I sighed. I knew he was eager to share his happiness. I also knew that when Jim was intent on something, it was really hard to say no to him.

I don't even answer the door in my bathrobe, so I wasn't wild about appearing before millions not only in my bathrobe but in a wheelchair. I realized, though, that despite the fact that I was not the elected official, as long as Jim was a public figure, my own privacy was going to be in short supply. I'd long since understood that the essence of the news was telegraphed through carefully selected texts and images, and I also understood, as Jim must have, that hospital scenes could play well in the press. I remembered back to the attempt on Ronald Reagan's life and how his press office made sure to tell reporters right away the joke Reagan was said to have cracked ("I hope you're a Republican") as he met his surgeon in the operating room. I also remembered the photos released of him three days later. Bathrobe, yes, but he was standing on his own two feet. Still, I wasn't the president, and I hadn't been shot.

Every politician makes a myth of his own life story for public consumption, and Jim was no different. In fact, over the years I'd watched as he honed and shaped his myth. Just as Bill Clinton sold himself as "the man from Hope," Jim's myth—as a true son of the red, white, and blue New Jersey Irish working class—began with his namesake, Uncle Jim McGreevey, and the day Jim had learned that his uncle had died serving his country at Iwo Jima. As Jim told me the story, seeing the letter honoring his uncle had been a moment of transformation in which Jim, true heir to his uncle, picked up the mantle of public service, setting his destiny in motion. As for his Irish-American roots—that was a half-truth, since his maternal ancestry was English, not Irish. And finally there was the myth I understood least—the myth of his father—the marine drill instructor who ran a tight ship, demanding his son make a bed so tight that the quarter bounced off the sheets. Now and then, for reasons I've never understood, Jim liked to hint that his father's instructions came at the end of a belt strap, but from everything I knew, Jim's father was a kind and loving man, generous in his praise of his son. And he'd been long gone from the military during Jim's New Jersey childhood. Actually, he was a traveling salesman, but that occupation didn't really lend itself to the mythic.

And now, just weeks before Christmas, here was Jim, the governor-elect of New Jersey. Still intact in his mind was the conviction that he thought had helped him defeat Torricelli the year before—that the governor of a state needs not only a face but a family. We weren't the Holy Family, but I'm sure it didn't hurt that we were right on the cusp of the Christmas season. At the very least, at just the moment that his hidden infatuation with Golan was at a boil, we established Jim as a family man, and he was eager to present his wife and child to the public.

In the end, I was too uncertain about the demands of my new role *not* to agree to the press conference, and on December 8, one-day-old Jacqueline and I—First Baby–elect and First Lady–elect—were wheeled into a conference room at St. Peter's where a crowd of journalists awaited us, cameras aloft, bulbs flashing. Jacqueline, who was characterized in later press reports as being the first young child of a New Jersey governor in thirty years, slept through the whole thing (probably the last time she was known to miss a photo op) while I sat by as Jim told reporters—in what was news to me—the most recent addition to the myth: that Jacqueline had been named after his father, Jack.

I spent the next few days learning to be a mother—handling such a small infant, feeling anxiety over her mild jaundice, and figuring out how to breast-feed. I had been told that she would probably be able to go home within the week, but Jacqueline was not gaining weight, and the pediatrician told me she now might have to stay even longer. I was not leaving that hospital without my baby. I hadn't wanted to add formula, but I did want to take my daughter home, so late one afternoon we settled into a rocking chair in the NICU and I introduced Jacqueline to the bottle. She didn't much like the bottle and liked the formula even less, but I said to her, "Listen, little one, we have to get you out of here, so drink." On December 14, the McGreevey family went home.

12 · FIRST LADY, SECOND WIFE

I HAD READ EVERYTHING I could get my hands on to prepare myself for Jacqueline's arrival, but I didn't have a clue about how to get ready for the role of First Lady. There was no *What to Expect When Your Husband Is Elected*, no *T. Berry Brazelton for First Ladies*, and there was no one around to tell me the rules. Just as well, because apparently there weren't any. But that would all have to wait. I didn't have the time, or the energy, to figure it out—especially not when I was also trying to figure out how to be a mother.

We were driven home to Woodbridge by a state trooper. Jim and I were sitting on each side of Jacqueline, who was in her car seat. In the front next to the trooper was Jason Kirin, Jim's traveling assistant, who was overflowing with pressing questions for Jim. Nevertheless, I noted happily that Jacqueline was more than a match for Jason, as she tightly gripped Jim's thumb with her tiny pink fingers, prompting him to lean down more than once to kiss her forehead.

When we arrived home, Jim carefully lifted Jacqueline out of her car seat and shepherded us both inside. I'd been gone for more than a month, and Jim was notoriously blind to disorder and clutter, so I wasn't entirely sure what to expect. But I needn't have worried. Knowing that neatness and cleanliness were important to me, he had taken pains to make the house presentable.

"What do you think?" he asked. "Pretty clean, isn't it?"

"Looks great," I said, relieved and also touched at the effort he'd gone to on my behalf. "I'm really glad to be home." He helped me off with my coat and placed Jacqueline in her bassinet, wrapping her tightly in her blanket, the way she seemed to like it. My close friend Freddie, who had driven me to the hospital when I went into labor, was already at the town house when we arrived. Freddie was going to stay over to help me because I was still so weak I could barely walk. My mother would be coming over later.

Home always feels a little strange to me when I've been gone for a while—and in fact everything *was* different now, very different—so I was grateful to finally begin the process of settling in, to sit around with nothing more to do for the next few hours than just be a family at home. This was the first moment when Jim, Jacqueline, and I were home together as a family, and I was looking forward to settling into the afternoon, to finding our rhythm. Jason and the trooper had followed Jim in, and I was hopeful that they'd be leaving soon, which they did. But after half an hour, Jim stood up.

"Well," he said, "I have to go to a meeting now." I could *hear* his gears shifting.

"A meeting?" I was incredulous. "We just brought our brand-new baby home, and you're leaving?" Was this what it was going to be like from now on?

"I'm governor now," he said, a phrase I would hear hundreds of times in the next two and a half years. "There's so much I have to do—a staff to assemble, a cabinet to put in place, an inaugural to plan," he said.

I must have looked as if someone had just slapped me. I guess Jim noticed, because he softened a bit.

"I'll try to be home as early as I can. Really, I don't think this will take too long."

"Why do you have to do it now?" I asked.

"If not now, when?" he said. "We're a month away from my swearing-in." There was no point in arguing. Jim was going to do what he was going to do. But that moment stayed with me. It wasn't dramatic or explosive, just one of those small, telling episodes that, paradoxically, really *doesn't* tell you what it means, at least not right away.

As I see it now, I'd been waiting for this homecoming, yearning for it, since we'd begun dating in 1996. Like many men, Jim had never participated in the life of our household at all, and I'd made my adjustments to that. When I first moved in, there was a hole in the dining room ceiling, a leak in the bathroom, soot in the chimney, and canned food in the cabinets that had been there since before Clinton was president. I took care of all of it, with the help of my father and friends. I was Snow White, and Jim was all seven of the dwarfs. But I hadn't really minded. In a way, we had been weekend nomads, most at home on the campaign trail.

But it was different now—for me, and I hoped for Jim as well. Even though we would be moving to Drumthwacket sometime in the next several months, for the present I needed this house to be *home,* especially after six weeks in the hospital that began less than two months after 9/11. Many people I knew, especially those of us who had once seen the Twin Towers daily as part of a familiar skyscape, were still recovering; we needed to be able to retreat into a sheltering home and a welcoming family. At the same time, we had to get on with the rest of our lives, our *new* lives. Now that we'd brought our hardy little daughter safely into the world, I wanted—and Jim should have wanted—time to consolidate, to take pleasure in her and in us, to come together as a family in our home. For years, he'd been running for office, and now, in my first hour on the outside with him, he was still running. And he was exhausted. I could see that. With all his secrets, how could he not have been?

FOR BETTER OR WORSE, all marriages have their chapters. In hindsight, our homecoming and Jim's instant departure marked the beginning of a new chapter for us, though not so much in terms of external events, which were all so exciting that they served to mask a feeling of disillusionment I didn't recognize until much later. During the years of campaigning, I'd found Jim elusive, maybe even evasive, but I'd never admitted it to myself and had chalked it up to the campaign; and that had worked pretty well to keep any discontent at bay. Now the campaign was over, and so my disappointment and diminished expectations took root, waiting for me to feel them whenever I got around to it. I tried not to get around to it.

Christmas was days away, but there was no sign of it in the house. I wasn't up to decorating, and Jim didn't care. Before we were married, he hadn't had a Christmas tree in the house since Kari and Morag had left in 1994. Thankfully, my friends went out and got a tree and decorated it. I was happy to have visible signs of the holiday. I had bought decorations the previous year—an angel for the treetop and some ornaments—and we'd gotten a bunch more ornaments as gifts for Jacqueline. One I still love says "First Christmas."

On Christmas Eve, Jim and I exchanged gifts. Thinking of a winter inaugural parade three weeks away, I got Jim a navy blue cashmere coat. For me, Jim got a 14-karat-gold charm bracelet with two charms—a Santa Claus and little golden booties engraved with Jacqueline's initials, JMM, and her date of birth, 12-7-01. I still wear it during the Christmas season.

A few days later, Jim stayed put for the afternoon because the three of us were the subjects of a photo shoot. Our photographer friend, Jerry Casciano (who later became the governor's official photographer), came over to photograph the new baby and the new "First Family." These were the official photos the governor's communications office would now start providing to the press. For variety, each of us, including Jacqueline, appeared in two different outfits. I finally got to wear the red maternity dress I had planned to wear on Election Day. Jacqueline was so tiny that Jerry had difficulty photographing her other than in the turkey-just-out-of-the-oven position. Finally we propped her up against a number of pillows so Jerry could get a decent shot of her.

The following week, I was scheduled—finally!—to visit the residential floors of Drumthwacket, where we expected to live for the next four years, and maybe even eight. I didn't know what that part of the mansion looked like or what furnishings I'd have to buy. I didn't know which rooms would have to be painted or which floors would have to be sanded. The only thing I knew was that Drumthwacket was Scottish for "wooded hill" and that the house itself was in the Greek Revival style.

Construction on Drumthwacket had begun in 1835 by Charles Smith Olden, who became governor in 1860. Later his widow sold it, and it hadn't returned to its stature as the official governor's mansion until the 1960s, when it was purchased by the state of New Jersey. It lay unrestored until the early 1980s, and since then only one governor—James Florio—had actually lived in it. He'd left office eight years earlier, and his successor, Christie Whitman, had preferred to live in her home in Oldwyck and commute to the statehouse in Trenton. For Jim, living in a two-bedroom town house in Woodbridge an hour and a half away from Trenton was going to be untenable, so we had to move. *How bad can this place be?* I wondered. *It's the governor's mansion.*

The mansion was under the auspices of the Division of Parks and Forestry, within the Department of Environmental Protection, so its director, with Diane DiFrancesco, the wife of Acting Governor Donald DiFrancesco, and a few other staffers were there to meet me and give me a tour.

As we walked up the steps to the residence, Diane turned to me. "You're going to hate living here," she said.

If she only knew.

It wasn't quite the Addams Family mansion, but it was dismal, faintly shabby, and down-at-the-heels—not what I expected a governor's mansion to look like. There were forty-two windows in the residence, and given that the house was more than 150 years old, I wondered about the presence of lead paint, since it hadn't been banned until 1977. The walls had likely been painted several times in the subsequent quarter century and thus were likely to pose no problem, but the windowsills had undoubtedly been painted less frequently, and while lead paint hadn't been used on the top coat, the chipping of the windowsills would expose it.

"This house was built in the 1830s," I said. "Has it ever been tested for the presence of lead paint?"

"Good question," said the director. "I'll look into it."

That evening, Jim arrived home and asked me about my tour. "So how'd it go? What did you think of the place?"

"There's lots of potential. First big question is where Jacqueline will sleep. There are two bedrooms in addition to ours on the second floor, but they're too far away for a nursery. We'd never hear her cry."

"So where will she sleep?"

"There are two options—an exercise room and our dressing room. I think the exercise room would be perfect. It's right down the hall and a little bit larger than the dressing room. But there's a possibility of lead paint, especially on the windows."

"I never would have thought of that," he said.

"But, you know, we just can't live there in its current condition, especially with a baby," I said. "It's not just the windows—it's the dirty rugs, the rusted stove top, the old refrigerator. Nobody's really lived there in eight years. The place is awful."

"But we have to live there," he said. "It's close to the statehouse, and it can accommodate meetings and large gatherings."

"If we're going to live there, we have to renovate."

"Well, what about the Foundation? Let's see how much money is available for renovations."

We put the question on hold.

THE DAY AFTER CHRISTMAS, Jim was going to Vancouver to see his daughter. Though I'd now been with Jim for five years, I still had not met Morag; but from the photographs I'd seen, she was a very pretty and demure little girl, often dressed in floral prints, with ribbons in her hair. While she didn't seem to shrink from being photographed, she never looked directly into the camera either. I wondered what she was like. I could see she looked very much like Jim. So did Jacqueline, from the very moment she was born. In fact, the two girls looked more like full sisters than my brother Paul's two daughters did.

Jim went to visit Morag at Christmastime every year, but I'd hoped that he'd have her come stay with us as I had suggested several times, or that he would go a bit later this year, perhaps after his inauguration. However, as he had all the other times, he said that her mother would not allow her to come spend time with us.

JIM'S RELATIONSHIP WITH Kari continued to make me uneasy. I suspected that he was still involved with her, maybe even in love with her. My misgivings dated back to Election Night of 1997, the night Jim had not returned my phone call, though the papers reported on his late-night conversation with Kari. Before Jim and I married, I often saw mail from Morag lying around his house. Usually the envelopes were written in an adult hand—Kari's, I assumed—but the contents, at least the contents I saw, were often drawings by Morag, or little cards or notes. But soon after Jim and I were married and I began living with him in Woodbridge, the envelopes mysteriously stopped. Later I learned that all of Kari's mail was being addressed to Jim's office—I assumed at his direction. I also noticed that whenever Kari called, Jim took the call as far away from me as he could. What was that about?

Jim went to Vancouver as planned, returning on New Year's Eve, which we spent at home with close friends, including Lori and Jimmy Kennedy, dining on take-out chicken from Boston Market. By now, Jimmy's 1997 Election Night worries—about what would happen to his friendship with Jim if Jim became governor—had resolved themselves. In hindsight, I wish I could have felt as resolved as he did. In any case, I was content to be spending one uninterrupted evening with my husband and new daughter. It wasn't intimate, but it was peaceful.

Meanwhile, ready or not, preparations for the inauguration were taking place, and I needed an outfit for the swearing-in and a gown for the inaugural ball. I liked St. John suits but had never owned one. Now that I was going to be the First Lady—one of fewer than fifty, since not all American governors are men—I decided that because I'd worked so hard to get to this day I deserved to treat myself. So I went to the local mall and purchased a red St. John suit. There was press grousing about the cost, but what business was it of theirs? It wasn't the taxpayers' money. Deciding on the inaugural gown would be a little more complicated. Although I'd be slimmer than I initially anticipated being, I worried about how I'd look.

Maria, the wife of one of Jim's supporters, worked for Vera Wang, my favorite designer, and Maria had called Jim's office to ask that I call her. The message had the annotation "inaugural gown," but I didn't know what that meant, though I did remember telling her that my wedding gown had been a Vera Wang.

When I learned that Vera Wang herself wanted to design my gown I was thrilled. I hadn't been thinking about an inaugural gown at all, just about how much pain I was in and how much sleep I needed. Before the chaos of the last month and a half, "inaugural gown" had been somewhere on my list, but since then I hadn't given it a thought. I knew that the gowns worn by presidential First Ladies were fodder for the fashion pages, but it hadn't occurred to me that the same interest might apply to gubernatorial First Ladies. Still, I was thrilled that Vera Wang wanted to design a dress for me and delighted that she was offering to send two of her employees for a personal consultation to find out my preferences in style, material, and color. I instantly and gratefully agreed. Who wouldn't want Vera Wang to design a gown for her?

It was a once-in-a-lifetime opportunity, and I felt like a celebrity, a few days before Christmas, when Maria came to the house to take my measurements. I felt I was about the size of Little Toot and wasn't exactly eager to reveal my dimensions, but she whipped out her tape measure and waved away my objections.

"Two weeks after you've had a baby, and you're a size eight? I don't want to hear any complaints!" she said, all business. "What color?"

"Black."

"We're going to make you a spectacular gown. Vera already has something in mind." And then she was gone.

A few days before the inaugural, Maria swept into our house again, this time with a magnificent strapless black gown, all silk and organza with beading below the waist. It was just like my wedding gown, only in black. As with the St. John suit, before the end of Inauguration Day the gown had become fodder for the reporters. When had I gotten these outfits? What had I paid for them? Was this an indication of things to come?

One of my first jobs was to figure out what a First Lady was supposed to look like, or at least how *I* was supposed to look now that I had become the First Lady of New Jersey. I thought about my hairstyle, my makeup, and how I carried myself. But more than anything else, I thought about how to dress. For longer than I care to admit, I felt as though I were playing dress-up, masquerading in someone else's costume, and I really needed every "ma'am" and ball gown and shred of protocol I could get my hands on to feel that I really was First Lady. I worked hard at it, but I knew I was making the rules up as I went along.

Hillary Clinton has said she thought of Eleanor Roosevelt—and, in her mind, talked to her—when she became First Lady of the nation. Before the inauguration, I'd been thinking about role models too, and I thought I'd found two: Hillary herself and Jackie Kennedy. I identified with Hillary as a Baby Boomer First Lady, the first to have her own profession and her own name, and to want to maintain her own distinct identity. In an altogether different way, I also identified with Jackie Kennedy. She was a First Lady in her thirties, an elegantly dressed woman with a brand-new baby and a mansion to renovate.

Being First Lady would become a big and gratifying job, but it would be different from my daily job. When you're First Lady, there's no such thing as a dress-down Friday. Far more often, it's about dressing *up,* and far more expensive! It turned out Jim would have a $70,000 budget for expenses, but when it came to clothing, all he needed was one pair of patent leather shoes and one tux (which he already had from our wedding), seven or eight suits, and several dozen shirts and rep ties. But there was no budget for the First Lady's wardrobe, and yet as First Lady I would spend quadruple what I had as a private figure who just liked dressing well. The Vera Wang gown I wore to the inaugural ball was only my second designer outfit. (The first was my wedding gown, not exactly a versatile garment.)

As I learned about functions I would have to attend as First Lady— fund-raisers, dinners, ceremonies—I realized I would need several suits, ball gowns, and cocktail dresses, not to mention shoes and accessories to match. More than that, I realized I had to establish my own style as a young First Lady who was also a working mother.

Clothes aren't just clothes, after all. If they make the man, they also make the woman—or help to. Jim was well aware of that, and as his term progressed—and perhaps as he began to need the cover of his "perfect family"—he would more and more often expect me to wear St. John suits and other designer items on a daily basis. Just weeks before what was to be his resignation speech, he even urged me to go ahead and spend $500 for a pair of designer shoes. It was an extravagance I couldn't justify, so I refused. Still, it was hard to keep up with it all.

OVERALL, IT WAS A dizzying time. There I was, a nursing mother of an infant barely a month old, wearing my Vera Wang strapless gown out to an inaugural ball. Would I leak milk and ruin my gown? And if so, would it show up in the photographs? Or, worse, on television? Who was there for me to consult on such matters? Jacqueline and I were now as attached as two strips of Velcro, and leaving her was wrenching, yet there was no way I could bring her along to any of the inaugural events. For the first time—and the hundreds more times that would follow—I was having to juggle motherhood and First Ladyhood. (And soon having a job would be thrown into the mix.) I found an experienced baby-sitter for inauguration night whom I knew and trusted—the mother of two children, one of whom required special care—but, nevertheless, a baby-sitter. I would have felt better if I were leaving Jacqueline with my parents, but they were going to be at the inaugural ball as well. So I worried, but now that I'd fallen down the gubernatorial rabbit hole, I had state troopers at my disposal every minute of the day, and if I needed them to, they could turn on their sirens and lights and whisk me home in minutes.

I was up at 4:30 A.M. on Tuesday, January 15, Inauguration Day, and took my shower before waking Jim at 5:00 so he could take his—there were two bathrooms, but I'd never gotten around to fixing the second shower, and I certainly wasn't going to put it on my list of household repairs now. The events of the day started quite early, with a prayer service at Princeton's University Chapel. Jim, in his customary uniform—blue suit, white shirt, and red-striped tie—was ebullient. From there, it was on to the War Memorial in Trenton for the swearing-in ceremony. There was gridlock galore, but with our trooper escorts we glided through. My parents and my brother Paul and his wife, Elvie, who'd had Jacqueline with them, barely made it. In the flurry of events, no one, including me, had made sure that they too had trooper escorts. Paul was irritated. "We should have had an escort," he said. "We had your daughter with us."

Jim and I were joined onstage at the War Memorial by three former governors; the chief justice of the New Jersey Supreme Court, who would swear Jim in; his parents; and fellow legislators. In the audience were Jacqueline, my family—including my brother Rick, Jim's sisters, brother-in-law, niece and nephew, and other relatives—and several hundred friends, supporters, and staff. After the benediction, given by the pastor of our parish church in Woodbridge, and after a few more assorted speeches, finally the moment we'd worked so hard for was at hand—the swearing-in of Jim as New Jersey's fifty-first governor. Just before he stood in front of Chief Justice Deborah T. Poritz, as we had planned, my mother climbed the steps to the stage to hand Jacqueline to me so that she could be onstage with us when Jim took the oath. I couldn't help but think, with a bit of a twinge, that this public moment was also our most moving family moment since Jacqueline's birth. At the same time, it was a moment of pride and magic, the next step of a journey that had begun with a wedding photograph, the White House in plain sight.

I'd never seen so many camera flashes as I did at that moment when Jacqueline was settling into my arms. There was a collective "Awww!"—that unmistakable noise made by adults in the presence of babies or kittens—when I took her from my mother's arms. Since my parents had been seated in the front row, few had seen that my mother had been holding a baby or that that baby was Jacqueline. This was the public's second glimpse of a little girl who to this day almost instinctively poses for the camera at a moment's notice, invariably giving herself a central place in the mix.

At Jim's inauguration, however, she was not yet capable even of holding up her own head, much less arranging the participants, so Jim's mother held the Bible and I stood to his right holding Jacqueline. His father, Jack, had tears in his eyes as he watched his son take the oath of office. Once Jim completed the oath, I handed Jacqueline back over to my mother and we sat down to listen to the rest of the speeches.

Next was the inaugural parade. On this clear and cold morning, we walked several blocks through downtown Trenton and then stood on the grandstand to view the rest of the parade, Jim in his new navy blue overcoat. After that, we went home to get ready for the inaugural ball, and Jacqueline and I were reunited for a few hours before I had to put on my Vera Wang gown and leave again.

The evening was a festive blur. We had seats but never sat in them. Instead we shook hands, dispensed hugs, posed for photographs. I've since been asked if Golan Cipel was there, and the answer is yes, he was. All Jim's staff and supporters were there, and though I saw Golan, it was only in passing.

It was an exciting day. Jim pulled me on through a crowd so thick that James Schedrick, the tallest and most muscular trooper on duty that day, was assigned the role of Protector of the Gown. My gown. In that capacity, he served as a human barricade, walking behind me everywhere I went, with his arms outstretched in order to keep the guests off the train. He was accompanied by at least half a dozen other troopers who, in that very packed ballroom, created a protective circle around Jim and me.

The ball continued at the Raritan Center in Edison until well into the night, with all of us exuding a sense of triumph and exuberance and high spirits. Jim and I danced the merengue and the samba together, and then later a slow dance or two. I was very proud of him that night and very excited about what I thought he was going to be able to do for the state of New Jersey. The papers the next morning described the ball as having an aura of Camelot, with all its youth, glamour, promise, and potential. At the end, back home, we collapsed into bed, and the next morning the newest chapter in our lives began.

13 · STICKS AND STONES

❧

IT WAS THE END of January, and I was trying to catch my breath. The election had been victorious, but the campaign had been grueling, as had the month and a half in the hospital and childbirth. I was exhausted. Jim and I both were.

The learning curve was steep for Jim, and for me as well. Jim was now charged with balancing a multibillion-dollar state budget, dealing directly with the federal government, and making cabinet and judicial appointments. As a legislator, he had been an advocate for his district, but now his point of view had to shift. He had to become an advocate for the entire state, a manager who would make sure that all the different systems, appointments, and priorities worked as harmoniously as possible.

As for me, the role of mother was brand-new, and I relished every moment. Well, almost every moment. When Jacqueline slept more than an hour, I did have to learn not to race to her crib and place my fingers under her nose to make sure she was breathing. I nursed her for the first few months but worried a bit about what would happen when she moved on to cow's milk, which, especially when heated, has always made me gag. Would I retch my way through Jacqueline's toddlerhood and childhood? Would I deny her hot cocoa? If I did, would that make me a bad mother? But I started to relax, and even warm milk became manageable. I soon came to think of the burp cloth I wore on my left shoulder as a fashion accessory and that only people with narcolepsy slept through the entire night.

By February, I was back at my job and had become an almost expert juggler. In the span of an hour, my phone might ring a dozen times—with calls from my assistant Cindy, at the hospital, reminding me I had to decide on the date for the fund-raising gala by tomorrow; from Jim, hoping my calendar was clear to attend the next Democratic Committee fund-raiser with him; from my assistant Nina, at the statehouse, wanting some dates when we could schedule a meeting on childhood obesity with various community leaders and health-care experts; from a contractor, asking whether I preferred tile or wood for the Drumthwacket kitchen floor; and from my father, who took care of Jacqueline while I was at work, worrying about what he thought might be a rash on her stomach. Meanwhile, in just about every one of these realms, I was aware of being watched and reacted to by the media.

Two weeks into Jim's term, he suggested we get away—"flee" might be a more accurate word—to Cape May, a lovely seaside resort town at the southern tip of the New Jersey cape, the oldest resort in the country, frequented by nearly half a dozen nineteenth-century American presidents. These days, Cape May is famous for its large Victorian houses richly adorned with gingerbread trim (now converted into quaint bed-and-breakfasts), for its summer jazz and music festivals, and for its trendy shops. In summer, its population swells to a hundred thousand, but in winter, with only the permanent residents, there are no more than five thousand souls. In other words, the perfect getaway.

We were reluctant to leave Jacqueline behind, but we both realized that exhausted parents didn't make the best parents, and also that we were in desperate need of time out and time together. We would never have left her with a sitter at that young age, but we knew that Jacqueline would be lovingly cared for by my mom and dad, and that we were reachable twenty-four hours a day. So we piled into the car with our luggage, our three troopers, and our four cell phones (I had one, and now that Jim was governor, he had acquired a third), and off we went.

We arrived in Cape May at teatime. The bed-and-breakfast where we had booked a room was an enormous Victorian with several towers. Inside, the tearoom was small, as most Victorian rooms are, with one dining table where four other guests were already seated. We ordered tea and scones from a pleasant waitress. I warmed my hands against the teapot as the tea steeped, then poured it into the lovely but endearingly mismatched bone china cups resting in their saucers.

"Cold?" Jim said, placing his hands on top of mine.

"What do you think?" I said, smiling. By now he knew that my hands were almost always cold.

This was our first time alone in public as governor and First Lady. The people at the table recognized Jim, and as usual he struck up a conversation, introducing me as well. It was teatime for the six of us rather than the two of us, but this was just the way things were. I was flattered at this first hint of celebrity status, though not quite comfortable.

After tea, as we were about to check in to our room, Jim asked the receptionist if we had a room with a view. "You can't see much of the ocean, but if you want an ocean view, I can check the owner's other property."

I wondered if she would be doing this for any customer and decided that since it was the dead of winter, she probably would. They had the spare rooms, so why not? But it was also star treatment and, for me, the beginning of a kind of divided consciousness where I was always wondering why people were acting as they were acting toward me. It was flattering, but it made me feel like a different person, not quite myself. They're doing this for me? This is me? After a quick phone call, she directed us to a second bed-and-breakfast. "It's right on the ocean, and they'll be able to put you in a beautiful room with a fireplace that looks out at the water."

Since we both loved the ocean, we headed back to the car to tell the troopers we were changing our location. They drove us a few blocks to the waterfront lodging and brought our bags in. "You guys can go. We're OK," Jim told the troopers. "We just want to be alone."

"Are you sure, Gov? We'll stick around," said one of the three. Actually, all of us were aware that it would be quite irregular to leave Jim unattended. By law, they were not supposed to do so. They knew it, I knew it, and Jim knew it. Still, he insisted.

"No," said Jim. "I want you to leave and come back and get us on Sunday afternoon. Besides, who's going to kidnap us in Cape May in the middle of winter?" They looked at each other, clearly uncomfortable with the request.

"OK, but call if you need anything," they said.

"We'll see you Sunday afternoon," Jim replied, and then the troopers took off. They were uneasy leaving us, but Jim was their boss and they wouldn't disobey his orders. Anyhow, two was company and five was a crowd.

OUR LODGINGS CONSISTED OF a large room done in Victorian floral wallpaper—red and blue florets on a white background—with the promised fireplace and spectacular ocean view. We settled in and then dressed to go for a walk on the beach before dinner. On the way out, we stopped to make reservations for eight o'clock dinner. The restaurant at the inn was very popular, and it was best to make reservations, even in the winter.

We crossed the street to the beach and began walking north, close to the ocean's edge. It was a cold but beautiful night. We walked hand in hand and stopped to gaze at the sky as we embraced. It was just great to be away from the rest of the world, so peaceful, with only the lulling sound of the waves and the cawing of the gulls. Not another soul was in sight, not even a car. After walking for about a half hour, we turned around and began to head back south in the direction of the inn, still walking on the sand.

The night was clear, and the stars filled the sky in a way they never seem to in the city. Jim and I were holding hands, looking up, stargazing, comfortable in our silence. The wind felt strong, but we were nonetheless enjoying its roar along with the sound of the waves.

Suddenly, though, Jim's Irish tweed hat was seized by the wind and carried off. He rushed after it, disappearing from my view into the dark. I couldn't see him, and I didn't hear him.

"Jim?" I called. "Where are you?"

No answer, or if there was, it was muffled by the sound of the wind and the waves. After a minute or two of calling "Jim!" and peering into the dark, I got scared. I couldn't imagine what had happened to him.

"Honey, where are you?" I called out again. I was probably *shrieking* by now, the panic rising in my chest.

Finally I heard a faint voice. "Dina! Help! Over here! I'm over here! I fell, and can't get up."

I still couldn't see him, but at least I could follow the sound of his voice.

"I think I broke something," he said. The sand was uneven, and the erosion had formed a small ditch of sorts. And that was where Jim had fallen.

"Are you OK?" I asked, relieved to finally reach him.

"I'm really in a lot of pain," he said. "And I think I might have internal bleeding." I grabbed Jim's arms and tried to drag him out of the ditch and through the sand, but I was unable to make any headway. On his own, he couldn't move at all.

"I'm calling 911," I said, taking my cell phone out of my jacket pocket.

"Wait," he said. "Let's think about this."

"What's there to think about?" I asked. "You're hurt and you can't move! I'm calling 911."

"No, wait. I don't want anyone to know I was running after my hat when I fell."

I couldn't believe my ears. "Why not?" I asked.

"I'll look stupid."

Poor Jim. Ever mindful of appearances, he seemed to be imagining the morning's headlines:

GOVERNOR BREAKS LEG
CHASING IRISH TWEED CAP

And then he backed down. "All right," he said reluctantly. Clearly, his pain was worsening.

I called 911.

"Hello, this is Dina McGreevey, the governor's wife. We were walking on the beach at Cape May. My husband fell. We think he might have broken his leg."

I guess the story was sort of preposterous, because the dispatcher's tone was incredulous. She seemed to find it astounding that anyone would be on the beach at this hour and in this weather. But she kept to protocol and asked for further details about our location. I really didn't have a clue. I had no idea how far north of the inn we still were. There weren't even streetlamps, so I couldn't see across the street to the houses and the hotels.

EMS was now sending an ambulance, the dispatcher told us. Meanwhile I called the inn to alert them, too. At least I didn't have to persuade them that I was Jim McGreevey's wife. It was cold on the beach, and I figured they might be able to come find us before EMS got there. But when they asked our location, I was unable to identify it. Jim, lying on the damp sand and unable to move, was now trembling from the cold.

My concern was that no one would be able to find us. It was so dark. I tried to comfort Jim, telling him that someone would be coming to get us soon, then attempting again to drag him farther away from the ocean, but I couldn't. That's when it occurred to me to hit the "send" button on my cell phone so that it would light up. Hopefully, the faint beam would be visible even two or three hundred feet away, where the beach met the street.

While we waited for help, Jim asked me to call Kevin Hagan, a member of his staff. He had realized that the troopers were going to be in big trouble and that someone had to notify them so they could turn around and get themselves back to Cape May as fast as possible. I hadn't even thought about the troopers. I wasn't yet used to having them around, and it hadn't even occurred to me that the essence of their job was to be with us for just this kind of emergency. Jim told Kevin Hagan what had happened and that he would call back once we'd gotten to the hospital, wherever that might be.

It took EMS only about ten or fifteen minutes to arrive and find us, but it seemed like hours. The dispatcher called back to tell me that while the ambulance would be in the area within minutes, we might be hard to locate. I told them that I would attempt to alert them with my cell phone's light, praying that my battery didn't die before they came. When I finally saw the ambulance as it attempted to drive north along the back edge of the beach, I waved my phone frantically.

They saw the light! And soon they reached us.

Jim was now trembling violently and in excruciating pain, all the more as they moved him onto a board so they could carry him to the ambulance. True to the narrative tradition of injured political officials—again I think of Reagan greeting his surgeons—Jim joked with the EMTs as he was loaded into the ambulance.

"You're lucky to have gotten the only two Democrats on the squad," one said.

Jim laughed, reminding them to "go easy on the bumps."

So once again, in this unimaginable life we were leading, one of us was in enough medical trouble to require an ambulance, for the second time in four months. We were headed to the nearest hospital, Burdette Tomlin Memorial Hospital, about ten miles north. I knew that Jim was in excruciating pain because he would let out a yelp with every bump, but the fact that he was able to kid around with the EMTs offered me a bit of relief. I held his hand and stroked his hair in an effort to comfort him. When we arrived, we learned that the state troopers, however they'd learned about Jim's whereabouts, were on their way.

A team was assembled to care for Jim in the emergency room. They took his vital signs and attempted to move his leg, but he gasped and cried out. Had he broken something? Fractured it? The medical staff said they wouldn't be sure until they saw the X-rays, but from my years of following my brother's leg injuries, including his fractures, it was pretty clear to me that something had to be broken for Jim to be in that much pain.

The X-rays showed that he had in fact broken his left femur, the bone in the thigh. The radiologist was surprised, telling me that the femur was the strongest bone in the body and very difficult to break, especially in someone as young as Jim, who had just turned forty-four. And in the sand, no less. By this time, two troopers had arrived. As the nurses cut one leg of his trousers, Jim joked about how they were ruining a new and perfectly good pair of pants.

It was clear that Jim would have to have surgery to set his femur as soon as possible. The question was, where? We were unfamiliar with this hospital and its staff. Jim's designee for commissioner of the Department of Health, Clifton Lacy, M.D., recommended that Jim be brought to an orthopedic surgeon at Robert Wood Johnson University Hospital in New Brunswick. It was an excellent regional trauma center and he was on staff there. But now the question was how to get Jim to that hospital.

The same wind that had swooped down to steal Jim's tweed cap was now proving perilous to helicopter travel. One of the troopers had heard from headquarters that the wind was so severe that the Federal Aviation Administration had grounded all small craft in the area, and that obviously included the MedEvac helicopter waiting to transport Jim. Finally, the FAA gave the go-ahead—apparently for this one flight only—considering his condition and the fact that a two-hour road trip would further aggravate his injury.

It had been decided that one of the troopers would drive to the hospital and the other would fly, because there was limited space on the helicopter and because someone had to get the car back to Drumthwacket. Under the best of circumstances, I'm a reluctant flier, and these circumstances—with the wind so strong that no one else was being allowed to fly—were hardly the best. But I knew I couldn't leave Jim.

"Come with me," he said.

So I did.

It was a terrifying flight. At one point, the helicopter dropped altitude precipitously. The trooper and I both looked at each other, and although neither of us spoke, we were both terribly afraid we wouldn't make it. Jim, meanwhile, was in so much pain that he could barely speak. Once we landed at the heliport at Robert Wood Johnson, Jim was immediately taken to the operating room where the orthopedic team was waiting. Kevin Hagan was already there to discuss the media strategy. There was to be no mention of Jim's runaway hat. The story would be that he missed the ditch and fell. Jim asked that Dick Codey, president of the state senate, be informed that for the next several hours he would be acting governor. As senate president, Codey was first in line to assume the duties of governor when the governor was incapacitated—a dress rehearsal, of sorts, for his assumption to the governorship when Jim stepped down in the wake of the Golan Cipel scandal. As Jim's wife, I signed off on Jim's surgery, and off he went into the OR, accompanied by two state troopers, who remained in the operating room the entire time.

It was a long night.

After the surgery—by now we were long past midnight—we went to see Jim in the recovery room. The surgeon had put two metal rods in his leg, which would be left in there permanently unless they bothered him. I listened as one trooper described the procedure in vivid detail. The doctor had drilled two holes in Jim's leg and inserted the rods and screws to hold them in place. I was sad for Jim. He was just beginning his administration and was now going to have to spend time in the hospital followed by months of physical therapy. I also knew that being on crutches would upset him. He never showed any sign of weakness, and in fact was intolerant of giving in to it. I knew that he would now perceive himself as weak.

The following day, reporters flocked to the hospital. Everyone wanted to know what had happened. Jim's communications director and his inner circle—including Kevin Hagan, Teddy Pedersen, Gary Taffet, Paul Levinsohn, and Golan Cipel—were in and out of his hospital room on a regular basis. The troopers were also stationed outside the room. I stayed in the hospital during Jim's entire stay, along with Jim's mother.

Because Ronnie had been a nurse her whole adult life and at the time was a nursing instructor, she felt especially equipped to care for Jim. She kept tabs on his medications and their dosages, making sure that they were all compatible with one another. She was also aware that he would need extensive rehab and conferred with the medical staff about exactly what sort of rehab was indicated.

"Thanks for being here, Mom," Jim said.

"I wouldn't have it any other way," she replied.

Ronnie and I were his private-duty nurses, both of us sleeping in his room in side-by-side recliners. During our downtime, while Jim was working with his staff, we chatted—mostly about Jacqueline and how she was doing. "You must miss her terribly," Ronnie said. "But it's so great that you have your parents to take care of her." I did miss Jacqueline terribly, even though I spoke to my parents several times a day. I knew that my mom and dad loved her and loved looking after her, so it wasn't that I was worried about her—it was that I was yearning for her. Nevertheless, during the period of Jim's hospitalization, I left only once— to go home to Woodbridge to get clothes and spend time with Jacqueline for a couple of hours.

After five days, we left for Woodbridge. But Jim couldn't sleep in our bed, because it was on the second floor and he couldn't negotiate the stairs. So he began the second month of his governorship sleeping in a hospital bed in our living room, which now also doubled as the state-house. The staff was in and out constantly with paperwork for Jim to sign or documents for him to review. The day started at 7:00 A.M. and didn't end until midnight. And the phones were always ringing.

Left to right: Cousin Jimmy, brothers Paul and Rick, and me. Our first summer in New Jersey, 1975.

Rick, Paul, and me—standing at attention in our scout uniforms. December 1978.

My eighth grade school photo— I remember feeling like a real Jersey Girl when this photo was taken.

High School Awards Ceremony, 1984. I don't remember what the award was for, but I know that my parents were proud.

At a New Jersey
Portuguese-American
Democrats fund-raiser for
Jim's first gubernatorial
campaign, 1997.

As Jim's date to the White House
Christmas party. A dream come true for a
proud American.

Posing in my Vera Wang
wedding gown. It was the
dress of my dreams.
(© Jerry Casciano)

Our marriage ceremony,
with Father Robert
Counselman. Jim's
parents, Ronnie and Jack,
look on, October 7, 2000.
(© Jerry Casciano)

My mom and dad at my wedding. It was a big day for all of us. (© Jerry Casciano)

One of our first photos as Mr. and Mrs. McGreevey. (© Jerry Casciano)

Meeting His Holiness Pope John Paul II on our honeymoon. I thought that his blessing would guarantee a happy marriage. (© L'Osservatore Romano)

On vacation in Portugal, August 2001. I was four months pregnant with Jacqueline and trying to hide my tummy.

Celebrating many months of hard work at the Governor's Inaugural Ball, January 2002.
(© Jerry Casciano)

Promoting literacy with Jacqueline in New Jersey, December 2003.
(© Jerry Casciano)

Drumthwacket
Princeton, New Jersey
08540

STATE OF NEW JERSEY
OFFICE OF THE GOVERNOR

DINA MATOS Mc
First Lad

From the desk of

To _____ Date _____

You are seated
Table No._____

DINA MATOS MCGREEVEY
FIRST LADY
OFFICE OF THE GOVERNOR

JAMES E. MCGREEVEY
GOVERNOR
STATE OF NEW JERSEY

P.O. BOX 001
TRENTON, N.J. 08625
(609) 984-9851
FAX (609) 394-7636
dmmcgreevey@gov.state.nj.us

My official First Lady photograph. Being in that position was an awesome responsibility, one that I took seriously. (© Jerry Casciano)

Jacqueline meets the press with her dad, October 2003. The spotlight didn't intimidate her. (© Jerry Casciano)

My girls! Jacqueline with her cousins Meagan and Nicole. Drumthwacket, December 2003.

Supporting John Kerry's nomination at the Democratic National Convention in Boston, July 2004.

With our friends Jim and Lori Kennedy, 2004.

As First Lady I had the privilege of meeting a lot of famous people. Here I am with Julio Iglesias.

With Jacqueline shortly before moving out of Drumthwacket, fall 2004.
(© Jerry Casciano)

At the Renaissance Ball with my brothers, Rick and Paul, honoring the owner of
my favorite team, the New Jersey Devils, November 2006. (© Jerry Casciano)

14 · THE OTHER MAN

DESPITE THEIR ROLES AS representatives of the public, political figures lead lives that are to some degree insulated. They often have people to buffer them from the experiences of ordinary citizens—people to make their reservations for them, to pay bills on their behalf, to stand in lines for them, to drive them any- and everywhere, and even to fill their gas tanks. But they're insulated in other, more profound, ways too. The fishbowl may be transparent from the outside—so many people can see in, after all—but those inside can't always see out quite as clearly. That's why political figures routinely misread their constituents, and perhaps it's one of the reasons Jim misread the implications of his actions.

It was ironic that, despite his enormous sensitivity to managing his image, Jim could be remarkably nearsighted when it came to anticipating how some of his decisions would be perceived. There was toxic fallout from several of the choices he made—his selection for state police superintendent, a costly state-sponsored trip to Ireland, a trip to a union convention in Puerto Rico underwritten by a union leader with alleged mob ties. But worst of all was his move to make Golan Cipel his "special counsel on homeland security."

Jim appointed Golan Cipel to his administration in January 2002, shortly after commencing the affair that, by Jim's own admission, began while I was in the hospital awaiting the birth of our daughter. It was unconscionable. I guess that people engaged in adulterous affairs think they're less obvious than they invariably are, especially in the beginning. Jim was no exception. When the news of Golan's appointment broke in January, the affair was still very new, which may have been why Jim was not in the best position to see how bizarrely inappropriate the appointment was or how instantly it would raise questions about their relationship.

Newspaper accounts from February 2002—Jim's second month in office—suggest that the press not only knew that the emperor wasn't wearing any clothes but had an excellent idea of whom he wasn't wearing them with. Reporters could stoop to the worst sort of smarmy innuendo to make known what they believed was going on but couldn't yet prove. The *Bergen Record*, for example, vigilant but often shrill in its reporting, hinted at the affair in a page-one story appearing February 21, 2002, entitled MCGREEVEY PICKS ISRAELI AS ADVISER ON SECURITY; CALLS EX–CAMPAIGN AIDE A "SUPER-BRIGHT INDIVIDUAL." Further down, the item read, "Democrats close to the administration say McGreevey and Cipel have struck up a close friendship and frequently travel together." Given that peculiar subhead (it's not generally big news that an appointee is considered bright by the person making the appointment), plus the paper's characterization of Jim and Golan's "friendship," any reader over the age of twelve would have instantly understood that the paper was suggesting that "super-bright individual" was Jim's term of endearment for Golan. Jim might as well have referred to him as "darling."

If the *Record* wanted to expose Jim's adulterous affair with Golan, they should have done so directly, without stooping to innuendo. In fact, in their role as protector of the public weal, however self-appointed, they *should* have wanted to. It was terribly dangerous for Jim to appoint Golan to a position for which he lacked the credentials and experience. Compounding the danger was the fact that the position Jim created specially for Golan was undefined and that it muddied the clarity of the chain of command, undermining the authority of others, especially in the event of another terrorist attack.

As the *New York Times* explained as tonelessly as possible in an article published on February 21, 2002, Golan reported to Jim, but Kathryn Flicker, an assistant attorney general whom Jim had appointed to head the new Office of Counterterrorism and charged with the job of coordinating responses to terrorism by local agencies, did *not* report to Golan but to the attorney general. So what exactly would Golan know that he could then report to Jim?

The *Bergen Record* elaborated on additional confusion in the same article the same day.

> Flicker, former director of the state's Division of Criminal Justice, is also chairwoman of the state's domestic security task force, which was formed by the Legislature less than a month after the terrorist attacks.
>
> But it is Cipel's, not Flicker's, name that appears on the federal Office of Homeland Security Web site as the person the governor appointed as New Jersey's homeland security contact. Flicker was not available for comment Wednesday.

When Jim was asked to explain, he couldn't.

> "Well, Golan is not the official representative, but he's my representative," McGreevey said.

It was clear to the *Record* that there was trouble and that in an emergency the results would have been devastating.

> When the FBI issued a terrorist alert last week, it was apparently Cipel who first contacted McGreevey, not New Jersey's newly appointed terror czar, Assistant Attorney General Kathryn Flicker.

Also true, and newsworthy, and deserving to be placed high up in the story, instead of being buried in the middle as it was, was another piece of news: Former FBI chief Louis J. Freeh had been willing to work in McGreevey's administration heading the state's Domestic Security Preparedness Task Force.

Why hadn't Freeh been appointed? "Cipel had argued strongly against the choice," said the article.

There are pork-barrel appointments all the time, and people in such positions have been known to do less than a heck of a job. By having an adulterous affair, Jim placed himself at risk of blackmail; but by having an adulterous affair and putting his lover in a position as sensitive as homeland security, Jim put at risk the lives of the people of New Jersey, and perhaps even the entire country.

In the next several weeks, Jim had more headaches over his appointment of Golan. First, members of the federal government said they would not share classified security information with Golan because he didn't have clearance. Then members of the New Jersey legislature—mostly Republican, unsurprisingly—complained that, at a time when fiscal belt-tightening was called for, Golan was being paid $110,000. As opposition to Golan continued to harden along partisan lines, a Republican in the state senate threatened to hold up all Jim's appointments unless Golan presented himself to the state senate's Judiciary Committee to be questioned about his qualifications.

All this was taking place less than six months after 9/11 in a state that had lost hundreds of its citizens and where thousands more had seen the smoke from the burning Twin Towers.

By March 7 it was clear that the opposition to Golan's appointment was not going to disappear, and so Jim moved him to another position as his "special counsel," a move that satisfied nobody and fooled nobody. Golan's tenure as a member of Jim's administration lasted for only seven months. By August 12, 2002, Golan would be gone from the government altogether. Less than two years later, in June 2004, he would begin his sexual-harassment suit against Jim, having by then gone through four jobs, each arranged by Jim or his associates, undoubtedly at Golan's behest. In each case, Golan was fired or asked to resign in a matter of months.

It was widely assumed that I knew all along about Jim's affair with Golan. Other people knew, or at least suspected, so how could I not? That's how the reasoning went. Yes, I'd once or twice heard the rumor that Jim was gay, but I dismissed it just as I dismissed many other stories, most of which I knew not to be true. There was the rumor that we were living apart, that news account of us "necking" on Election Night 1997, and then the most ridiculous one of all—the rumor that he was having a gay tryst in Cape May the night he broke his leg and that I'd been flown in to cover for him. If I'd known that my husband was seeing someone else—man or woman—I would never have agreed to cover it up. I have my integrity. That story was completely fabricated.

The simple truth was that Jim's affair with Golan, which in hindsight so indelibly colored not just our marriage but his whole tenure as governor, was then so far beneath the surface of my daily life that it didn't even roil the waters. Even looking back, I can't see now what I didn't see then, perhaps because even the very surface of our daily lives was so tumultuous.

Unlike most public figures, I was a working mother, having returned to my job at the hospital when Jacqueline was two and a half months old. I was checking for spit-up on my suit and to make sure my daughter had enough diapers. I wasn't checking Jim's shirts for hints of another woman's perfume, and I certainly wasn't checking them for the scent of another man's aftershave. As for the odor of rumor of his affair with Golan? Not even a whiff came my way, despite the fact that, unlike many political spouses, I lived a major part of my life outside the goldfish bowl in the real world. Later I asked some of my friends what they'd known, what they'd heard, what they'd thought. They'd heard some of the rumors about Jim's interest in young men but either discounted what they heard or thought I already knew. A few knew and did think I didn't know. So why didn't they tell me? When is the last time you knew someone who was being betrayed, in whatever way, by his or her partner? Did you run to tell? I didn't think so—and the last time I was in that position I didn't either.

As to the newspapers? I don't know what I would have thought if I'd been reading the news closely. But I wasn't. And if my trusted ABC News or *Good Morning America* had reported those rumors about Jim, what would I have done? I don't know. But they didn't. Jim and I would talk— "Oh, the press is giving me a hard time about Golan," he might say, but at the time I was also overwhelmed with everything else that was going on in my life. Did I think Golan was qualified to be an adviser on homeland security? No, I didn't. He struck me as a lightweight, self-important and self-absorbed. And I can't even count the number of times I heard members of Jim's staff complain to each other, or to Jim himself, about how "demanding" or "arrogant" Golan was. But I certainly didn't think that he was having an affair with my husband.

Here's what I did think, though. One of Jim's major supporters was real estate developer Charles Kushner, and I thought that Jim was beholden to him because he had underwritten so much of Jim's campaign. I won't haul out my soapbox, but I'll pause to offer my conviction that any candidate who isn't personally wealthy enough to underwrite his own campaign is every bit as likely to be as beholden as Jim was—whether to an individual or to an industry or to an interest group. I believe that this pattern of beholden politicians will continue, often preventing them from doing the right thing, until we have public financing of campaigns, thus eliminating the debt owed to special interests and big donors. Public officials should be beholden only to the citizens they represent. They should do what's right for their constituents, without the fear of repercussions from special interests and powerful individuals.

Jim was a good fund-raiser, but he arrived at Drumthwacket heavily indebted to Charles Kushner, and that meant Jim owed Kushner. Furthermore, from everything I knew, saw, and heard, Kushner wanted Golan in Jim's administration. Kushner had arranged for Golan's visa and had given him a job when he first arrived. Knowing Kushner's interest in the Jewish community of New Jersey, I assumed that Golan's appointment as a liaison to that group was done with Kushner's support and perhaps at his urging. I assumed then that Golan's position as a consummate insider in Jim's administration was at Kushner's behest, that in fact he was there to represent Kushner's point of view and his interests.

That's what I thought. Besides, during that time, there were other things on my mind. Life was more exciting than it had ever been and yet more difficult as well. Shapes were shifting. Things were not as they had been, nor as they'd seemed.

15 · SECRETS AND LIES

❧

AS WE ROLLED OUT of January and into February, I was far more concerned about my family having a roof over its head than I was about Golan Cipel or any of Jim's troubled associates. One evening during that period, Jim said to me, "It looks like the Foundation has a hundred thousand dollars to spend on the residence. So you can start selecting carpeting, paint colors, and window treatments."

I was combing through samples within days.

Then Jim came home with an update. "Well, the Foundation doesn't have a hundred thousand dollars, after all. There's only about thirty thousand set aside."

"What happened?" I asked.

"I don't know, but that's all you have to work with."

"That will never be enough," I said. "We're lucky if we get the nursery done and maybe carpeting in our bedroom."

"We're just going to have to do a little bit at a time, there's no money."

"We'll see about that," I said. I hadn't been a fund-raiser for nothing. "I'm going to find a way to do the whole thing."

"What are you going to do?" Jim asked.

"I'm going to call some of my board members from the Columbus Foundation, to start with."

This was a Thursday. I started making phone calls, and by Monday I had assembled a group of fifteen people who were interested in donating money, materials, or time to renovate Drumthwacket.

Then I got the answer to the question I had asked a month earlier about the presence of lead paint. As I'd suspected, there was lead paint throughout the house in the walls, but it didn't pose a health threat because it had been covered by several coats of new paint or wallpaper; however, all forty-two windows in the private residence had tested positive for extremely high levels of lead and they would have to be stripped, treated, and painted. Thank heavens I asked.

In the end, it took three weeks to remove all the lead from the windows, all done by workers in getups that made them look more like astronauts than the craftsmen they were. As soon as they were finished, the work crew moved in to start renovating the entire second floor—fifteen rooms in all. They gutted the kitchen and two of the bathrooms, removed old furniture, replaced the floors, and painted. By the beginning of April, it was ready for us to occupy.

Immediately the media started nattering about the renovations. One reporter, for instance, quoted at great length Governor Whitman's view that Drumthwacket Foundation funds should be used only for the public areas, not the governor's private residence; a few others darkly noted that Charles Kushner had contributed funds to be used for the renovations to the residence; another noted—as if there were a whiff of scandal—that Jim had once worked for Merck and now some of the support for renovation had come from Merck. They thought that in light of the fiscal crisis facing the state, the resources should have been put to better use. But I had not spent a dime of the taxpayers' money. I had secured donations to the Foundation worth $500,000 of labor, materials, and cash from private individuals. It was another taste of life in a fishbowl, without so much as a fake coral reef to hide under. Was the media going to watch and criticize everything I did from now on?

I thought Jim should have defended me in the face of such criticism. Instead, he invited the press on a tour of the private residential area of Drumthwacket. I was furious.

"How could you invite them?" I asked.

"We can make them feel part of the process and, hopefully, they'll stop criticizing," he said.

"They're not going to stop just because you give them a tour!"

Jim wanted me to join the tour, but I refused. I was not going to welcome the very people who criticized us for transforming the governor's mansion into a place that my daughter could be safe in and that all New Jerseyans could be proud of. So, Jim gave them the tour himself. He wasn't happy that I went AWOL, and I wasn't happy that he was playing tour guide. So we were even.

Jim and I had been married for barely a year and a half when the work on Drumthwacket was completed in April 2002. We were little more than newlyweds. And yet, perhaps because my expectations had changed, perhaps because his behavior had changed (or maybe it was both), I started to see him in a different light. It was during this time that I began to view Jim as secretive rather than private and to wonder if he lied rather than omitted. I guess you could say I started to see the shadows.

As I look back on it now, Jim spent a great deal of time accruing secrets and arranging his life to conceal them. The affair with Golan may have been Jim's biggest secret, but it wasn't his only one. Or even his only sexual secret, as I've already indicated.

Fundamentally, I don't think being gay was the prompt for Jim to keep secrets. I think Jim's inclination to keep secrets is at the core of who he is, and maybe part of the reason it took him almost half a century to come out of the closet. Secrets are Jim's currency; they're how he moves through the world. Keeping secrets was his default position. In fact, sometimes his secrets—or evasions, or ellipses—were so oddly pointless that they struck me as bizarre. Once, for example, during Jim's time as governor, he told me that he wanted to go to dinner at Mediterra, one of our favorite restaurants in Princeton. That was all he said. *Oh, good,* I thought, *a quiet dinner.* A little time to catch up with each other. But when we walked into Mediterra, we were greeted by about a dozen other people. It turned out that Jim was throwing a party that night to celebrate the birthday of his staffer (and former driver) Teddy Pedersen. Why the omission?

Another time, he let me believe he was going to work, but later I found a single movie stub for that date in his jacket pocket; and still another time he told me he was going to meet with a particular politician, whom I later learned had been out of town on the day in question.

More serious was the time Jim told me he was going to visit Morag. I assumed—why wouldn't I?—that he would be heading to British Columbia. But later I found an e-mail that his secretary had printed out and learned from it that he had instead gone to Las Vegas. Kari, Morag, and a few of their relatives were all spending the week there living under the same roof as Jim at the home of one of Jim's friends. Later I asked Jim why he'd let me think he was going to Vancouver and left me in the dark about Las Vegas, never mind the living arrangements. "I went to see my daughter," he said defensively, seeming to be annoyed that I had asked at all. "What difference does it make where I see her?"

To this day, I have no idea why he kept these pieces of information hidden. If I asked for an explanation or clarification, as I often did, either he ignored the question altogether, as if I hadn't just asked it, or he gave me an answer that made no sense.

Though I continue to believe that acquiring money is not central to Jim, he was, and is, incredibly secretive about the subject. During our marriage, he kept his finances secret from me. Aside from Jim himself, only his secretary, Cathy McLaughlin, had access to his bank accounts. She even signed his checks for him. It was she who paid his bills and made purchases for him. He told me that she had always done it and that he preferred it that way, because he wasn't good with finances.

It would have been no effort at all for me to manage our combined finances. Although I lived with my parents for years, I was financially independent, keeping my own bank accounts—checking, savings, a 401(k), a certificate of deposit now and then—and while I didn't have a written budget, I always knew the balance in my checking account. To this day, I've never once bounced a check.

When we moved out of the town house in Woodbridge, Jim sublet it to someone we knew. Months later, quite by accident, I learned that not only had the tenant moved out but that Jim had put the town house on the market and sold it.

"Why didn't you tell me any of these events as they were happening?" I asked.

"I just forgot," he said.

"You forgot?" I asked, incredulous. "How is that even possible?"

He shrugged.

"Well, who did you sell it to?"

"I don't know."

"How much did you sell it for?"

"I don't remember," he said. "Cathy handled all that. I'll have to ask her." Of course, he never asked. If he did, he never told me about it. Later, when a real estate agent reported that Jim had accompanied Golan on a walk-through of a town house Golan was buying, a number of friends and acquaintances even suggested that Jim had given him money toward the purchase of the home. I have no idea whether this is true, even now, but it sure would have explained it. Despite the fact that I have asked repeatedly and despite the fact that it is information necessary in the process of arriving at divorce terms, neither I nor my lawyers have seen any documentation at all regarding the sale of the house in Woodbridge.

But even these sorts of secrets, with the obvious exception of anything relating to Golan Cipel, would never have led us to divorce. I was committed to Jim. I loved him and had a child with him. Sure, I was apprehensive of the way he dismissed his omissions as miscommunications or forgetfulness or poor judgment, but I still wasn't going to make his secrets a marital deal breaker. Did I like it? No. Did I understand it? No. I did know it was odd, but I also knew I didn't want to get into a fight every time he hid something. I had made a decision early on in my relationship with Jim to pick my battles, and that's what I did.

WHO KNOWS WHY JIM was so secretive? Maybe it made him feel powerful to know something that others didn't. Or maybe he kept secrets because it made him feel less fragile or vulnerable, more in control. If he felt he couldn't hold his ground in the face of pressure or requests or demands from others, maybe his secrets acted as an anchor, something to give him weight and substance. Whatever his reasons, Jim's tendency to secrecy was reinforced by his family. The McGreeveys played everything very close to vest. I remained an outsider, and I suspect that my brother-in-law did also. Significant family conversations never took place in my presence. I dated Jim for four years and was married to him for another four. We never lived more than five or six miles away from his parents during our time in Woodbridge. And yet while Jim would stop by at their place from time to time and they certainly came to our house, in all those years I was never in his parents' home. Not once. Jimmy Kennedy once observed that Jim's parents never seemed to have anyone over, but Jim explained it away by saying that they were "very private." *Why all the privacy?* I wondered.

I noticed more secrets once we moved to Drumthwacket. When Jim was campaigning, his time was his own. But when he became governor, his life was central to a network of other lives and his schedule was a matter of importance to all of them in relation to their own jobs or how they might plan their own lives. In order to conceal his whereabouts, at least from me, Jim kept me in the dark about his schedule. Actually, he had three schedules—a long-term calendar that was prepared three to six months in advance, a monthly agenda, and a daily timetable. All of these, especially the daily schedule, were available to his inner circle and were supposed to be distributed to my assistant Nina, who was the director of the office of the First Lady, as a matter of routine. But they weren't, no matter how many times I brought it to Jim's attention. This was a constant source of anxiety for me, in part because I was not kept informed of events I was expected to attend. Often, the day before an event, sometimes even on the day itself, someone would allude to it, thinking I knew all about it, and then I would have to scramble, change plans already in place, get a baby-sitter, or simply not go. And often I did scramble, because I was embarrassed at not being in the loop and didn't want anyone to know.

Whenever I complained loudly enough about not being kept informed, Jim would say that it was an oversight and would promise to correct it. For a few days, I'd receive a schedule, and then it was back to the same routine. For a while, I persuaded one of his staffers to e-mail me with Jim's schedule daily. When she left, I asked her replacement to continue the practice, but she out-and-out refused—I suspect at Jim's instructions.

All Jim's secrets started even before we were married. The secret I was most threatened by, and which kept me from ever considering the nature of Jim's relationship with Golan, was Jim's relationship with Kari. Although I didn't expect to be privy to the terms of their divorce—especially the financial terms—I was kept in the dark as to his custodial agreement. Jim evaded the question anytime I asked, and I did ask, because I wanted to meet Morag. Before we were married, Jim would plan trips to Vancouver and not tell me until the day before. The evasion continued after we were married, and once Jim actually informed me that he was going to visit Morag only when he was already sitting on a plane.

Everything I knew about Jim and Kari's separation led me to believe he still cared for her. He'd told me that she couldn't handle political life, and he'd said that he'd attempted to salvage the marriage by asking her to go to counseling with him, but she refused. I didn't know what to think.

Very early on, Jim turned away my efforts to meet Morag or speak to her on the phone. Then there was that business of having mail from Morag and Kari delivered to his office when I moved to Woodbridge, and to his secretary once we were at Drumthwacket. Did he think I was going to throw them away before he got home? Or maybe hold them over a kettle and steam them open?

I didn't know. I had accepted that I couldn't do anything about whatever Jim's relationship was with Kari, but I was determined to establish a relationship of my own with Morag or perhaps to join him in his. This was important to me before Jacqueline was born and even more so after-ward. I wanted the girls to think of each other at least as friends, if not as sisters. Still, Jim rejected my efforts to meet Morag. I tried to show my interest by asking questions or offering to go shopping for her before his trips (or for Christmas or her birthday) but he always waved away my offers. "Don't worry about it. Cathy will go out and buy something," he'd say. After a while, I stopped offering.

Jim always kept the most current photos of Morag on his refrigera-tor, so I had watched her grow over the years. When I first met him, the photo on the fridge showed Morag as a sweet little girl just out of toddlerhood. Over time she grew more distinct, a pretty child, but shy. Then came the school photo of Morag, then another of her wearing the costume she wore for her Irish step-dancing competitions. During all these years, I imagined how it would be, or could be, if we met—I could take her shopping at the local mall, we could get our nails done, we could have lunch or go to the movies. I could find out if she was a popcorn girl or a Gummi Bear girl. I knew it would take work on my part. I imagined that she would be a bit shy with me as well as a bit resistant to getting to know me, but I thought with time we would connect. And I wanted to connect. Not only was she Jim's daughter, but now we had a blood relative in common: I was the mother of her half sister.

Now, in 2002, Morag was almost ten. Jim and I had been together for six years, and still I'd never met her. In fact, I'd never even spoken to her. Jim simply wouldn't allow it. Not that he ever refused outright—not in so many words anyway. Sometimes, while we still lived in Woodbridge, I would hear Jim talking on the phone as he approached the front door, but he always finished the conversation outside the door, before coming in. If I happened to have come home after Jim and he was on the phone with Morag or her mother, he would wander out of the room I was in and into another. After we moved to Drumthwacket, if he wanted to call her, he would go downstairs, out of the residence to the offices. Now and then, if I went downstairs for whatever reason, I might overhear him. For years, whenever I raised the subject of finding some way to connect to Morag, he gave me a nonanswer or simply no answer.

I hadn't given up, though, and I'd tried various ways to get to meet Morag, all to no avail. Jim even opposed my suggestion that she attend our wedding.

"If Morag comes, Kari will have to come also, and it will be awkward," he said. He made it clear that he wouldn't budge on the issue. But he had a point, so I let it go.

I had also suggested to Jim on several occasions that Morag spend some time with us in the summer or during holidays.

"No," he said. "Her mother won't allow it."

"She's your daughter," I'd said. "She needs to spend some extended time with you."

"I don't want any problems," he'd told me. "If I fight with Kari over Morag visiting, I'm afraid Kari and her mother will poison her against me." For a while, quite a few years, I didn't push because I didn't want to complicate his relationship with Morag. I had no immediate knowledge of Kari myself anyhow, so I had no basis on which to believe or disbelieve him, though eventually I became suspicious and thought Jim's fundamental motivation was to keep Kari and me apart because of what I believed his relationship might be to Kari.

More than once, though, I asked to go with Jim when he went to see Morag in Vancouver. He went three or four times a year and stayed for a period of five to seven days each time—at Easter, sometime during the summer, for her birthday in late October, and during the week between Christmas and New Year's. I didn't expect to tag along with them every minute they were together. I just thought that gradually Morag and I could get to know each other.

"No," said Jim. "I want to spend time alone with Morag. Besides, having you there would be uncomfortable for her." What Jim said hurt me and made me feel rejected, but I could understand how, seeing her as seldom as he did, he might feel possessive of his time with her. Still,

I always felt I was there in spirit. He stayed at the Inn at Westminster Quay in New Westminster, British Columbia. After we'd been together awhile, I knew the hotel phone number by heart.

THE EASTER AFTER JACQUELINE was born, I became more insistent. "This time Jacqueline and I are going to Vancouver with you," I said to him late one night. He was already in bed, and I was about to climb in beside him.

"No, you're not," he said, suddenly erupting. He was so furious that he got out of bed. It was now a month or two after our Cape May visit, and Jim was still on crutches, so he picked them up off the floor next to his side of the bed and began to head toward the stairs. When I followed to ask why he didn't want us to go with him, he spun toward me, flinging one of his crutches at me. Thankfully, he missed. Then, picking it up, Jim hobbled down the stairs in a fit of anger and went out the front door, slamming it behind him. I was shocked. I had never expected this reaction. What's more, I couldn't understand it. I went back to our bedroom, where Jacqueline, awakened by his screaming, was now crying, and I cried with her as I held her. *What was this all about?* I wondered. *Why didn't he want me to go to Vancouver? What was happening to our marriage?*

For the next few hours, I alternated between weeping and nursing Jacqueline. By midnight, when I went to bed, Jim wasn't back. The last time I remember looking at the clock, it was close to 1:00 A.M., and he still wasn't back. When I woke up, Jim was next to me in bed. I had no idea what time he came in.

"I'm sorry I lost my temper," he said, more defensively than apologetically. "But it would just be too complicated if you came. When Jacqueline's older, she can meet Morag."

Jim and I rarely disagreed, and when we did, one or the other of us would apologize, and then we'd kiss and make up. In fact, Jim's trips to Vancouver and his unwillingness to have me meet Morag were one of the only issues we quarreled about. We didn't quite kiss and make up, because the issue wasn't resolved and was by now a sore point, but if nothing else, I was willing to have this particular fight end. Still, the damage was done.

Whether I chipped away at Jim's resistance over time, or whether something else happened, I just don't know, but in June 2002, Jim told me that Kari and Morag were coming to New Jersey.

It was about time. Maybe he wanted to show off his new life—the Princeton mansion and the state troopers who escorted him everywhere—or maybe he realized it was time for Morag to meet her new baby sister. Whatever it was, arrangements were made for Morag and Kari to visit at the beginning of July 2002.

It was a good time for their trip. The campaign was long since over, and Jim was settling into his new role as governor, which meant that he wasn't being besieged by reporters. Besides, if the press did intrude, the troopers could always intervene. And with Jim as governor, the problem of comfortable accommodations for Morag and her family was resolved.

The governor of New Jersey has the use of two secluded beach houses in Island Beach State Park, ten miles of otherwise-undeveloped land on the long barrier island off the Jersey coast. Referred to as the Ocean House and the Bay House for their location, the two cedar-shingled houses are right across the road from each other on the island, which at that point is no more than a quarter of a mile wide. Generally the governor uses the sprawling six-bedroom Ocean House, whose back door leads to a beach on the Atlantic Ocean, while guests or cabinet members use the Bay House, the back door of which leads to a beach on the bay side.

Jim had planned something of a family reunion for Morag's visit. Morag, her mother, her grandmother, her aunt, and her uncle would stay at the Bay House, while the ten members of the extended McGreevey family—Jim, me, Jacqueline, Jim's parents, his two sisters, his brother-in-law, and niece and nephew—would stay at the Ocean House.

Still, despite all Jim's new options, whatever concerns had pushed him to keep his life with me totally separated from his life with Kari and Morag all these years continued to gnaw at him. As the visit drew closer, Jim retreated into the emotional state that always indicated he was anxious: He brushed aside, evaded, or otherwise short-circuited any question and every effort I made to discuss the details of the visit. Just days before Morag and her family arrived, Jim's parents and his sister Sharon had come to Drumthwacket for dinner, and we sat around the dining room table as Jacqueline played on a mat on the floor between us. None of the McGreeveys had seen Kari or Morag at all since the two had departed for Vancouver ten years earlier, and, perhaps in an effort to alleviate their own anxious feelings, they wanted to talk about the visit, learn all the details, anticipate some of the events.

"So next week we'll all be down at the shore," said Sharon. "It'll be good to see Morag. She must have gotten so big,"

"Yes," said Ronnie. "Christopher and Catherine"—Caroline's children—"haven't seen her in years. I wonder if they'll remember her."

Jim didn't say much and looked uncomfortable.

"Are you planning to take her anywhere?" Ronnie asked.

"Oh, we'll plan some day trips," Jim said vaguely, before he abruptly changed the subject. "Hey, Mom, look at Jacqueline. Look at how she's trying to reach for all those toys on her mat."

The talk then turned to Jacqueline. But Ronnie hadn't forgotten what was on her mind. When Jim left the room, she looked at me and said, "So Kari is coming."

"Yes," I said, as noncommittally as possible. I had never discussed my misgivings about Kari or Morag with Ronnie, though Jim had once told me that his mother never really cared for Kari. Not so surprising, I'd thought. Regardless of what had prompted Kari's sudden departure, no mother is likely to feel great warmth toward a woman who flees a marriage to her son and whisks her granddaughter thousands of miles away.

"It'll be OK," Ronnie said, as if she were comforting me. "Kari will be cordial to you."

"I'm sure she will," I said. That was the end of the conversation, but clearly she had her own unease not only about the visit but about how Jim seemed to be handling it. Or not handling it. After dinner, likely at some subtle signal from Ronnie, Jim followed her outside to the gardens for a walk around the grounds. They were out in the back for about half an hour—undoubtedly discussing Kari's visit, which Ronnie would never have done in front of me—while my father-in-law, Jack, and my sister-in-law Sharon remained upstairs with me and Jacqueline. Eventually Ronnie and Jim came back upstairs.

"We were just catching up," Jim volunteered.

The July Fourth weekend came around, and Morag and her family arrived. As Jim planned, they would be at the Bay House, while we would be across the road at the Ocean House. I thought we'd spend most of our time at one house or the other and that we'd see one another on a regular basis for meals or at the beach. I was especially looking forward to having Jacqueline spend time with Morag. Jacqueline, who was now seven months, wouldn't remember the visit, but Morag would, and I hoped it would be the start of their lifelong relationship. I imagined that Kari would be as interested in having Morag know Jacqueline as I was in having Jacqueline know Morag. I didn't think that Kari and I would become best friends, but I thought that since we were the mothers of half sisters, we might spend time together with both girls. I was curious about Morag simply because she was Jim's daughter, and I thought Kari might be curious about Jacqueline in the same way.

Early in the afternoon on the day of Morag's arrival, the troopers drove Jacqueline and me from Drumthwacket to the shore. All the McGreeveys would come that day too. Meanwhile Morag and her family would come to the Bay House straight from the airport—the troopers would pick them up, and if Jim could get away, he would go too. That was the plan. Then, early in the evening—joined by Jimmy and Lori Kennedy—we'd go out to a local restaurant for dinner, and that's where we'd all meet for the first time.

Jacqueline and I arrived at the Ocean House before anyone else. Then we waited. And waited. And waited. Eventually one of the troopers told me that Jim was waiting for me outside. I had no idea how long he'd been on the island. Had he just arrived? Had he arrived with Morag and her family? I carried Jacqueline outside, and there stood Jim, more nervous than ever.

"Hi," I said. "I didn't know you were here. The troopers just told me."

But Jim was so tense he barely greeted me. I suspected that he was feeling nervous not only about the visit but also about shouldering the burden of being the event planner as well.

"My mom and dad and the others are going to meet us at the restaurant," he said.

"Where are Morag and Kari? Did they get in OK?"

"Yes," said Jim. "They've already left for the restaurant. We have to hurry to get there." He was pacing, like an animal in a cage.

"It's only a couple of minutes away," I said, trying to calm him down.

"We have to leave right now," he said, his tone impatient. "Are you ready?"

"This very second?" I asked. "No."

"Well, why not?"

"Because I didn't even know you were here till the troopers told me. I'm changing the baby and getting her ready."

"Well, really you have to hurry. We need to go." His voice revealed his strain.

As I rushed back in with Jacqueline to pick up the diaper bag along with my purse, he walked over to the car where the troopers were waiting.

When I got out, I saw that Jim and Lori Kennedy were now outside as well, talking to the troopers.

"I didn't know you were here," Lori said, greeting me.

"Yes, I got here two or three hours ago," I said.

"Jim asked us to stop by the Bay House to say hello to Kari and the others," said Lori. "So we did. When the troopers left with them for the restaurant, we came over. We knew we'd find Jim here, but we didn't know you were here. I don't understand why Jim didn't tell us you were here, or tell you that we were."

I shrugged. I didn't know either.

"He told us no one was here," she added. "And he asked us to stop across the street." She sounded apologetic.

This was all too strange.

Suddenly I realized that in my hurry to get out, I'd forgotten Jacqueline's bottle. "I have to go get something," I told Lori. "I'll be right back."

Jim, who'd been waiting at the car for me to join him, was furious. "We can't keep them waiting. It's disrespectful," he called over to me peevishly. He was almost shouting.

"Well, you go ahead then," I snapped back. "I'll just stay home with the baby."

This was one of the first times we'd truly shouted at each other, and it was shocking to both of us that we did so in front of the troopers, who tried very hard to act as if we weren't there—or they weren't.

It takes a lot to get me angry. And now I was angry.

Though Jim's behavior would get even more bizarre before Morag and her family left, for the moment he seemed stunned at his own mixture of anger and obliviousness, and he promptly went into damage-repair mode.

He started to follow me as I walked toward the house. "Can I get the bottle for you? Or help you with something?"

"No, I'll get the bottle myself."

"Look," he said, "it's just that I don't want to keep them waiting."

"What's the big deal?" I asked. "We're not that late, and the restaurant is two minutes away." I wasn't quite ready to forgive and forget.

He knew it would look really awkward if I didn't show up, so he continued to pursue me into the house while trying to placate me. "The visit is awkward, and so I want everything to be as smooth as possible."

In the interest of having the evening go as well as it could, I calmed myself down. I got the bottle, and then we headed to the restaurant.

When we arrived, everyone else, including Jim's family, was already there. I was most curious about Kari, and looked for her immediately. She pretty much looked as she did in her photographs—an attractive woman in her mid- to late forties with a pleasant smile. She was seated, but later when she stood up, I could see that she was relatively tall for a woman—maybe five-seven or five-eight. Certainly she was much taller than I was! When we were introduced, she greeted me pleasantly, though since we weren't seated near each other, there was no opportunity to make even small talk. Everyone looked settled; Jim, however, whose need to micro-manage is always a clue to how uncomfortable he's feeling, felt the urge to determine where each of the sixteen of us—seventeen if you counted Jacqueline—should sit. After several minutes of chair legs scraping, guests moving, and already-sipped water glasses being passed along to their next place setting, the dinner got under way, with Jim and me seated on either side of his mother and therefore not being in a position to talk to each other. Jim had also seated Kari and Morag next to each other and near Jimmy and Lori, all of them too far away for me to chat with any of them. Amid the clatter of the silverware and the pleasantries of the wait-ers, we made our way, via small talk, through a carefully pleasant dinner. I was disappointed not to get much of an opportunity to talk to either Morag or Kari, who both seemed quiet and reserved. What I did see was that Kari was most at ease around Jim, and he, in turn, was very solici-tous toward her. I also noticed that Kari was wearing—on the fourth fin-ger of her right hand—what seemed to be her engagement ring and wedding band.

After dinner, Jim's sister Caroline spoke to me privately. "Did you notice the rings?" she asked.

"Yes," I said. "They look like a wedding ring and an engagement ring."

"What the hell is that all about?" she wondered aloud.

I just shook my head and shrugged.

"Those are the rings she wore when she was married to Jim!"

Lori Kennedy, who as the wife of a jeweler was attuned to such matters, later told me she remembered those rings as well.

The next day we got up and were sitting at the breakfast table when we received a phone call from the Bay House. Because of Jim's comments, which seemed to be about what kind of time an unnamed "she" had had that morning, I suspected he was talking to Kari about Morag. As the conversation drew to a close, he said, "OK, sweetheart, see you later." I stared at him but didn't say anything. He glanced at me quickly, registering my look, and then looked away. Ronnie, who had overheard Jim's conversation with Kari, gave Jim a look of disapproval. I saw her take him aside and talk to him earnestly and intensely. I'm sure she was reprimanding him, though I didn't hear the conversation and neither of them mentioned it to me. It made me more certain than ever that something was happening between Kari and Jim.

Later in the morning, Jim muttered something about "meetings" and went off with several of the troopers. During his absence, I overheard two of the remaining troopers talking about a helicopter ride that seemed to be in the works. There was a helipad near the Ocean House, but that wasn't the context. It was something about a helicopter ride in New York.

When Jim returned several hours later and didn't say anything about his "meetings," I figured he had a new secret. "So how was the helicopter ride?" I asked him, with something of an edge.

"I wasn't on any helicopter ride," he said.

"Well, if you weren't on one today, you have one planned."

He blew up at me. "I don't have to tell you where the fuck I'm going or what I'm doing!"

I was furious, but before I could respond, his sister Caroline heard the shouting and came into the kitchen, where we were. "What do you mean you don't have to tell her?" she said indignantly. "Dina's your wife!"

"This is none of your business!" he said, and stormed out.

I began to cry, and Caroline put her arms around me and patted me, before following Jim. I heard their voices, although I couldn't hear what they were saying.

A few minutes later, Jim came into the family room where I was sitting with Jacqueline and asked if I would go for a walk with him so we could talk.

"I'll watch Jacqueline," said Caroline, now walking in.

We went out the back door and over the dunes and headed toward the water. It was a private beach, and except for the occasional walker, there was no one around.

"I'm sorry," he said. "I really am sorry. It's just that I've been nervous and on edge about their visit."

"Why?" I asked.

"It's Kari's first time here since she left, and I didn't know what to expect."

"That's not a reason to treat me this way. I don't get it."

I wondered if Caroline had mentioned to Jim that I'd noticed that Kari was still wearing her wedding and engagement rings. And had Ronnie mentioned to Caroline overhearing Jim call Kari "sweetheart"? I didn't know. But I did know that I had made Jim aware—repeatedly— that his efforts to keep me in the dark about his relationships and plans with Morag and Kari were hurtful.

There was something really odd going on here.

Of course, it's obvious now that Jim wasn't having an affair with Kari, but still I believe that there was an intensity to their relationship that neither time nor distance seemed to affect, and that it too constituted a kind of unfaithfulness, which, after all, is as much about the heart as about the body.

But I've come to understand Kari's visit east in a different light. Looking back, I can see that whenever any situation arose that presented Jim with the hint of conflict—conflict between two people (me and Kari), or between two lifestyles (being gay and being straight), or with the reality

that he would have to disappoint someone—instead of trying to recon-
cile or integrate, or resolve, he kept the two elements as far apart as possible. It could be anything from keeping us on opposite coasts to
keeping us at opposite ends of the table. But I think that his efforts to
position us were a reflection of his struggle to evade any and all experience of conflict internally, in his own mind. When a conflict threatened
to overwhelm him or immobilize him, he was perfectly capable of suddenly rendering himself blind to one part of the conflict or the other.

Walking along the beach now, Jim wanted to reassure me about his
relationship with Kari. "I don't know what you think, but there's nothing
going on between us," he said. Then he proceeded to tell me about his
visits to Vancouver over the years to see Morag.

"In the beginning, I wasn't even allowed in the house. I would pick up
Morag at the door to take her to the park or some other public place," he
said. His eyes were watery. He continued, "When I went there for Christmas once, I spent the day alone in a hotel room. They didn't even invite
me for dinner. It was painful."

I felt sorry for him. I even began to shed tears. We'd been walking side
by side, but suddenly he stopped walking, grabbed both my arms tightly,
and turned me toward him until we were face-to-face, our bodies touch-
ing. He pulled me closer and hugged me. "You have a husband who loves
you." He said it emphatically, trying to erase my doubts. He had a catch
in his voice and tears in his eyes as well.

Although I was still upset, I felt better that we'd had a heart-to-heart
of sorts. Jim then went on to tell me about the planned helicopter ride
over Manhattan. He also told me about a planned trip to Philadelphia
and asked if I wanted to go. He said a friend with an office in Philadelphia had called and suggested Jim visit.

I'd already overheard the troopers talking about the trip and was glad
that Jim was now telling me about it, so I agreed to go.

Jim's sister Caroline was so upset at Jim's behavior both toward me
and Kari that she decided to leave. She had planned to stay with us for
the week but simply packed up and left. She and my brother-in-law

rented a place for them and their two children farther south on the shore for the rest of the week. I was worried that this might take away one of the reasons for Morag to visit us at the Ocean House, but she did come over the next morning. She was a pretty and very quiet little girl who didn't say much. There were some gifts for her, and she opened them appreciatively, taking the paper off very carefully and folding it neatly into squares. "She's her mother's daughter," said Jim, looking on.

After an hour or so, Kari appeared at the kitchen door to fetch Morag, but didn't come in.

The following day, Jacqueline and I went along when Jim took Morag to Manhattan for the scheduled helicopter ride. He had somehow gotten another ticket to *Beauty and the Beast* so I could join them.

Only three passengers plus the pilot could ride in the helicopter at a time. Jim said, "If you want to go, you can go. I'll stay behind."

"No," I said. "You go ahead." I didn't want to prevent him from enjoying the experience with Morag. Jacqueline and I waited with the troopers and Morag and Kari's family while Jim, Morag, and Kari toured Manhattan. Following the ride, we went to Broadway for the performance. Jim didn't appear very comfortable with the arrangement, and neither did Kari, but after our recent argument he had been careful to invite me along. We brought Jacqueline into the theater, but she was cranky, so Jim spent most of the time outside with her.

The next trip was to Philadelphia, with a stop at Betsy Ross's house. As we were walking into the house, I tried to hold Jim's hand, as we often did, but he brushed it away. "Don't hold my hand now in front of them," he said. He didn't want any display of affection in front of Kari. That was something else I never forgot. Dinner was cordial but awkward. Kari was remote, Jim was ill at ease, and I was more and more suspicious of their relationship.

We ended the week with a trip to Washington, D.C. This trip had also been planned well in advance, though I learned of it only after our argument. In Washington, we stopped at a few historic places and even had lunch in the Senate Dining Room. This was a big deal. Private citizens were seldom allowed in there. Admission was by special invitation from a senator. In our case, we were guests of Bob Torricelli, who by now had resumed diplomatic relations with Jim, despite the contest between them two years earlier.

We stayed overnight, and the next morning Jim had meetings scheduled in his Washington office. He had arranged for Morag, Kari, and the entourage to visit the White House. He asked if I wanted to go with them, and I said no. I knew they were uncomfortable with me around, and I decided to go with Jim to his office instead.

The entire time she was there, Kari and I never exchanged more than a few sentences. Partly, it was because we traveled separately, with Jim and me in the car driven by one trooper, and Kari, Morag, and their family in the second car driven by another trooper. When we were out of the car, Kari seemed uneasy, and reluctant to talk. During the whole visit I think the only personal interchange we had was when she asked me if Jim ever changed Jacqueline's diaper. I said on occasion he did. "Oh," she said, "he never changed Morag's." After that the conversation seemed to run out of steam.

After Washington, Jim and I went back to Princeton, and that was the last I would see of Kari and Morag. The next morning Jim left for a meeting. I was to meet him in South Jersey later in the day, at a funeral for a firefighter, one of four who had been killed in a Fourth of July fire. Jim flew down in a helicopter, and I drove down with a trooper. It was a very somber ceremony. It was so sad to see a young woman who by all accounts had a great marriage lose the man described as her best friend. I couldn't imagine myself as a young widow, without Jim.

Despite the recent crisis, I was determined to make the best of my marriage. I had felt closer to him since our tearful walk on the beach, so I resolved to put aside my suspicions about him and Kari. Even when there was not conflict, I mused, he seemed, reflexively, to keep elements of his life separate. Any elements. All elements. He had always dealt with his relationship with me and his relationship with Kari separately. He just didn't know how to merge the two.

Back in Princeton, we were to attend the annual Governor's Tennis Tournament—participants were members of the business community who had played annually for the last twenty years. Traditionally the tournament was played at Princeton University, followed by a luncheon and the final round at Drumthwacket. I had learned recently that it was customary for the First Lady to be photographed with the players at the beginning of the tournament. So I took Jacqueline with me, and we spent about an hour with the players. One of them was Warren Wilentz, Jim's good friend and supporter. The Wilentz family was well known in New Jersey's political circles. In fact, Warren's brother, Robert, had served as chief justice of the New Jersey Supreme Court, and Jim's campaign headquarters were housed in the Wilentz building in Woodbridge.

"I don't know how you put up with all this stuff," Warren said, greeting me with a hug. I didn't know what "stuff" he was referring to. I thought that he might be talking about being at the tournament. But I wasn't sure. I just shrugged it off and said, "I do what I have to do."

"Are you going to the party?" he asked. I thought he was referring to the luncheon and said, "Yes, I am. I'll see you there." He also introduced me to one of his associates, David Wildstein, and said, "If you ever need a divorce lawyer, he's the best."

"Don't hold your breath," I said. Ironically, David Wildstein's path and mine would eventually cross again only two years later, when Jim retained him as *his* attorney in our divorce proceedings.

Later that day, Lori Kennedy asked me if I was going to the party the next day.

"What party?" I asked.

"You don't know about the party?" she said.

"No, what are you talking about?"

"The party Jim is throwing for Kari at the Sheraton in Woodbridge before she leaves for Canada."

I just looked at her. I didn't know what to say. I knew they were leaving that day, though he hadn't told me the exact time. I just assumed that if he were out in the evening, it was because he was now resuming his regular work schedule.

Lori was stunned.

"He didn't invite you?" She shook her head. "He didn't even tell you?"

I still couldn't say a word. In fact, I could barely catch my breath. This must have been the party Warren Wilentz had been alluding to.

"If you're not going, we're not going," Lori declared.

Later that day, Jim's sister Sharon called. She too said she'd see me at the party.

Obviously, Jim hadn't told anyone *not* to mention the party to me. *So just how was he going to explain my absence?* I wondered. Would he tell people that I was tired or that I had a headache? Or would he come up with a more pathological excuse? Whatever his intentions, I wasn't going to let him get away with it.

"No, you won't," I said. "I wasn't invited. In fact, I just learned of the party."

Sharon, with her strong streak of integrity, had the same response as Lori. "If you're not going," she said, "I'm not going." And neither of them did.

The following day, I went into work at my hospital in Newark but left to head back to Drumthwacket much earlier than usual. When I was just six or seven miles from home, Jim's car and security detail passed us heading in the other direction. He had waited until I was gone to give Kari, Morag, and the others a tour of Drumthwacket and made sure to leave before I returned.

That was the last straw.

Jim's trip to Drumthwacket with Kari—behind my back—made me angry, and it came on top of my anger that Jim had planned a party for

Kari and Morag in Woodbridge that night without telling me. And both of *those* came on top of his original failure to tell me about the traveling plans he'd made for Kari and Morag to go to New York, Philadelphia, and D.C. It wasn't that I wanted to go to the party in Woodbridge. I didn't. But I was Jim's wife, and he should have let me know what he was doing, especially when it came to making plans with his ex-wife.

I didn't think of myself as a particularly jealous person. In fact, I prided myself on my independence. I'd had other boyfriends over the years; most had had girlfriends before me, and some had stayed friendly with those girlfriends. It never really bothered me, as long as I felt I wasn't being toyed with or deceived. I wasn't clingy, nor was I insecure. I knew that Jim found me attractive, and while Kari was a lovely woman— thick curly hair, dark brown eyes—it wasn't his ex-wife's physical appeal that threatened me. It was her ex-husband's lack of candor and his secrets. Besides, what woman wouldn't feel troubled if she overheard her husband call his ex-wife "sweetheart," especially an ex-wife who still wore an engagement ring and wedding ring from a defunct marriage? Maybe that marriage wasn't so defunct, after all?

Unhappy because of what I knew and uneasy because of what I didn't, I had watched them with particular attentiveness whenever I could. They seemed at ease together—certainly more at ease than Jim and I were with each other that week. At the same time, they seemed reserved with one another, a reserve I didn't quite believe. After my heart-to-heart with Jim, however, I'd tried to put aside my suspicions about their relationship.

The secrets of the last few days had left me drained, but at least I had thought we'd arrived at an understanding. And now here we were, back in the same dreadful place.

As the trooper drove the last couple of miles to Drumthwacket, I called Lori on my cell phone and told her I'd just seen Jim's car heading away from Drumthwacket, and I was upset.

"You know what I'm going to do?" I continued. "I have a plan. I'm going to the Sheraton with Jacqueline tonight, but I'm not going to Jim's party, I'm going to have dinner in the hotel's dining room."

"Dina, why do you want to do that?" said Lori.

"I don't know. I just don't want Jim to think I don't know what he's doing. I want him to *know* I know. I'm sick of all his secrets. And I can't believe he's doing this to me *again*."

"I'm not so sure this is a great idea," said Lori, slowly but sympathetically. "You're really making me nervous. I feel like I should go with you."

"You don't have to," I told her. "I'm going to call Paul and Elvie and ask them to bring Meagan and Nicole. It won't be a big deal. They live right there in Woodbridge."

"Dina, I feel so caught!"

Knowing how much Jim cared about appearances and propriety, I confess I also wanted to make him uncomfortable, as uncomfortable as he'd made me. *More* uncomfortable than he'd made me. I wanted all his guests to see me at the Sheraton. I wanted them to be aware that no, I wasn't coming to Jim's party, and I wanted them, one after the other, to express their confusion over this to Jim.

"I'm really nervous about what you're doing," Lori said again. "I want to go with you, but I feel I can't, because Jim will be furious."

"Don't worry about it. Just don't try to talk me out of it."

Back at home, I called Paul and Elvie, who said they could meet me for dinner. Then I changed and told the troopers that I was going out alone. They were concerned about my driving myself and wanted to drive me. I refused. I told them that I would drive myself and would be OK. They asked how long I'd be, and I told them just a couple of hours. But none of them asked where I was going. I'm sure they knew that if I didn't want them along, it was because I wanted my privacy and didn't want them to know my whereabouts. The trooper assigned to me said, "Are you sure you don't want me to drive?"

"I'm sure. I'll be OK," I said.

"Please call if you need anything, ma'am."

I promised I would. Anyhow, they had my phone number. I took off, with Jacqueline in her car seat, and headed to the Sheraton in Woodbridge, on the phone the entire time with Lori Kennedy, who continued to be both concerned and sympathetic. When I arrived, I described the scene to her. I hurried out of the car and into the hotel, worried that Jim's security detail would see me. As I entered the lobby, I ran into a few people from Woodbridge who were on their way to the party. They greeted me and said, "We'll see you inside."

"Oh, I'm not here for Jim's party," I said. "I'm just here to have dinner with some other people." I could see the confusion in their expressions, but they didn't ask anything.

I was successful in avoiding the troopers and waited for Paul and Elvie and the girls. When Paul arrived he said, "Do you know Jim is here?"

"Yes," I said dismissively. "It's just another Woodbridge event."

I'm not proud of lying to Paul, but I didn't want to tell him that I hadn't been invited.

Just as we were finishing dinner, my cell phone rang. It was Jim. Obviously, someone had mentioned seeing me.

"If you were in the hotel, why didn't you come to the party?" He said it in his no-big-deal voice, but clearly he knew he was in trouble, and this call was his effort at damage control.

"Why didn't I come?" I repeated. "If you recall, I wasn't invited."

"You could have come to say hello."

"I don't go anywhere I'm not invited," I said.

"I'm going to an event in Jersey City," he said. "Do you want to come with me?"

"No. I'm going home when I'm done."

"Come on, why don't you come with me?"

"No," I repeated. "I'll see you at home."

"I won't be late," he said. He knew I was furious. He also knew, and I knew, that whatever story he'd cooked up to explain my absence had been exposed as a lie once the first guest who had seen me appeared in the room. Even those who didn't know either truth or lie in any detail had to know that something was off.

Jim arrived back at Drumthwacket just as I was preparing to go to bed. When I asked how the party went, he said, "It went well. You should have stopped by."

"If you wanted me to stop by, you would have invited me," I shot back.

"It wasn't a big deal," he insisted. "Kari hasn't been here in ten years and probably won't be back for another ten, and I wanted to give people an opportunity to say hello."

"Oh, that was nice," I said sarcastically, and went to bed.

16 · THE BEGINNING OF THE END

꧁ ꧂

IT WAS JIM'S THIRD year in office and I was feeling that I had hit my stride as First Lady and also as a working mother. I was one of millions of women juggling the responsibilities of career and family, but in my case I felt as if I had two careers, as well as two families—my immediate family and my extended family, the residents of the state of New Jersey. I was never as proud as the time I heard myself described as "the mother of all New Jersey."

Some days I might attend a function or play First Lady in the morning and go to work afterward, or perhaps I'd go to the office in the morning and attend a function in the afternoon or evening. As is the case with many working mothers, I often felt guilty at leaving my daughter behind, so I'd take Jacqueline with me whenever possible. If I was going to cut a ribbon, visit a school, or attend a breakfast or some another function where her presence would not be a problem, my little girl would accompany me. If I was expected to make a speech, Nina, my assistant, would keep an eye on her. And of course, there was always a trooper present, which eased my concerns about her getting lost in a crowd. Usually, the guests were all too happy to get a glimpse of Jacqueline and even play with her. She was a sociable child, accustomed to having people around her all the time. She was more than comfortable with Nina and the troopers—my troopers, she called them—and felt at ease with strangers, too.

Of course, it wasn't always smooth sailing. More than once she'd interrupt me during a speech or when I was reading aloud to a group of children, which I did frequently to promote the governor's literacy initiative and the "Book of the Month Club." I remember one embarrassing occasion when she asked me for money just as I was preparing to give a speech. All I wanted to do was to keep her quiet, so I gave her my wallet. What a mistake that was. She ran down the aisle of the room, credit card in hand, shouting, "Yay! I have Mommy's credit card!" I needn't have worried about her causing a scene. Who could do anything but laugh? What I still don't get, though, is how my little munchkin, then just two years old, understood what a credit card was. (I shudder to think what's in store for me!)

Sometimes having Jacqueline around while I assumed the responsibilities of First Lady in addition to working mother served to remind me of the importance of having a platform. I had gotten involved in the March of Dimes to promote awareness of the dangers of premature birth, its impact on families and health care costs, and the need for funding for education to prevent the increase in premature births. On this particular occasion I was speaking about my experience at a press conference in a hospital in South Jersey—the goal was to promote a new program for parents of premature children—and as I mentioned Jacqueline's name, she ran up to the podium as if to say "I'm here!!" Watching her run around as a normal and spirited child gave parents of premature babies hope that their child might also thrive in spite of the current challenges facing them. It was during that same event that Jacqueline accompanied me to the NICU. She never forgot that visit, and for a while talked endlessly about the tiny babies she saw at the hospital, and the nice doctors who cared for them. More than once, however, she has reminded me that while she may have been one of those tiny babies, that was once upon a time ago. She's a *big girl*! I guess that's why it's been ages since she's let me call her *my baby*.

IT WAS DURING THIS time—the early summer of 2004—that Jim was evaluating his bid for reelection. And he was on edge. From the time he became governor, he carried three cell phones, and though I'd often seen him juggle more than one call at a time, I now saw him pacing from room to room with a phone at each ear, the tension in his voice audible.

Jacqueline was two and a half by this time, and to her, Daddy was a treat, because he was so rarely there when she was awake.

One evening, while Jacqueline played in the nearby family room, I walked toward our bedroom as Jim was coming out of his dressing room. "Let's sit down," he said as he sat on the step outside the dressing room and patted the spot right next to him. "Let's talk." I sat and waited for him to speak. For a second, Jim said nothing, lowering his head and running his hand through his hair over and over—always a sign that he was upset.

"What would you think if I didn't run for reelection next year?"

I didn't know what to say. This was the first time Jim had ever said anything like that. Both of us were fighters, not people who folded. "I don't know," I said. "Why?"

"It's just not fun anymore," he said. "It's vicious. Not what I expected. It's all crises and scandals."

I had no idea that in just a month a crisis and a scandal of Jim's own making would force him to resign as governor on nationwide television and that life as we knew it would be over. For all I know, he saw the beginnings of that crisis emerging when he spoke to me that day. However, I also knew about the rash of scandals, past and present, that had beset his administration, and those alone would have been enough to account for his distress.

Jim had run for governor vowing to clean up Trenton, but much of the dirt was either his own or from people in or close to his administration. It had begun with Gary Taffet and Paul Levinsohn. Both men had played major roles in Jim's campaign, Gary as campaign manager and Paul as finance director. When Jim formed his administration, he appointed Gary as his chief of staff and Paul as his governor's counsel. Unbeknownst to Jim, however, during his 2001 campaign Gary and Paul had used their position and influence to make shady deals by buying and selling billboard space. By the time Jim's administration began, they had made themselves millionaires. Both were now under investigation and had left the administration by early 2003, a year and a half earlier. As a result of their actions, Jim's governorship had begun on a sour note. Jim had been furious at Gary and Paul and thought they should have known better.

The dirt had continued with Joseph Santiago's appointment as superintendent of the state police. Santiago had stepped down in October 2002, after months of charges against him, including the allegation that he had friends in organized crime, an allegation Jim had known about from the beginning. There was more. Not only had Santiago created a bogus organization on paper that would allow him to qualify for a higher rank, but there was also a disorderly persons conviction in his past. I didn't know what was true and what wasn't, but when Jim had asked me my opinion of Santiago, I told him that according to what I'd heard he'd been effective during his tenure as police director in Newark. It was widely recognized that he had reduced crime and made the department more efficient.

And then there had been the messes Jim made for himself. One was a trip to Ireland that had played in the media as a junket and a McGreevey family reunion at the taxpayers' expense. That was followed by a trip to Puerto Rico to speak to the longshoremen's union. That had caused Jim problems because some of the union officials were rumored to be under investigation for alleged mob connections. And then, worst of all, of course, there had been his unconscionable appointment of Golan Cipel as his homeland security adviser, an appointment so ill-advised that it had rekindled rumors about his sexual orientation. By August 2002, Golan, too, was gone from Jim's administration.

Now, in the last two weeks, the news had been full of fresh scandals. On June 30, Charles Kushner, who had donated $1.5 million in total to Jim's gubernatorial campaigns, was fined $500,000 by the Federal Election Commission for improper campaign donations. A week later, on July 7, David D'Amiano, another major donor and fund-raiser, demanded $40,000 from a Middlesex County farmer in return for helping him to get a favorable sale price for his land. Shortly before D'Amiano was indicted, my mother-in-law, Ronnie, had called looking for Jim, saying that

D'Amiano's mother had called her to say that her son was "missing." I don't know if Ronnie and D'Amiano's mother knew each other, but they were from the same part of New Jersey. Perhaps D'Amiano was taken in for questioning, because a week later it was all over the papers that he was under indictment. The indictment against him, written by a Republican prosecutor with gubernatorial ambitions, seemed worded to make an unnamed "state official"—obviously Jim—look as guilty as possible, although there were no charges against Jim and none pending. Jim pushed the prosecutor to make the D'Amiano indictment public so he could clear his own name, but the prosecutor refused. Nevertheless, the press had weighed in, criticizing the prosecutor for smear tactics. The prosecutor eventually had to make a statement saying Jim had no involvement in the D'Amiano case. Though the issue quickly became a nonissue, it certainly kept alive the idea that Jim's judgment was not to be trusted.

The D'Amiano scandal had taken a toll on Jim, even though he wasn't under investigation himself. But then Charles Kushner, who had also been Golan's sponsor for a work visa, was back in the news with another scandal, the worst so far. On July 13, Kushner was arrested (and would later plead guilty and go to jail) for obstructing a federal investigation into his business dealings. That's the sanitized way to put it. Actually, Kushner had hired prostitutes to entrap two witnesses—one of them his own brother-in-law, his sister's husband—who were cooperating in the investigation. The plan was that the prostitutes would lure the targets to a motel room equipped with a hidden video camera to record what Kushner hoped would ensue. One of his targets had refused the woman's solicitations entirely, but Kushner's brother-in-law had merely taken a rain check, and on his return the encounter between them was videotaped. Kushner subsequently sent his sister the videotape, threatening to make it public if her husband testified against him. Instead Kushner's sister and brother-in-law had alerted the police.

I didn't believe that Jim was involved with Kushner's or D'Amiano's wrongdoing. Yes, he cared about power, but he had never much cared about money, or at least not personally. He was disappointed in both men, and I knew this because he told me so. "How could they have been so greedy?" he wondered aloud. "How could they have been so corrupt?" But in the media coverage of each new scandal, Jim's name was invoked—the innuendo being that birds of a feather dirty their nests together.

However, shortly after Jim's "Gay American" speech, various stories broke pointing out that Jim's staff—almost all young men whose average age was twenty-eight—were paid an average salary of $77,000. This was at a time when the average New Jersey civil servant was forty-four years old and earning $58,800 after twelve years of employment. "McGreevey's penchant to surround himself with young men of questionable experience only reinforced dark rumors that Jim McGreevey was a gay man on the make," wrote the *Bergen Record* reporter who broke the story, adding that eleven staffers had received raises averaging $19,000 over the preceding three years. Golan had made $110,000 annually.

IN ALL SORTS OF ways, the Jim I thought I married turned out to be someone that I don't recognize now, and the fact is that I don't know if he was involved in any wrongdoing. But on that July night when Jim sat there on the hallway step in our residence at Drumthwacket telling me that the scandals were taking a toll on him, I believed him. I didn't want to see him hounded out of government service for problems I didn't think were of his making.

Whatever else I feel, I continue to think that Jim accomplished a lot in the two and a half years he was governor. He provided funding for stem-cell research; he made the Department of Motor Vehicles functional for the first time in anyone's recollection; he fixed the E-ZPass system, which had been beset by technological as well as bureaucratic glitches; he reduced class size and overcrowding by funding school construction; and last, but certainly not least, he succeeded in lowering consumers' auto premiums. By making regulations more favorable to auto insurers, he increased their number in the state, and the resulting competition among them prompted lowered costs.

Still, I had long wished that Jim would leave politics. I'd been with him through two all-consuming campaigns, and though I'd signed up for both of them with my eyes open, I also thought that once Jim was no longer campaigning, we would have more time together. Now, almost four years into our marriage and two and a half years into Jim's governorship, we had less time together than ever. At least when he was a candidate, I'd often been on the road with him all weekend. Now I barely saw him. He continued to conceal his schedule from me, and when he told me he had "appointments" on the weekend, there was nothing for me to do but accept it.

If Jim left politics, I wanted it to be a choice, not because he was cornered. That was what I thought, though I doubt Jim knew what I thought, about this or anything else. Once in a while he would ask my opinion—as he had about Santiago—but it was more as if I were the public's representative or a one-woman focus group rather than his partner. Otherwise he seldom asked my opinion on anything. During the campaigns, I'd felt like more of a participant. He had consulted me about his speeches, his appearance, and fund-raising strategies. On occasion, he found my political contacts useful. I always envisioned marriage as a partnership and believed that a couple should share everything, but this, unfortunately, was not the experience I was having. I didn't know what was going through his mind, but I was in it for better or worse.

"It's your decision," I told him, "and I'll support you in whatever decision you make. But don't let them run you out of office. If you want to fight for the job, I will fight right alongside you."

AS THE WEEKEND OF July 17 drew near, Jim asked me my plans, and I told him that I was preparing to take Jacqueline with me to the Ocean House for the weekend. As our routine had evolved, I generally made my own weekend plans, since Jim wasn't including me in his. He would come to the beach whenever an event on his political calendar was to be held there, and on occasion he would come down to the shore Saturday night and stay till Sunday morning, but mostly, especially that summer, he didn't make it at all. Though summer was supposed to be a slower time of year, and Jim was supposed to have more free time, we often wound up apart for much of the weekend. I didn't like it.

"Why can't you take some time off?" I had asked him more than once.

"I'm the governor," he said. "I have work to do."

"Even the president of the United States takes a vacation. Why can't you?"

"I'm thinking that maybe Morag will come again in August," he said. "Or maybe we'll go to Vancouver to see her."

I didn't take the proposal seriously. Jim often changed the subject when I confronted him, attempting to evade by attempting to appease. This dance—where I'd say, "More time!" and he'd say, "How about a vacation?"—was an old and familiar one to me.

I hadn't quite recovered from Kari's visit, though I would have been willing to accept either travel plan. When Morag—now almost twelve— came east the previous year, Jacqueline had been too young to have any real interaction with her sister or to remember her. But in the course of the year, Jacqueline had become a full-fledged person (and then some), and I thought again that the two girls could begin to forge a relationship. I had put a framed photograph of Morag in Jacqueline's bedroom, on her dresser where she could see it from her crib. "That's your sister, Morag," I told her. Sometimes when staff came into her bedroom, Jacqueline would point to the picture and say, "That's my sister."

Just as Jim devoted time to Morag, I wanted him to do so with Jacqueline, and with us as a family. Jim was also my husband, and I wanted some time for just the two of us, as well. But clearly, on this particular July weekend, he wasn't in a state of mind to be able to relax with anyone. "This is the most difficult week of my career, and you're taking off?" Jim snapped. I assumed he meant that on top of the scandals that had been on his mind, he was nearing the date where he had to decide one way or another whether to run in 2005 or not. Since he was the incumbent, the candidacy was presumed to be his, but if he decided against running, he had to let others know to give them time to organize a campaign.

"If it's a difficult week, then why don't you come with us to the shore?" I said, as evenly as I could. My annoyance at his neglect of Jacqueline, who was so eager to be with him, vied with my compassion at seeing how upset he was. I relented. "Do you want us to stay home? If you do, we will."

"No, that's OK," he said, more sad than sullen. This was Jim's way of saying he knew he shouldn't have snapped at me.

THE 2004 DEMOCRATIC NATIONAL convention, at which John Kerry would be nominated as the Democratic Party's presidential candidate, was in Boston from July 26 to 29. The night before we left, Jim—who rarely went to bed before midnight—did something I'd never seen him do before: He climbed into bed at 9:00 P.M., saying he was exhausted. Later I discovered that a day earlier, on July 23, he'd learned that Golan Cipel was planning to blackmail him. Unless Jim came up with a multi-million-dollar "settlement," Golan's lawyer said he would file a sexual-harassment suit against him. Ignorant of any of this, I was up doing Jacqueline's packing and my own, choosing outfits for myself from my walk-in closet. Beyond my closet door, I could hear Jim's restless tossing.

"Why don't you stop with that and come to bed!" he yelled finally from the darkened bedroom. "You're keeping me up with that light and with all that noise!"

"It can't be more than ten P.M. now, and I have to finish packing."

"Well, do it in the morning!"

He was in such a dark mood that I didn't argue with him. Once he was asleep, I got up to finish.

Over the next three weeks, Jim would more than once take to his bed at an odd time of the day or night.

At the convention in Boston, Jim saw—and heard—how badly the D'Amanio and Kushner scandals, as well as all the previous missteps, had weakened him. As the governor, he was the head of the New Jersey delegation; nevertheless, all the talk that had gone on behind closed doors about who might run against him in the primaries was now right out there in the open, right in his face. Democrat Jon Corzine, the former CEO of Goldman Sachs who had used millions of his own funds in his successful run for the U.S. Senate in 2000, was said to be interested in the governorship (and in fact would be elected governor in 2005). He was something of an ally of Jim's, so it was unlikely he would be considering a run against Jim in the primary. But now . . . who knew? Corzine was also connected to former Democratic senator Bob Torricelli, and everyone knew that Torricelli and Jim were not the best of friends.

The more Jim saw that his control of his public life—or perhaps I should say his public self—was collapsing, the more hysterically he tried to micromanage how his family appeared in public. Dress at the convention was casual much of the time, but Jim wanted Jacqueline in frills and me in a suit at all times. When I was getting Jacqueline ready on that first morning of the convention, he said, "Let me look at what you're putting on her. She has to be wearing a pretty dress." It was ninety-five degrees! He himself wore his suit-and-tie uniform at all times.

If you're comfortable with who you are, and if you really are who you say you are, then you can just *be* who you are. But Jim was living a lie, and because of that, he couldn't ad-lib. He didn't dare. Consequently, every single word, every glance, every outfit had to be scripted, and all his energy went to learning the script and sticking to it. I believe it was why, in interviews and in his extemporaneous talks, he was so good at staying "on message."

However, although Jim could control his words, increasingly he couldn't control or conceal the revelation of his interior life as it informed some of his more controversial decisions. The public reaction to his appointment of Golan Cipel to the homeland security position was just the first among many. But by July 2004, Jim's interior life seemed hell-bent on jailbreak. And so, as the script shredded and the costumes frayed, the public Jim fought against the private Jim by marching in the perfect family—or at least the perfectly dressed family—which he hoped would provide cover.

This was my second convention. I had attended the 2000 convention with Jim shortly after we became engaged and just days after Jim unequivocally derailed Torricelli's effort to make himself the front-running Democratic candidate for the 2001 governor's race. I had looked forward to the 2004 convention for months, because as a delegate I would have a role in selecting the person who might be our next president. But none of it was turning out as I'd expected.

One morning during the convention, Jim, Jacqueline, and I were having breakfast with Jimmy and Lori Kennedy in the hotel restaurant. "See those guys there?" said Jim, gesturing with a toss of his head to a nearby table where Jon Corzine and a few others were sitting. "Bet you anything they're talking about who they should run against me."

At a breakfast meeting the next day, Corzine said he was 100 percent behind Jim. Jim wasn't convinced. "Well, he said all the right things," Jim told me, "but he had to say all that." Much of the time, it was a whirlwind of events: breakfast speeches, lunch speeches, cocktail parties. Jim and I—and often Jacqueline—rushed from one event to another, starting early in the morning and not stopping until late in the evening. Wherever Jim went, he took us with him, as if we were his magic amulets.

One day during the convention, I left Jim and Jacqueline in the hotel room to go shopping, and after an hour or two away I returned. The three of us had been to a breakfast, all of us dressed up, despite the heat. When I got back, my first wish was to shed my suit and get into something cooler. There, sleeping on our bed, was Jacqueline, in her undershirt and diaper, with her head nestled in the crook of Jim's arm. She looked peaceful, her breathing easy. But even asleep Jim looked weary. Seeing him there in midday was like watching a fighter down on the mat just giving up before the count was done.

Another day, toward the end of the convention, the troopers dropped

us off near the restaurant where we were to have dinner with some of
Jim's supporters. As we got out of the car, Jim said to me, "Let's walk
around the block before we go in." I was happy to have some time alone
with him during this whirlwind of a week. It was now two weeks after
our first conversation about Jim's not running again.

As we walked, he again asked me whether he should run for reelection. Even though I have come to accept what a sham Jim's marriage to
me was, my marriage to *him* was not a sham. So there are still moments
of reflection when I am stunned anew, not only by Jim's capacity to
exploit me emotionally but at his willingness to do so. At this point, as I
now know, Jim and his staff had already agreed, at a meeting during the
convention, that because Golan's suit would expose him as the adulterer
he was, he would absolutely *not* run again. In fact, to protect himself,
he'd considered resigning immediately.

Jim knew—*had* to know—that I would be devastated by his unfaithfulness, traumatized by the end of my marriage, shaken by the recognition that I hadn't been able to tell the difference between appearance and
reality, and scarred in my ability to trust. Nevertheless, in asking me
whether he should run again when he knew for sure that he wasn't going
to (and even thought he might resign), Jim was toying with me, knowingly depriving me of time I desperately needed to prepare myself for
the debacle soon to come. That kind of selfishness is hard to forgive.

But I was still operating from within my marriage, not his. So this time
when Jim asked me whether he should run for reelection, I said, with an
inadvertent irony that couldn't have been lost on him, "I will support any
decision you make, but if you decide not to seek reelection, you will
appear guilty. People will think that you have something to hide."

We had planned to spend a few days in Newport, Rhode Island, with
Lori and Jimmy Kennedy following the convention. Jim planned to stay
until Monday, and Jacqueline and I would stay until Wednesday. One
night during the convention, he told me that he was not coming to Newport. He told me there was too much going on, I assumed in regard to

potential primary opponents. Then, a couple of days later, he changed his mind and said that he would come after all. I didn't know it then, but Jim's announcement of his resignation from the governorship was barely two weeks away.

In Newport, Jim remained anxious. Later, on Saturday, as we were walking to dinner, he got a call from Tom Ridge, the secretary of homeland security. Secretary Ridge told Jim that the terrorist threat level had been elevated to high alert for New York City and New Jersey as a result of the discovery of a plan to attack two financial institutions—Prudential in Newark and Citibank in New York City.

"I'm going to have to head back tomorrow morning to take care of this," Jim told me. He had decided to hold a press conference Monday to reassure the public, which was the right thing to do. But I knew as well as Jim did that it didn't take a day to organize a press conference. He had a Communications Department charged with such duties. Jim didn't really have to head back on Sunday morning at all, but he was in such a foul mood that I preferred to stay on without him.

On Wednesday, August 4, Jacqueline and I returned to Drumthwacket from Newport. It was two days before Jim's forty-seventh birthday and just eight days before he would resign on national television. I asked him what he wanted to do for his birthday.

Maybe a quiet dinner at Jimmy and Lori's, he said, adding that he really didn't want to go out.

The next day, Thursday the fifth, Jim was already in bed when I came home from work at 5:30 P.M., and he stayed there for the rest of the night, trying to sleep.

We did go to the Kennedys' for his birthday dinner the following evening, but it didn't feel like a celebration. Everyone was subdued, especially Jim. I had bought him a beautiful sweater and shirt in Newport, which I gave to him. He liked the gifts but didn't make a big deal of it. After dinner, while Lori and I played with Jacqueline, he and Jimmy went out to the backyard and stayed there for almost forty minutes. When they came back in, Jimmy had a concerned expression on his face and was quieter than usual. I noticed Lori register Jimmy's expression, although she didn't say anything.

Lori later told me that whatever Jimmy had learned that night about his old friend, he was adding it to what Jim had already told him the previous week. On reflection, I've come to think that Lori was also in on the secret. She just wasn't herself that night. If my speculations are correct, Jim told Lori and Jimmy more than he'd told me, and more than he would ever tell me directly.

The following morning, Saturday August 7, I left with Jacqueline for the shore at about 10:00 A.M. Sunday evening, when I returned, Jim was again in bed and again on the phone with an attorney, I think from Washington, D.C. He was visibly depressed, now leaden rather than agitated. During this month, I had often asked him what was bothering him, and he generally put me off by telling me he was under stress from the scandals or just tired. This time when I asked, he told me that he was "trying to figure things out."

"What do you mean?"

But his answer was vague, as his answers often were when he didn't want to discuss something, and I didn't press him.

MANY HAVE SUBSEQUENTLY ASKED me whether all these phone conversations didn't tip me off, especially ones such as this, which I knew to be with an attorney. Of course I knew that something was going on. I could see it in Jim's irritability and in behavior that was unusual for him, like taking to his bed, which he'd never done before. But a call to Jim from a lawyer didn't strike me as odd, especially given that both of the new scandals—involving David D'Amiano and Charles Kushner—involved legal matters. Jim was the governor, governing is about the law, and law requires lawyers.

Even my awareness that Jim was talking to a lawyer from Washington, D.C., didn't raise my own homeland-alert system to orange. Jim had an office in D.C., as all governors do. He also had pollsters and advisers in

D.C. I'll go even further and say that I'm sure that over this six-week period I heard the word "lawsuit" in Jim's conversations with his chief of staff and with his governor's counsel. But "lawsuit" didn't strike me as unusual either, especially in regard to D'Amiano's case.

I have been asked, What did I know about Golan Cipel and when did I know it? What did I know about Jim McGreevey, and when did I know it? But shouldn't the question be "What did Jim know about himself, and when did he know it?" Or "What did he and his staff know about Golan and about Golan's suit, and when did they know it?" I have no answers. Only questions and newspaper clippings, which no one in political life ever fully believes in, and for good reason. Should I have known? Should I have figured it out? You tell me. I was married to a man who had lied to himself for a good part of his life, who lied to others for the rest of it, and who lied to me in word and in deed, in mind and in body, in acts of commission and omission. I was married to a man who invented stories he hoped would aerosol away the bad smell of the truth, who committed adultery (never mind the sex of his partner), who withheld truths central to his being, and who had done so from the first day we met.

Should I have known?

How should I have known?

17 · ENDGAME

~ ·~·~

THE ENDGAME HAPPENED QUICKLY.

On Monday, August 9, 2004—he would resign just three days later—Jim called me after I had left work. I was running errands at a local mall.

"Dina? When will you be home? I need to talk to you."

I told him I could be back within an hour and a half.

He was silent for a moment. "I also asked Jimmy and Lori to come over and they said they could be here by seven thirty P.M." As I hung up, I felt my mind go blank and my body go numb. I knew for certain that whatever had been happening for the past six weeks was now coming to a head. My body began to shake. I called Lori before I got to the car.

"It's me."

"Oh. Dina. Hi."

"Jim just called. I know you're coming over tonight. But what's going on?"

She'd known before I did when Jim wanted to marry me, so perhaps she knew this.

"I don't know," said Lori. "Jim did call, but he was very evasive. He didn't say much."

Ordinarily, Lori would have been eager to figure this out with me, but I could feel her reluctance and her discomfort. I wondered what she wasn't telling me.

I got the trooper who was assigned to me that day to get me home as quickly as possible, and I hurried to the family room, where Jim was watching Jacqueline. Since Jacqueline was happily involved with her newest *Sesame Street* tape, Jim and I went into the sitting room. Jim sat in a chair, and I sat on the couch to his right. He was very tense.

"I want to tell you that what I'm about to say has nothing to do with you."

I nodded. He had obviously rehearsed this moment.

"I want to thank you. You've been great. You've been a wonderful wife, and I want to thank you for everything, especially Jacqueline. I want you to know that I love you." Then he repeated what he'd begun with. "This isn't about you."

I nodded but I didn't say anything. I couldn't.

"I'm being blackmailed."

"Who's blackmailing you?"

"Golan."

"Golan?" I didn't get it.

He nodded. "For fifty million dollars."

"What do you mean? Why is Golan blackmailing you?"

"I had a relationship with him."

"A relationship? What kind of relationship?" I still wasn't getting it. I wasn't allowing myself to get it.

"Not sexual . . ." he said.

He paused. I must have given him a puzzled look, a stunned look.

". . . but sexual."

I still was having trouble comprehending.

"Not sexual . . . but sexual . . . ? What does this mean? What does this mean for us?"

"I need you more than ever."

I started to cry, feeling a tangled mixture of bewilderment, injury, fear, sorrow, uncertainty, and, at the same time, relief that he still valued me. I sensed that Jim had done profound damage to our family, irreversible damage. Still, I pitied him, knowing that he knew that whatever the scope of the destruction, he was its agent. He looked forlorn. Jim got up from his chair, came over to the couch, and sat next to me. Then he just held me. "Don't worry," he said. "We'll get through this together. I just want this to go away."

All I could do was cry.

"Golan's demanding a lot of money, but I'll start begging people for money in the morning." Actually, the plan was for Jim and his advisers to solicit private money for Jim's "defense fund." Because the funds would be private and not public, they could be used however Jim wanted without his being accountable to the public. However, as I would learn sometime during that week, the real goal was to accrue enough funding to pay Golan's bribe. Just then Jimmy and Lori Kennedy walked in. They tried to comfort me, and they tried to comfort Jim, embracing both of us, and then they started to cry. Now we were all crying, the four of us.

Jim and Jimmy started talking about whether they could bargain Golan down. "Maybe two million dollars?" said Jimmy.

"Maybe three million," said Jim.

"Yeah, maybe three million," said Jimmy, nodding.

"What do you think it would take to make it go away?" said Jim.

"I don't know. He could always come back for more, I guess."

It was futile. They were spinning their wheels, grasping at straws, having the kind of conversation you have when nothing you can say or do will make any difference at all.

I couldn't stop crying, and I didn't want Jacqueline to see me in this state. I didn't want her to sense that anything was wrong. I wanted to protect her, so I asked Lori to put her to bed.

Jimmy and Lori left at about ten o'clock, and Jim and I stayed up to talk awhile. We discussed whether or not to try to pay Golan off to make the threat go away. "This is a difficult decision, and one that we will make together," he said. We went to bed, but neither of us slept.

The next morning, Tuesday, Jim again brought up the issue of agreeing to Golan's demands. "If I pay Golan off, we'll be in debt for the rest of our lives," he told me, bleakly. "We'll never own our home, we'll never be able to send Jacqueline to college. Nothing." It seemed to me that Jim was thinking that he could announce he wouldn't be seeking reelection, but that if he found a way to pay Golan off, he could see his term through to 2005.

At this point, all the particulars of the damage still hadn't gotten through to me—at least not steadily—and so my emotions slid and skittered every which way. I was in tears, then I was numb, and then I was convinced we could find a solution. But wait. A solution to what? Jim's governorship? Because he was my husband, his problems were my problems too. But where was our marriage? Was there a marriage? Had there *ever* been a marriage? Jim's words rang in my ears ". . . relationship with Golan, *"not sexual but sexual."* Had I missed signs of his *relationship* with Golan because I'd been concentrating on what I suspected was his *relationship* with Kari? Could I have recovered if that had been the case? Not that it mattered now, but I thought so. During the time I'd suspected Kari, I'd never threatened to leave. But Golan?

Never mind, I needed a respite from this. I needed a respite from myself. I took my shower, got dressed, but then felt exhausted by the effort. Still, I forced myself to go to work as if it were the kind of ordinary day I thought would never come my way again. At least there might be some distraction at work. Besides, if I stayed home, the house staff would know something was really wrong and, most importantly, Jacqueline would sense my despair. On the way to my office in Newark, I just sat in the car, not chatting with the trooper who was driving me as I usually would have.

Once I was at work, though, I couldn't function. I lurched through the day, grasping my situation and then losing my grasp on it. I stayed bunkered in my office, my door closed and calls to my office going to voice mail, as my thoughts continued to skid around my mind. The fact that the events of my life were taking place on a public stage amplified my pain, but my pain wasn't about Jim's job; it was about our marriage and our family.

Jim was signing the Highlands Preservation Bill that day and had called my office at 11:00 A.M. as he was about to board a helicopter. He told me that he was probably going to hold a press conference later at the statehouse in Trenton to announce that he would not seek reelection, and that he wanted me there with him.

"Call me back and let me know," I said. I couldn't have thought through a cogent response, but if anything was routine in our relationship, it was that Jim's plans were always in flux, and so my call-me-back response was automatic.

"OK," said Jim. "I'll call you back to confirm."

When I hadn't heard from Jim by noon, I thought maybe he'd canceled the press conference, but he called again at one thirty asking me to get to the statehouse as soon as I possibly could. He didn't explain the delay. An hour later, thanks to having a state trooper driver who could speed with impunity, we were fifteen minutes from Trenton.

Then my phone rang. It was Jim again, only now he was telling me *not* to come.

"Are you going ahead with the press conference?"

"I don't know. I have to go," he said. "I can't talk to you now. We'll talk more later."

It was no use asking him his thinking; his major political decisions were never made by him alone, but in consultation with his advisers. In fact, I thought he too often succumbed to his advisers. I was exhausted, wiped out, and red-eyed. I had barely been able to control my crying on the ride from Newark to Trenton. I needed refuge and, literally, a shoulder to cry on. Although I was just minutes from home, I couldn't face going to an empty house, so I asked the trooper who was with me to turn around and take me to Lori Kennedy's in Rahway, and when I got there I cried some more.

JIM DID NOT HOLD a press conference that day after all. When I got home later in the evening, he was again in bed and on the phone. He registered my presence, but he didn't say much of anything to me. He spent most of the night on the phone, talking to various people, including a rabbi whom he had asked to talk to Golan, or maybe to plead with him.

In fact, Jim was directing the rabbi to Golan's apartment. ". . . Yes, that's the right apartment . . . No answer? OK, just wait . . ." This conversation lasted more than an hour.

Jim got off the phone and got up to go to the bathroom. As he came back into the bedroom, I could see he was having difficulty making his way back to bed, as if he had taken several sleeping pills. He could barely walk. If I hadn't known better, I would have thought that he was drunk. At one point, his foot got caught in a lamp wire and he tripped, knocking down the lamp on his nightstand. Perhaps as a reflex, and almost to my surprise, I got up to help him as he stumbled about. I was suffering myself, and I was angrier at Jim than I'd ever been at anyone in my life. But I also felt pity for him. In fact, I felt pity for all of us. *Such a tragedy*, I thought.

Once he was back in bed, Jim took the phone and called the rabbi back again to ask if he'd succeeded in convincing Golan not to pursue the lawsuit. He hadn't. Jim was distraught. Hours on the phone, and nothing to show for it. We tried to sleep, but all we did was toss and turn.

On Wednesday, August 11, for the first time during this crisis, Jim paid a visit to his parents and his sister Sharon, who were staying at the Bay House. I don't know what he told them, but if it wasn't the whole truth, or nothing but the truth, my guess is that it was more of the truth than he'd ever dared tell them before. He also called me to say he wanted to talk that evening when he got back.

I thought he might want to reopen yesterday's conversation about paying off Golan. Maybe he'd been able to come up with the funds? But Jim never even mentioned Golan. Instead, once he was home, we sat at the kitchen table and talked, which we'd done so rarely during our marriage. Jim's irritability was gone, and he seemed almost calm.

"This is not easy, but we'll get through it," Jim began. "We have our health and our daughter." He told me that he was confused about who he was, confused about his sexuality. "I think I might be gay," he said. However tentatively he phrased it, this was the first time he'd ever used the word "gay" to characterize himself, at least to me.

Confused. Might be gay.

I began to cry. "If you thought you might be gay, then why did you marry me?"

"I fell in love and was attracted to you. You were smart, beautiful, and talented."

"This marriage was all a lie."

He said, "No, we have a beautiful daughter."

Suddenly, I was reeling, like a punch-drunk boxer—the blows had come so fast and furiously, I couldn't absorb each one in time to ready or steady myself for the next one. I'd had a few weeks to prepare myself for the possibility that Jim might not seek reelection, and I knew I could stand by his side and look poised, and maybe even relieved, as he made that announcement. But now, in the last three days, he had told me that Golan was planning to sue him for sexual assault and harassment unless he could come up with $50 million. Then he told me this had come about because of his "relationship" with Golan, which was "not sexual but sexual." As recently as dinnertime, I had little crannies of hope that at least, at the very least, Golan's attempts at extortion would disappear if Jim announced he would not run again. That way he could finish out his term, and if our marriage was dying, it could at least die in private. Now another blow: It appeared Jim would be making more revelations at this press conference. He didn't tell me what he planned to say, but I assumed he would reveal the fact that he was being blackmailed.

Another sleepless night. I was locked up in my body, a small cramped cell of dread. What I felt was akin to physical torment. I knew, my body was telling me, that my marriage to Jim was over, and my life as I'd known it was over too.

"You fell in love with a very confused man," Lori Kennedy had said to me earlier that day. Maybe so, but for a "confused" man, Jim now seemed to be finding his way. In a span of less than twenty-four hours, he would move from telling me, his wife, that he "might" be gay to telling the world that he was. I couldn't see it from my vantage point at the kitchen table in Drumthwacket that Wednesday night, but he had been traveling to this moment of self-acceptance for a good part of his forty-seven years, and was almost there, almost in the driver's seat. But the rest of those close to him, and no one more than I, were lost and disoriented. Once again, I was in the dark, in a storm, in a skid on black ice.

18 · MY DAY OF INFAMY

꙳ ⸱ ꙳

THANKS TO AMBIEN, I was able to sleep for a few hours, but I still woke up early, weary and listless, not knowing what to do or how to do it. Jim was awake but still in bed, already on the phone planning for his press conference later in the day. I walked to the kitchen to make my morning coffee, grateful for the tiny shred of routine. With the press conference looming, going into the office or even working from home was completely out of the question, and I called Cindy to tell her I wouldn't be in. What else of the life I had recognized as my own would survive?

As if she were reading my mind, Jacqueline called out to me from her room a dozen feet from ours.

"Mommy! Mommy! Come get me!"

"Good morning, sunshine," I said to her, kissing her as I always did when I got her out of her crib and hugging her, today maybe a little more tightly than usual. Did she notice? I deliberately relaxed my grip, hoping I was hiding the sorrow in my voice as well. I wanted to shield her from all of it—my grief and confusion and the uncertainty ahead. I wanted her to feel as if the day were ordinary.

My father was still taking care of Jacqueline while I was at work, but my parents were vacationing in Portugal for the month, so my friend Freddie would be baby-sitting Jacqueline today at home. They were comfortable with each other, so there wouldn't be a problem.

Jim came into the kitchen while Jacqueline and I were eating break-fast, telling me he'd be working downstairs in the first-floor library with his staff on the statement for his press conference, scheduled for this afternoon. They would work out the details of the press conference, as well as the wording for the announcement. In it, he would say that he was not running for reelection and acknowledge that he was being blackmailed. As for what he was being blackmailed about? I had no idea how he planned to handle it or if he planned to elaborate in any way.

"Why don't you come down and say hello," Jim said. Then he was gone.

Half an hour later, now dressed, I went down to the library. Around the table with Jim was a tense huddle of men, about half a dozen of them, arguing in audible but constricted tones. Among them were Jamie Fox, his chief of staff; Michael DeCotiis, his governor's counsel; Jim's political boss and mentor, Ray Lesniak; Curtis Bashaw, whom Jim had appointed to chair the Casino Reinvestment Authority; as well as political strategists Joel Benenson, Steve DeMicco, and Brad Lawrence. And there they were, sitting downstairs from our bedroom, apparently debating our future or lack thereof.

As I walked into the room, one or two got up to greet me with a kiss or a hug, and the others greeted me from their seats, their expressions sympathetic or uncomfortable or both. A couple of people just gawked at me, clueless as to how to react. I wished they would all disappear. I went back upstairs.

Later Jim came upstairs, telling me he would like me to be at the press conference that afternoon.

"I'll think about it."

"But if you come, you can't cry," he said. "You have to be strong."

"I can't promise that."

"You have to."

While Jim was downstairs with his advisers trying to figure out how to spin the fact that there was a multimillion-dollar lawsuit against him, I went back upstairs to try to figure out how in the world to tell my family. They would all have to be told one way or another.

Now it was about 8:00 A.M., not too early to call my family. First I called Paul and Elvie. Elvie picked up, and I told her that I needed both of them to come over right away.

"Is anything wrong?" she asked.

This was not a conversation I could have on the phone. "Just come over as quickly as you can. Please." I waited while Elvie repeated to Paul what I was saying.

"Dina, what's wrong?" said Paul, now on the phone himself.

"Nothing's wrong. Just come over."

They said they would get Meagan and Nicole in the car and head down to Princeton. Then I called Rick and asked him to come over. He told me it was going to be hard for him to get away from work, but if I needed him, he would come. Knowing he was there for me was enough for the moment. I said, "No, don't worry about it. I'll call you later." Lori and Jimmy Kennedy also came down from Rahway to be with me.

At this moment, only the downstairs hub of Jim's inner circle knew what was going on. Now the news would end its quarantine and begin to travel. First it would make its way upstairs to my family and friends. Then it would make its way into the world. While I didn't think Jim's announcement would make the news in Portugal, I had to be sure that my mother and father didn't learn via the TV what their daughter was going through. Jim was a public figure. He had no way of fully protecting our privacy, and therefore I had no way of protecting or shielding my parents. But I continued to search for a way to tell them.

But how do you tell your parents that just the day before, a lifetime ago, your husband, whom you've known for almost ten tears, told you that he's "confused" about his sexuality and thinks he might be gay? How do you tell them that he's had an affair with another man? I didn't want to put it into words. To do so cemented it, made it real, collapsed my life. I wasn't going to tell my parents that part, at least not yet.

Odd as it may seem, I had not given the fine points of homosexuality much thought either. As someone who considered things politically, I had long been in favor of domestic partnerships for gay couples. I thought that a lot of the legal impediments homosexual couples faced were unfair and needed to be eliminated. If one member of a couple were ill, the other should be permitted to be informed of and involved with health-care decisions. If a couple had a stable and ongoing relationship, one part-ner in the couple should certainly be able to use his or her health plan to cover the other partner. I also didn't believe that homosexuality was a "lifestyle choice" and thought it was likely to be inborn. I was, and am, also a practicing Roman Catholic. I attend mass every week, get ashes on Ash Wednesday, and go to church on Christmas Eve; and while I don't share the church's views on birth control, abortion, or stem-cell research, I did feel, and continue to feel, that marriage is a sacrament reserved for a union between a man and a woman.

When I counted the number of gay people I knew, I didn't even have to use both hands. Three were members of Jim's staff, and another was among the troopers assigned to me—a favorite, someone I liked and trusted immensely. In the previous twenty years of my life, there had been three other people I knew to be gay—a former teacher of mine, a nurse at the hospital, and a hospital volunteer. That was seven. Eight, if I counted Jim. There were probably others in the administration and in other areas of my life, but, just as I'd been in the dark about Jim, I was probably also in the dark about them.

Jim had people around to advise him both politically and emotionally, and even cheer him on. I sensed even then that while there would be many people whose hearts were with me, their sympathy would be so spiked with their discomfort that I would feel done in by it. And I didn't know anyone in whose eyes I could see not so much sympathy but empa-thy, a recognition that they had walked—"staggered" may be more accu-rate—in my shoes. No one I knew was comfortable even broaching the subject with me.

Luckily for me, Jacqueline was too young to need an explanation at this point, because I couldn't imagine how I could have gotten her through the shattering of her family, the removal from her home, the news—sudden and unexpected—that it was happening because her father had admitted he'd had a "not sexual but sexual" relationship and might be gay. And that didn't even include how he had tangled and knotted the homeland security chain of command by putting his lover in a position that, in the event of another terrorist strike, might well have risked the safety of millions. My God. Any one of those elements would have been devastating to a slightly older child.

Waiting for Lori, Jimmy, and my family to arrive, I was waterlogged with tears. But I pushed them back for Jacqueline's sake. She played and watched *Barney* in the family room, and I stopped in to sit with her during the moments I felt in control. At one point, before my family arrived, Ray Lesniak came upstairs without Jim. He sat down next to me, looking uncomfortable, and said that he had the name of a good therapist he thought I should talk to. He told me he had already called her—I assumed after consulting with Jim—and had asked her if she was available to speak with me on the phone this morning.

I should have realized what this signified. When Jim and I had spoken the evening before, the plan was that he was going to announce he wouldn't be running for a second term and possibly that he was being blackmailed. And that was all he was prepared to say, as far as I knew. But I now recognize that bringing a therapist, a stranger, into this secret was a prologue to a more devastating announcement that was surely coming. The downstairs crowd was already in the know, but I wasn't and Jim didn't even have the courage, or maybe the decency, to tell me himself.

I called the therapist, because I knew that I alone could not prepare myself for whatever was coming. She told me how bad she felt for me and talked me through my feelings a little bit. We spoke a little about Jim's affair, a little about the press conference and whether I would go or not. For the life of me, I can't recall more than that, probably because at that moment my mind was going in several different directions simultaneously. I was waiting for my family and trying to determine how I would tell them, trying to figure out when to tell my parents, worrying about Jacqueline, and trying to predict the future and what life would be like from this moment on. Somehow the con-

versation with the therapist came to an end, and I agreed to speak to
her again later.

When Paul and Elvie arrived—this was sometime between ten and
eleven—it was obvious to them that everything wasn't all right at all. My
eyes were puffy from crying and from lack of sleep. I hadn't done more
than run a brush through my hair, and I didn't have any makeup on. I
have no idea what I was wearing. By now Lori had arrived as well, and
since she was a kindergarten teacher, I asked her if she would take
Jacqueline and her two cousins into the playroom or outside. Once they
were gone and Paul, Elvie, and I were seated, I tried to find a gradual
way into what I had to tell them, but there wasn't one.

So I leaped.

"Jim's being blackmailed," I told them. "A former employee of his is
accusing him of sexual harassment, so he's not going to be running for
reelection."

"Who's blackmailing him?" Paul asked.

"Golan," I said.

"What, that Israeli homeland security guy?" asked Paul.

"Yes."

"He's the one that's blackmailing him?"

"Yes," I said. That was it. Paul looked puzzled and upset, but knowing
me as well as he did, he didn't ask any further questions. He just told me
he and Elvie would support me in any way they could.

I couldn't bear to be completely candid. Some people deal with devastating pain by sharing it. They try to surmount trauma by telling it over
and over until it doesn't hurt so much. Talking seems to lessen their
agony. But that's just not the way I'm put together. Trauma leaves me
speechless. Literally speechless. Call it denial, but although I now knew
exactly what was going on, putting it into words made it worse. My ability to speak was only as great as the pain I could tolerate. And right now,
I was bearing about as much pain as I could stand.

Paul was going off to work, with my blessing. After I walked him to the
door, I returned to the family room and to Elvie.

"There's more," I said. Then I repeated what Jim had said to me the night before. "Jim is confused about his sexuality. He thinks that he might be gay."

Like me, she was incredulous. "I can't believe this is happening." She just lowered her head and didn't say anything more.

I was reeling from Jim's disclosures of the last two days and what they meant for me privately, as a woman, a wife, and a mother. Could I have gotten beyond Jim's having an affair with a woman? I don't know. I had been suspicious of his relationship with Kari without threatening to leave. But I had no proof, and she did live thousands of miles away. As for how I would react if I'd learned that Jim had had an affair with a woman who lived close by? I like to think that with counseling and effort we could have gotten beyond it. But my sense of how I might react to such news is merely hypothetical. I don't know what I would have done. But I do know that I could not get beyond what, as of Wednesday night, I wasn't entirely willing to let in: My husband had had an affair with a man.

I had lunch prepared for the girls and attempted to play with them in between escaping to my bedroom to cry. At about two o'clock, two hours before the scheduled announcement, Jim came upstairs to the residence living room with Ray Lesniak to show me the statement that he and his advisers had crafted for the afternoon press conference. I knew he would announce that he would not seek reelection and was being blackmailed by a former employee, and I'd been preparing myself all morning to handle that. I was First Lady, and these were matters the public was entitled to know. I might be near tears, but I thought I could hold them in.

Jim handed me the statement. "I want you to look at what I'm going to say." He didn't say anything more than that. I started reading, not expecting to come upon anything I didn't already know.

"My truth is that I am a gay American." I stopped cold. In less than a day, he had resolved his confusion?! How could that be? Where had this come from? I said, "You mean you *think* you are." How could Jim be so sure he was gay? We were married. We had a child together. And what had happened to his reassurance that we would make decisions together, that we would get through this crisis together?

Jim didn't answer and instead looked at Ray, who then responded for him. "That's what he is. There's no more pretending, and we all have to accept the truth."

We do?! Easy for him to say. I was hanging over a very deep pit, holding on to a very thin branch. And, methodically and coolly, he was sawing the branch off from the trunk while Jim looked on. No more hope. In slow motion, I watched myself fall.

I read on and just a few lines later saw that Jim was going to resign as governor of New Jersey as of November 15. I said, "How can you resign November fifteenth? It's only three months away. What are we going to do? You won't have a job, and we don't have a home. Where will we go?"

"Don't worry," Ray said. "You'll have a place to live. I have three houses. You can live in one of them, and I'll get him a job."

I was crying again. All I could do was cry.

"You have to pull yourself together for the press conference," Jim said. "You have to be Jackie Kennedy today."

Jackie Kennedy?! Her husband was murdered. Someone had killed him while he was riding along in a motorcade in broad daylight. He didn't humiliate her in front of the world as Jim was about to do to me.

I was stunned at what I'd just learned and at war within myself, not sure whether to go to the press conference with Jim or not. How could he even ask me to go with him? This was the man who had betrayed me, and my knowledge of the betrayal was so new and so raw I didn't think I could bear to stand next to him. And yet . . . and yet . . . Even then, I thought of this moment, still in the future, as a moment that Jacqueline would look back on one day. In an odd way, I wanted to be there, not for Jim but for my daughter's father. The man who was leaving office in disgrace was her father, and I wanted her to know that I'd been there for her father.

There was more still. I had stood by Jim's side for so many years because I believed in him, and because I loved him, and because I had promised to be with him "in good times and bad times." I didn't particularly want to love Jim at this moment. I didn't want to feel it, and I didn't want anyone else to know I was feeling it. But love doesn't evaporate overnight, and however reluctant I was to feel it, and though I don't love him now, at that moment I still did love him. If there was ever to be a bad time, this was it. I had to be there.

Ray Lesniak was talking to me. What was he doing in this room anyhow? He shouldn't have been here—but I could barely hear him over the distraught voices inside my own head. Ray was saying, "Dina, you need to do whatever you're comfortable with. No one is going to force you one way or another."

Jim remained silent, as he had at so many other important junctures in his life, again letting others speak for him. He'd gotten someone else to find out if I would marry him, and now he was getting someone else to tell me the marriage was over. What was it with this man? He could talk to strangers, and he could talk to crowds, but he couldn't talk to me.

I walked away from both of them and went to call the therapist again. We talked about the press conference and tried to anticipate the welter of emotions I would feel with cameras popping and pointing while Jim exposed our marriage as a hoax in front of millions. Did the therapist know all this? Did she know more than she'd known a few hours earlier? She reminded me that I didn't have to do anything I didn't want to do.

When I hung up the phone, I decided unequivocally that I would attend the press conference, and I went into my closet to figure out what I was going to wear. For my own sake, I had to look put together. Jim had been playing a role and wearing a costume for most of his life, and ironically, on just the day he was shedding his costume, I understood his need for one and wanted one myself. If ever there were a moment when I had to look like a First Lady, this was it. So I decided to wear my blue St. John suit. It was one of my favorite outfits, and I felt I looked good in it. I got dressed, brushed my hair, and put on makeup. I could hear Jim showering, shaving, and getting dressed in his bathroom on the other side of our bedroom. What was going through his head as he prepared to give a single speech that would signify the end of the job he'd worked for all his life? I pitied him. As someone who had watched his career for nearly ten years and worked with him to support his goals, I wondered how he could so carelessly, so thoroughly, have destroyed what he'd achieved. How could he have let himself down like this? How could he have let *us* down?

IT WAS 3:00 P.M., time to leave for the press conference. Jim and I met in the bedroom.

"You look beautiful," he said.

I didn't respond. I couldn't.

"Let's go," he said. "We're going to be late."

We walked past the family room and told Elvie, Lori, Jacqueline, and my nieces that we were leaving.

"Are you going with Uncle Jimmy because he's going to get a new job?" my niece Meagan asked.

That was one way of looking at it. "Yes," I said, and gave all three girls a kiss and a hug. I hugged Jacqueline especially tightly. Jim and I walked down the stairs and went out through the first-floor kitchen. Olga, the residence manager; Freddie, my friend who worked in the Office of Protocol; and a few other staffers who were in the kitchen just watched us. Freddie had tears in her eyes when she hugged me. "We love you," Olga said.

Outside, the state troopers were waiting at the car. We rolled down the driveway and through the black metal gate, past reporters' cameras, and headed toward the statehouse twenty miles away in Trenton, where Jim would make the announcement. We hardly said a word during the car ride.

"Are you OK?" he asked.

How could he ask such a ridiculous question? It was now Thursday afternoon. Jim had first mentioned his "relationship" with Golan on Monday, first voiced that he *might* be gay the night before, and just two hours ago had stood by silently while I first read words on a page in which he defined himself as a "gay American" and announced that he would be leaving office in three months. Now we were heading to a press conference where he would reveal this to the world. And he wanted to know if I was OK?

As we were in the car leaving Drumthwacket, Jim told me again that I had to be Jackie Kennedy. "You have to smile," he said.

I just looked at him.

"And if reporters ask you why you're here, you should tell them, 'I'm here because he's my husband and I love him.'"

I didn't answer.

"And if the reporters ask you what you think of gay marriage, you should say, 'I'm sensitive to the issue.'"

I was trying to summon the courage—and the energy—to make it through the press conference, and he wanted me to discuss policy with reporters?

We arrived at the statehouse. Sure enough, reporters and photographers were outside snapping photos as we were helped from the car by the state troopers. The assemblage seemed both hostile and voyeuristic to me. *Snap, snap, snap.* They don't call it the "glare" of publicity for nothing. We went in through the side entrance, which was typical, through a "secret" stairway, and through the governor's outer office, out of sight of the media that had assembled for the press conference. As we made our way to Jim's office, we walked past two secretaries and through the office of Cathy McLaughlin. They looked stunned. My in-laws were already waiting for Jim in his office. They looked dazed and distraught. Jack appeared incredulous. We hugged and cried. My sister-in-law Sharon arrived a few minutes later and asked how I was and hugged me. They all looked depleted and drained.

Jim went into another office to discuss the logistics of the announcement. I paced around the office, meanwhile, looking at photos—of Jacqueline, of our wedding—and some gifts that I had given Jim. Two items stood out—one was a card with a poem about believing in yourself, which I had given him after he lost the 1997 gubernatorial election. The other, wrapped in an American flag, was a bronze eagle—a bird he was especially fond of, for obvious reasons—which I had given him for his birthday a year earlier. That eagle, I had thought, might one day sit in the Oval Office. Many thought that Jim would make it to the White House. Although we never discussed it, he would smile whenever someone mentioned that he was "going all the way to the top," and we'd just look at each other. It would have been a huge accomplishment, and if he'd decided that it was what he really wanted, I would certainly have helped him get there.

IT WAS CLOSE TO four o'clock, and we were all anxious to get this over with. While we waited, my mother-in-law, Ronnie, approached me. "Is Jim announcing that he is resigning?" she asked.

"Yes," I told her. "He's resigning as of November fifteenth."

Ronnie's eyes widened. She hadn't known this? How could he have failed to tell her? Ronnie walked over to Jack and Sharon to tell them.

Jim came back into his office. "Let's go," he said. He grabbed my hand, and we walked into the outer office, where the media awaited us. He looked over at me and said, "Make sure you smile a little more when I ask for forgiveness and thank you for bringing joy to my life."

I didn't reply. All I could think about was trying to be brave and not break down. I had thought I could do it, but now I didn't know. I pasted something meant to indicate a smile on my face and vowed I would keep it there as long as we were in public. Jim walked up to the podium and I looked out at a sea of reporters and photographers. I glanced at my in-laws, standing behind me and Jim. Their expressions were fixed and blank.

Then Jim began to speak:

> Throughout my life, I have grappled with my own identity, who I am. As a young child, I often felt ambivalent about myself, in fact, confused. By virtue of my traditions, and my community, I worked hard to ensure that I was accepted as part of the traditional family of America. I married my first wife, Kari, out of respect and love. And together, we have a wonderful, extraordinary daughter. Kari then chose to return to British Columbia.

I then had the blessing of marrying Dina, whose love and joy for life has been an incredible source of strength for me. And together, we have the most beautiful daughter. Yet, from my early days in school, until the present day, I acknowledged some feelings, a certain sense that separated me from others. But because of my resolve, and also thinking that I was doing the right thing, I forced what I thought was an acceptable reality onto myself, a reality which is layered and layered with all the, quote, good things, and all the, quote, right things of typical adolescent and adult behavior.

Yet, at my most reflective, maybe even spiritual level, there were points in my life when I began to question what an acceptable reality really meant for me. Were there realities from which I was running?

Which master was I trying to serve? I do not believe that God tortures any person simply for its own sake. I believe that God enables all things to work for the greater good. And this, the forty-seventh year of my life, is arguably too late to have this discussion. But it is here, and it is now. At a point in every person's life, one has to look deeply into the mirror of one's soul and decide one's unique truth in the world, not as we may want to see it or hope to see it, but as it is. And so my truth is that I am a gay American. And I am blessed to live in the greatest nation, with the tradition of civil liberties, the greatest tradition of civil liberties in the world, in a country which provides so much to its people.

Yet because of the pain and suffering and anguish that I have caused to my beloved family, my parents, my wife, my friends, I would almost rather have this moment pass. For this is an intensely personal decision, and not one typically for the public domain.

Yet, it cannot and should not pass. I am also here today because, shamefully, I engaged in an adult consensual affair with another man, which violates my bonds of matrimony. It was wrong. It was foolish. It was inexcusable. And for this, I ask the forgiveness and the grace of my wife. She has been extraordinary throughout this ordeal, and I am blessed by virtue of her love and strength.

I realize the fact of this affair and my own sexuality, if kept secret, leaves me, and most importantly the governor's office, vulnerable to rumors, false allegations, and threats of disclosure. So I am removing these threats by telling you directly about my sexuality. Let me be clear, I accept total and full responsibility for my actions.

However, I'm required to do now, to do what is right to correct the consequences of my actions and to be truthful to my loved ones, to my friends and my family and also to myself. It makes little difference that as governor I am gay. In fact, having the ability to truthfully set forth my identity might have enabled me to be more forthright in fulfilling and discharging my constitutional obligations.

Given the circumstances surrounding the affair and its likely impact upon my family and my ability to govern, I have decided the right course of action is to resign. To facilitate a responsible transition, my resignation will be effective on November fifteenth of this year. I'm very proud of the things we have accomplished during my administration. And I want to thank humbly the citizens of the state of New Jersey for the privilege to govern.

Each word, fewer than seven hundred of them, was a knife piercing through my heart. He had told me about the affair, and I had read the statement before we left Drumthwacket, but hearing it now in public gave it finality. I glanced around the room, not focusing on anyone, and saw stunned expressions, sadness and tears. It was all out in the open now. The lives we'd known were over. There was no turning back.

As soon as Jim completed his statement, we walked back into his office. I was relieved I'd been able to keep from breaking down on camera, but now I dissolved in tears, and Ronnie and Jack did too. We were all in disbelief. Jim walked into an adjacent office, that of Jamie Fox, his chief of staff, where others were gathered. He appeared relieved. His charade was over. He didn't have to pretend anymore.

Shortly thereafter, I could hear the laughter and applause as I sat in Jim's office in anguish, saddened, stunned, and lost. I grew angrier and angrier with the sound of the laughter. It felt like the end of my life, and these people were laughing and applauding. This was no laughing matter. I wanted to walk in there and yell, "Just shut up! All of you just shut up!" I thought of what would happen to my precious Jacqueline. What would this do to her? I thought about how my parents and friends would handle this. I didn't know how I would survive it. A parade of people came through to ask how I was doing—Jim's assistant, Cathy; Kevin McCabe, Jim's good friend who had been his chief of staff in Wood-bridge, and his best man at our wedding, and was now his assistant commissioner of labor; Kevin Hagan, Jim's deputy chief of staff; and half a dozen others. Another staff member handed me a note from my friend Celia saying that she and her sister Maria were outside and wanted me to know that they were there for me if I wanted to talk. I said, "No, I don't want to talk to anyone."

Soon Ronnie and Jack left, while Sharon stayed behind with me. We just sat there, not saying much. Jim was still in Jamie's office, waiting to hear if his announcement had succeeded in derailing Golan's lawsuit. Golan's threat of disclosure was now no threat, since Jim had exposed the relationship himself.

Meanwhile Jim walked into his office a couple of times to check on me. I told him I was going home. "No," he said, "don't go without me. We have to wait a little longer to see if this lawsuit is filed." The laughter continued in the other room. I just wanted to get out of there. I couldn't stand to hear those voices anymore. After about an hour and a half (what felt like five or six hours), Jim said, "We still don't know about the lawsuit, but let's get out of here." We walked out to the car with the state troopers, who were quiet. I was numb on the ride home. I don't remember saying anything. I didn't know how to deal with the situation. As we entered the gates, there were photographers outside snapping photos. I looked away.

WHEN WE ARRIVED AT home that evening, Jim went into the library on the first floor to wait for word about the lawsuit, to assess the situation, and to discuss the political implications of the announcement with the consultants. I went upstairs to Elvie, Lori, and the girls. I tried not to cry, because I didn't want any of them to see me that way. Your child is your child, but your very young child is also the most vulnerable and exposed flank of yourself. When I looked at Jacqueline—she was chortling about something—I felt such despair, sadness, and loss for her. . . . I knew that what I was feeling for her at that moment, I was also feeling for myself. She didn't deserve this. We didn't deserve this.

The girls were playing, and I walked into the kitchen because I couldn't bear to hear the sound of their voices or laughter. *How will I go on?* I wondered. My sister-in-law Sharon also came back to Drumthwacket. Freddie came upstairs with pizza for everyone. I had no appetite.

Jim came upstairs later. At some point in the evening, I answered a phone call from Bill Clinton. I recognized his voice immediately but didn't identify myself and only said, "Please hold on," when he asked for Jim. I heard part of Jim's conversation with the former president. Clinton must have congratulated him on his courage, and Jim referred to something in Clinton's book that he said had motivated him during the announcement. Later, John Kerry called as well.

Elvie and Freddie had both tried unsuccessfully to reach my mother in Portugal and had instead left vague voice mails, in order not to alarm her. But my mother knew that something was up and had called Drumthwacket as soon as she got the messages. Jim answered the phone, but at that moment I couldn't bear to talk to her. As much pain as I was in, telling her what had happened felt too much like delivering a blow. I just couldn't do it. "Tell my mother I'll call back," I told him. He relayed the message, and I asked Elvie if she would tell my mother for me.

Later in the evening, my mother called again.

"Did you ever get my mother?" I later asked Elvie.

"Yes," she said. Somehow Elvie, who was still at Drumthwacket, got to the phone, although I didn't know it at the time.

"What did you tell her?" I could see that Elvie didn't really want to repeat the conversation. It was upsetting to her, and she knew it was upsetting to me.

I persisted just a bit. "Well, how did my mother take it?"

"She's upset but OK. I think she was relieved that she'd finally talked to someone. God knows what she thought was going on."

"She probably thought I was dying or dead," I said.

Jimmy Kennedy came over late that evening. Elvie and my nieces left. Freddie ordered dinner for us—me, Jim, Lori, and Jimmy. She bathed Jacqueline, and I put her to bed. I kissed my little angel and waited until she fell asleep. Then I went back into the kitchen when the food arrived. I was hungry but couldn't eat much. I sat at the table, but I didn't feel like I was there. I don't recall the conversation. I just couldn't make sense of any of it.

I finally went to bed and tried to sleep, but I tossed and turned all night. Throughout the month of this developing crisis, Jim seemed to have no sense that this was a catastrophe looming in my life and Jacqueline's, as well as his own. There was no compassion, only self-absorption. I had given so much and worked so hard for Jim, and for goals I believed in as much as he did. Nevertheless, soon I would have no home, no husband, no marriage. And throughout all this, Jim had never once told me he was sorry.

19 · FRIDAY THE THIRTEENTH

AFTER THE SPEECH THAT ended my marriage and life as I knew it came Friday the Thirteenth. I had never been especially superstitious, but even if I had been I figured there wasn't much more in the way of bad luck that could happen to me. For the first time in my life, I understood the feeling of dread and doom that prevents some people from getting out of bed at all. Jim was already up, though, dressed and about to head downstairs for more meetings. He was all business, avidly focused on the to-do list in his head, seemingly oblivious to anything else.

I looked at him and at the familiar surroundings of our bedroom, which to the uninformed eye would seem almost a shrine to our now-desecrated marriage. There was a poster-size black-and-white photograph of me in my wedding gown still on the wall and a Lladró figurine of a bride and groom on our dresser, a wedding gift from Jim's sister Caroline. Elsewhere there was a photograph of Jacqueline as an infant, with me holding her. The whole room had been done in cool earth tones—beiges and some greens—because I had meant for it to be our refuge, a private space away from public life.

I tried to come to terms with the events of the last few days, tried to understand what had really happened and who Jim really was. Was this the man I fell in love with? The man I had married and the father of my child? It didn't seem possible. Everything felt distant and vague, as if it were somehow happening to someone else. At the same time, it felt all too real—too close—as if the pain were now a part of me, something I couldn't turn away from or deny. Jim's speech of the day before kept playing a loop in my mind. I tried to shut it out, but it was no use: *adult consensual affair . . . another man . . . wrong . . . foolish . . . my own sexuality . . . allegations . . . threats . . . disclosure.* I grasped for something, anything, to keep me going, but if I found any hope in Jim's assertion that he was going to take *total and full responsibility* for his actions, it was slipping away moment by moment, with Jim's flurry of activity and his business-as-usual manner.

"Oh, Dina," he said, less focused on me than on the first item he was now about to cross off his list, "I meant to tell you. You'll have to get health insurance through your job—for yourself and for Jacqueline."

I just stared at him.

He appeared pained, and his voice softened a bit. "You'll just have to. I won't have any money or any job after November fifteenth."

And then, looking at his watch, the White Rabbit was off.

Jim had just derailed my life and Jacqueline's, and rather than rush to assure me that he would lead us through this traumatic change that had been thrust on us, he seemed to be saying, "You'll have to fend for yourself." Our daughter suddenly seemed to be *my* daughter, at least when it came to taking any responsibility for her. Was this what his stance toward us would be over the next three months? Had he no notion that this was an upheaval in anyone's life other than in his own? I felt as if I had just sustained another body blow.

Jacqueline was still asleep, and I didn't want to talk to anybody, so I wandered out to the kitchen for coffee and then back to the bedroom. I clicked on the TV—more out of habit than anything—and turned on *Good Morning America,* today just for the comfort of the familiar voices. I noticed without paying much attention that Diane Sawyer was onscreen talking with two women, one blond, one with darker hair, about being a "straight spouse." In those first few seconds, I had no context for what the term meant—maybe a spouse who didn't cheat? And then, suddenly, my picture was flashed across the screen. Oh, my God, it was me, the day before, wearing that blue suit, standing silently beside Jim. That's what a straight spouse was. *Me.*

I'd been so deep inside myself as Jim had made his announcement that while I was concentrating on not falling apart, I wasn't really thinking about what I looked like. I saw this morning that I'd been clenching my teeth and resisting tears the way one resists nausea, acutely conscious of needing to stay in control of myself and my expression. I was amazed to see that I looked as composed as I did. I was also amazed that it was my experience—not even twenty-four hours old—that had prompted this morning's segment.

The women Diane Sawyer was talking to were "straight spouses," a term I would now never forget, and they were revealing what it had been like for them when they first learned that their husbands were gay. That morning, I couldn't have written my own name, much less theirs, so the names of Diane's guests floated by me. It had never occurred to me that there were other people in my position, but of course there had to be. And here were two of them. Miraculously, they seemed able to talk about their experiences without falling apart.

I couldn't watch, and yet I couldn't not watch, so, in a not-very-effective compromise, I hit the "mute" button on the remote while I stared unblinkingly at the screen. I didn't know what these women were saying, but I could see compassion, sympathy, acceptance on their faces. If they had once been angry, they no longer were, or at least they weren't showing it. I'd been thinking that surely it wasn't going to be possible to survive, but now here were these women wanting me, and anyone in my position, to know that I *would* be able to survive.

At some point, I wandered away from the television into my office. Each morning, news clippings from the daily papers were faxed to Jim through the fax machine in my office. Today the pile on the tray was thicker than I'd ever seen it. Over and over, I saw the headlines and photos of me standing next to Jim with Ronnie and Jack standing behind us. This was national news—international, even.

My assistant Nina arrived at the residence and hugged me. "I'm so sorry," she said. "Everyone from all over Trenton's been calling since last night to ask about you—people from Treasury, Communications, Education, Human Services. The phone just hasn't stopped and . . ."

She trailed off and looked at me. "How are you doing?" she asked.

I shrugged, while nodding to signal it was OK for her to continue.

"I spoke to Cindy, and there are news vans outside the hospital. When I spoke to Communications, they told me that the phone hasn't stopped ringing there either and that there are news vans at the statehouse too."

There was no point in either one of us settling down to work, so Nina, Freddie, and I sat around doing nothing more demanding than trying to entertain Jacqueline. My First Lady days had come to a sudden end. Scheduling meetings or appearances at events was pointless.

A little while later, the phone rang, and Freddie picked it up.

"It's your mom, calling from Portugal," she said, handing me the receiver.

"How are you?" my mother asked. She doesn't cry all that easily, or at least not as easily as I do, but this morning I could hear the catch in her voice. I realized she was holding back tears because she knew that if she cried, I would cry.

"We're coming back right away," she said. "As soon as we can get a flight."

"I don't want you to do that," I told her, and I meant it. I didn't want them to have to deal with the media circus. I already knew that reporters were at the hospital, and if they were at the hospital, I suspected they were staked out at my parents' home too.

"We don't want you to be alone," she insisted.

"I'm OK," I said. "I'm not alone. I'll go to therapy, and I'll be fine."

"Are you and Jim talking?"

"Yes."

"How is he toward you?"

"No different."

"He must be suffering also."

"I know he is."

"If you love him, do whatever you think is best." She was saying she would support me whether I chose to stay with him or whether I chose to leave. It was all so new to her that she didn't know what to say or how to understand the implications of hearing that her son-in-law was gay. My mother didn't raise the issue of his sexual orientation during that conversation or for many conversations afterward. But voicing her support for any decision I would make, including staying with Jim, was brave and loving, knowing as she did that the observant Roman Catholic community—and she and my father attend mass every week—is not accepting of homosexuality.

I remained concerned about Jacqueline. Even at two and a half, she was very perceptive. She already sensed that something was out of the ordinary—she was clingy, irritable, not sleeping well, and asking for "Daddy" more frequently than usual. I wanted to mask as much as I could by removing her from the fray and putting her in situations that felt familiar to her. And the truth was that I needed to escape from Drumthwacket myself. I decided to call Elvie to tell her that we were coming over so that Jacqueline could play with her cousins.

"Don't," she said, the tension in her voice obvious.

"Why not?" I asked. "It's unbearable here. I desperately need to get out. We both do."

"There are reporters staked outside the house, Dina. Trust me. You don't want to be here."

I felt like a prisoner. I couldn't even leave the house. I wanted this nightmare to be over so that I could get my life back, but I had the feeling that the nightmare was just beginning.

I checked in with Cindy, my assistant at the hospital. We knew each other very well; we'd worked together for the last eight or nine years and had had children at about the same time too. She had twins, a boy and a girl, less than a year older than Jacqueline, and we were fixtures at the children's birthday parties.

"How's Jacqueline doing?" she asked.

"Fine," I told her. It wasn't really the truth, but I just didn't feel able to go into it. I couldn't say much of anything, in fact. I guess I just wanted to hear her voice.

"And how are you? Lots of people have been calling and stopping by to ask about you."

"I'm fine," I told her, knowing she knew better.

Meanwhile Lori Kennedy, who had stayed overnight, was getting ready to go back to Rahway. Jim stopped upstairs before leaving for the statehouse. He said that it would be a good idea for all of us—him, me, Jacqueline, and the Kennedys—to get away for the weekend. He meant especially to get away from the reporters who were surrounding him like so many fruit flies.

"That's a good idea," I said. In the months to come, Jim and I would begin to spend less and less time together, but this was the day after a mammoth blow, and the knowledge that daily life would change, and would have to change, was understandably delayed. Besides, I knew I couldn't survive an entire weekend cooped up in Drumthwacket.

"How about Annapolis?" he asked.

"Fine," I answered. It seemed like I was on autopilot, with "Fine" my only response.

After Jim left, I called Jimmy Kennedy. A relative of his had just been to Annapolis and would be able to recommend some hotels. He told me not to worry about reservations, that he would take care of them.

More of my rat pack came by—first Celia, who'd been my wedding attendant, and her sister Maria. We hugged and cried.

"How could this have happened?" Celia asked. Just the question that I had repeated thousands of times in my mind.

I was glad to have them there to join Nina and Freddie. Among the four of them, they would keep Jacqueline fed, clothed, and entertained, covering for me during my helpless sieges of tears.

Meanwhile, for various reasons—including a NASCAR event—getting reservations at Annapolis was proving impossible. Calls went back and forth between Jimmy, me, and Jim's assistant, Cathy. At first the reservations were firm, and then they weren't, so more phone calls ensued. Then the phone rang again. This time it was Jim, and he was angry.

"Why did you ask Cathy to make the reservations? Why didn't *you* make them?" I tried to explain that I hadn't even spoken to Cathy, but he would neither listen nor be appeased.

Now it was my turn to be angry. Why was he upset with *me*? This was a very difficult time for him, and his career was over, but *I* hadn't done it. He'd done it to himself. He had done it to us. If anyone had a right to be angry, it was me.

Jim was still in a foul mood about the reservations when he came back later that afternoon, and he proceeded to bark at me some more. By that time, Celia and Maria, who had once owned a travel agency, were both on the phone, trying to find us a place to stay.

Cupping the mouthpiece so the hotel reservation clerks at the other end of the line couldn't hear, they just looked at Jim in disbelief. Maria later told me that she felt like hitting him.

Finally, after further back-and-forth and with Annapolis looking less likely by the minute, Jimmy Kennedy suggested we go to Connecticut instead. I agreed. I liked Connecticut. By that point, Stamford, where we finally got reservations, seemed almost as desirable as Tahiti. I tossed some clothes in a bag, and at 7:00 P.M., we took off—caravan style as always—with Jim, me, and Jacqueline in one car with two state troopers, and two more state troopers in a second car for backup. In Rahway, we stopped for the Kennedys, who piled into the second car.

Coincidentally, just as we were driving into New York, Governor George Pataki called Jim to offer his support. Just as Jim hung up, he suddenly realized that we had crossed the New York State line without his having transferred power to Dick Codey, president of the state senate. Under New Jersey law, the governor is required to transfer power to the senate president when he leaves the state so that an official would be present with the power to act in the event of an emergency. There was no reason this transfer of power couldn't be done across state lines, but

Jim—perhaps because he would so soon actually lose power—immediately ordered the troopers to turn around and head back to New Jersey. It was clearly a hysterical reaction.

"Why are we doing this?" I asked. And really, what did it matter?

I was in no mood to consider this calmly or in a more nuanced fashion. This was a weekend when we needed to be together, or at least that's how I thought of it then. We'd been through a trauma, and maybe this wasn't the weekend when we could map out the future, but at least we needed peace, a moment to catch our breath with friends we trusted.

Jim placed a call to Jimmy Kennedy in the other car to tell him why we were turning around. Jimmy didn't know how to respond, so he repeated it to Lori.

"It's not necessary for him to turn around," she said. "What are they going to do to him? Force him to resign?"

Ultimately Jim agreed with her, or calmed down anyhow. He again told the troopers to turn around, and again we were headed to Stamford.

Once we had actually made it to the hotel, our goal was to get inside unrecognized. Not an easy task when you're traveling with four state troopers. They may have been in plainclothes, but still, four men in suits with spiral phone cords disappearing down their shirt collars are hardly inconspicuous, even when they're not holding up their arms and muttering into their wrist microphones. We left a couple of the troopers at the desk to register for us. Meanwhile I pulled out a scrunchie, stuck my hair in a ponytail and, though it was dusk, threw on my sunglasses. Then I picked up Jacqueline while the others gathered the bags, and I headed for the elevators.

Jacqueline was not any happier today than she'd been for the last few weeks. She was clingy and cranky. As much a sponge as any toddler, she was undoubtedly absorbing the tension and stress from Jim and me. As I tried to soothe her and settle into the room, Jim went across the hall to Jimmy and Lori's room. Earlier I had told them with some bitterness that during this week of acute crisis Jim had never, not even once, apologized or even acknowledged the collateral damage he'd inflicted on my life.

Jimmy, or more likely Lori, must just have said something to him, because as he walked back into the room, he said, "For the record, I apologize."

His face was expressionless. His tone was flat. And that was it. One single sentence. This is the way you apologize to your wife for lying and cheating on her, for humiliating her in front of the entire world? It was such a pitiful, perfunctory specimen of a throwaway apology that I would have preferred none. I didn't dignify it with a response. It didn't deserve one. I turned away in disgust.

IT WAS NOW LATE in the evening, and none of us had eaten. Jim, constantly on the phone, didn't want to leave the hotel room. "Bring something back for me?" he asked as Jacqueline and I left with Jimmy and Lori. I wasn't in the mood to go to a restaurant, because I didn't want to be recognized, so we went in search of the hotel lounge, which we hoped might be somewhat quiet. I was relieved to see that the lounge was dimly lit, but all the same I noticed that the four troopers were sitting at the bar, watching the first day of the Olympics from Athens. I propelled Jacqueline to a table in the corner, where I sat her in a booster seat with her back to the troopers. They were among her favorites, and I knew she would shriek if she saw them. That would surely call attention to our group, the last thing any of us wanted.

Sitting next to Jacqueline, I couldn't see the television and wasn't paying attention anyhow, but when I heard "McGreevey," it registered loud and clear, as your own name always does. I glanced over my shoulder, and all of a sudden there was footage of Jim making his announcement, with me beside him in the blue suit. I turned immediately to Jacqueline and began talking to her just a notch louder than the voice emanating from the TV. I knew that if she saw the images of Jim and me on the television, she would have called attention to us by shrieking about Mommy and Daddy being on TV. Luckily, we made it through dinner without being spotted.

Back in the hotel room, I handed Jim the takeout I'd brought back.

He was lying in bed now, under the covers but still dressed and still on the phone, and he took the bag absentmindedly, though with a nod of acknowledgment. He was arguing vehemently with his staff about a forthcoming series of issues and meetings, despite the fact that some of the meetings would take place after his resignation. From what I overheard on Jim's end, it seemed that decisions were being made without his consent or approval. His tone had an unfamiliar note of urgency, even desperation. It seemed obvious to me that his anxiety was not about the meetings at hand but about the enormous power he would be stripped of three months from now. The hysteria in his voice had also been there a few hours earlier when he recognized he'd left New Jersey without turning power over to Richard Codey. (It was Codey who, as president of the state senate, was in line to succeed him as governor.) Everywhere Jim looked, he could feel his power and control draining, and he was resisting it because it scared him.

I put Jacqueline in the crib in the room, and then I got ready for bed myself. I took a sleeping pill to try to get some sleep, and Jim did the same. Neither of us was able to sleep, and as we lay there in the dark, he asked if I'd made any plans for the next day.

"No," I told him. "I'm taking one day at a time. I can't think beyond that."

The following morning, when the Kennedys, Jacqueline, and I went downstairs for breakfast, Jim stayed behind—in bed and on the phone, looking pale and deflated. When we came back, I gave him his breakfast and told him we were going out for the day. Did he want to join us?

"No, I think I'll just stay here," he said. But he had some news: *People* magazine wanted to do a cover story on us, and Ray Lesniak was negotiating the terms. He wanted to know whether I was willing to go forward with it. I told him that I'd think about it.

We got in the car, and I suggested that we go to New Milford, a town I'd been to before and remembered as scenic. But it was a longer drive from Stamford than I'd remembered, and we were in the car with the troopers for well over an hour. We arrived in the center of town, and as the troopers pulled into a parking spot, I once again put on what I would come to think of as my Gidget getup—scrunchie, ponytail, shades—and we were off. We watched a band play (although all that was playing in my mind were the events of the last six days) and then strolled around the town with Jacqueline as we tried to work up an appetite for dinner. As we were walking, Jacqueline asked for crackers, so we went into a CVS store to buy them. Standing in line to pay, I was confronted by a tabloid bearing a huge picture of Jim and Golan, with the word "Predator" in bold, bellowing letters. I didn't want Jacqueline to see the photo—another opportunity to shriek out "Daddy!" and blow our cover—so I quickly got Lori and Jimmy to take her from the store while I remained in line.

This was the second time in less than twenty-four hours that I'd had to protect her from images that represented the devastation of our lives. Hundreds of times would follow in the next months. Images of Jim and me or Jim and Golan would appear on television like sudden sniper fire, or I'd find them lurking behind what seemed an innocent enough newspaper or magazine page. I had never thought much about Golan one way or another, but now I hated the sight of him.

We walked around a little while longer and then found a place to stop in for dinner. Jim called while we were having dinner to talk to me about the *People* story, which he now thought would happen on Monday, with a reporter coming to do an interview. Would I go along with it? "Sure," I said, not really caring. By that point, nothing seemed to make a difference one way or another. That was the last I heard about it, and I don't know whether the interview ever took place or if the article was written. To me, Jim's concern over whether *People* magazine did an article about him was bizarre. Here he was, still spinning, while I was worrying about our daughter's well-being, the collapse of our marriage, and where Jacqueline and I were going to live when he was no longer governor. He was on Mars, and I was in a tailspin.

He asked where we were, and why we hadn't told him where we were going. Not that it would have made a difference. I don't think he would have accompanied us anyway. He asked me to bring him back dinner. I felt pity for him. He sounded so lost. This was a man who lived in and for the future even more than he did the present. Now everything was up in smoke, charring the present and blocking any glimpse of a future.

We arrived back at the hotel late, and he was lying in bed waiting for his dinner. What a pathetic sight, I thought.

Once we'd settled in for the night, again I couldn't sleep, even with Ambien, and neither could Jim. In the crib across the room, Jacqueline, who was a night owl, couldn't seem to settle down either.

The next morning, we checked out of the hotel and headed back home, stopping on the way at Bear Mountain in New York. It was a beautiful scene, a vista offering serenity and peace. But not today. I was carrying Jacqueline, and even she felt unusually heavy to me. As we stood there, one of the troopers approached.

"Ma'am, that family over there seems to have recognized you."

The dark glasses and ponytail hadn't provided the disguise I'd hoped for. We got in the cars as quickly as possible and headed back to the Kennedys' in Rahway, stopping on the way for take-out pizza. At the Kennedys', however, we encountered two reporters who'd been lying in wait for us—one from the *New York Post* and the other from the *Philadelphia Inquirer.* Jim acknowledged them with a wave, and we went inside, where we hastily gobbled down our pizza so we could leave as soon as possible. Both Jim and I were worried that now that the reporters knew where we were, they would put in a call to photographers and they would all be lying in wait for us when we left. Telling Jacqueline she could finish her pizza in her car seat, we took off.

For the past two days, we'd been living like escaped felons, and though Drumthwacket seemed a sad and sorry prison, we were actually eager to return there. At least there, the reporters could be kept at more of a distance. I felt locked in, but the press would be locked out. When we arrived at the gate to Drumthwacket, sure enough a small crowd of reporters and photographers awaited us.

At Drumthwacket, it was another sleepless and sad night. All I could do was cry. As for Jim, he told me his adversaries were trying to force him out of office earlier than he wanted to leave so that an election could be called for November rather than allowing for Democrat Richard Codey to succeed Jim. Some Democratic bosses wanted to put their own person on the ballot, and of course all the Republicans favored an election. "I'm fighting for my survival," he said, "and I need you to be strong. You can't fall apart."

Easy for him to say.

THE NEXT FEW DAYS were a spin cycle of despair, anger, pain, and uncertainty. I wandered around Drumthwacket aimlessly. I contemplated going to work but quickly decided against it, because I knew I would be beset by reporters' phone calls or possibly even surprise visits from reporters themselves. As for other employees in the hospital—people who'd known me by sight for years—I didn't know how to face them. How could I? I was ashamed. How could I have allowed something like this to happen to me? What did people think? Did they think that the press speculations about me, even accusations, were right? Many journalists were convinced that I'd known all along that Jim was gay and that my marriage had been a contrived political arrangement. Some took gratuitous swipes at Hillary Clinton while taking swipes at me, saying that, like her, I was an opportunist, and that I'd married Jim knowing he was gay because I wanted to be First Lady and wanted to advance my own political future.

Reading those stupid speculations made me angrier and even more depressed. I couldn't stand what was being said by people who didn't know me or anything about me. I would never have married Jim knowing that he was gay. And, as much as I'd enjoyed politics before I married him, I wouldn't have married him as a way of advancing my own chances of becoming a successful candidate for office myself either. Who needed Jim? I would have done it on my own if I'd wanted to.

Most of all, I would never have had a child with Jim if I'd known he was gay. I had a mother and father who loved each other deeply, as they loved me. As much as I wanted that kind of steadying love for myself, I wanted it for my child even more. So for people to say that mine was an arranged and cynical marriage was insulting and stupid. What woman in her right mind—and believe me, I *am* in my right mind—would while away the best years of her life with a man who cannot really desire her? Or who cannot respond wholeheartedly to her desire? Not only would I not knowingly have married a gay man, but I would never have allowed a gay man to father my child. A marriage between a straight person and a gay person is by definition unstable, and the last thing I wanted was for my daughter to suffer the consequences of a broken home, as in fact she has.

One of the only places I felt remotely at peace was at my computer—my own little Panama Canal, where I could control what got through to me and when it got through. During those first days, when even sleeping pills didn't work, I would get up out of bed and wander over to my computer in the middle of the night. In the middle of one night—was it the day after Jim's announcement? the day after that? who even knows?—I found an e-mail from Dan Mulhern, the husband of Jennifer Granholm, the governor of Michigan, whom I'd once met at a National Governors Association conference. He was writing to tell me that one of his staffers had, like me, discovered that her husband was gay and thought I might want to know about an organization called Straight Spouses Network.

I went to the Web site instantly and started to read up about the organization. It sounded suddenly familiar, so I found a photograph of its founder, and sure enough Amity Pierce Buxton, Ph.D., was the woman Diane Sawyer had been interviewing on *Good Morning America*. I wrote to Amity immediately at her Web site, and two weeks after Jim's announcement, in one of my first trips beyond work or Drumthwacket, I met her at the Boathouse restaurant in Central Park. In public, I was still trying to disguise myself, and in general I was succeeding. Because I'm so tiny—barely five feet tall—when I have sunglasses on and my hair in a ponytail, I can pass for someone not quite old enough to vote. Still, though my disguise was pretty reliable most of the time, it was better not to push it and for me to keep moving, just in case. But Amity and I wanted to be able to sit and talk. During the past few weeks, I'd learned that it was easier to hide in plain sight than to hide indoors, so we sat on the deck outside the Boathouse, where we were able to talk comfortably and yet privately.

Amity offered me a great deal of support and comfort that afternoon, for which I was, and am, grateful. I still was in unrelenting pain, but at least I didn't feel so alone. Amity mentioned to me that she had received hundreds of e-mails from spouses in my position and that many told her that through me they felt as if their anguished experience had been given a face. That knowledge didn't end my pain, but I was consoled by knowing that at least it had done someone else some good.

Back at Drumthwacket, I continued to wander around the house, washed by waves of more despair, more anger, more pain, and more uncertainty. I couldn't imagine surviving this calamity. I didn't know how. While I was trying to deal with the betrayal and humiliation, Jim continued to act as if Jacqueline and I were no longer of any concern to him. At least, that's what he did much of the time. It made me so angry. One day, after putting Jacqueline to bed, I tried to talk to him, to tell him what I was feeling. "My life has fallen apart," I told him. "I sacrificed so much. I loved you, and now I have nothing."

"I had dreams," he said, by way of dismissing my feelings and turning the spotlight back onto himself. And then, addressing my feelings only to critique them, he added, "We can't fall apart. We have to fight, we have to stay busy and make a to-do list." How could he be so emotionally deaf? There was no point in talking to him.

I was on my own. Who else could I talk to? Aside from Amity Buxton, there was only one person I could even think of. A day or two earlier, I'd received a note in the mail from a childhood friend of mine who had discovered that his wife was a lesbian. We'd lost touch over the years, and I hadn't known before of his situation. He had since remarried and was trying in his way to tell me that I would heal and recover.

But learning that there were others in my circumstance did not make me feel any better—most of the people I'd heard from were still suffering and still trying to make sense of their lives, even years after their spouses came out. Would that happen to me, too? Also, all of them had been able to deal with their betrayal privately. They could tell whom they wanted to when they wanted to, or they could choose to say nothing at all. Everyone—friends, acquaintances, and strangers alike—knew what had happened to me. My exposure—and my humiliation—was public.

Besides, as much as I tried to take solace in the fact that I wasn't alone, that there were others who had suffered as I was suffering, I kept coming back to the realization that Jim must have deliberately deceived me from the beginning of our relationship. I had kept away from newspapers during Jim's administration; but while I often find the press intrusive, I generally don't believe they fabricate quotes, so the following interchange between Kari Schutz and *New York Times* reporter Michelle O'Donnell, published on August 14, 2004, two days after Jim's announcement, was not only damning but at last made it clear why it was that Jim was so eager to keep Kari and me apart.

> In a telephone interview, Ms. Schutz said she thought her former husband's announcement [that he was a "gay American"] was courageous, and that it did not take her by surprise.
>
> "We knew this was going to happen," she said. "We are always in touch. He phones frequently, and always asks about our daughter."
>
> Ms. Schutz was asked if she was concerned about criticism of the circumstances surrounding the governor's involvement with a former aide, Golan Cipel.
>
> "We are just trying to support him in any way we can," she said of the governor, adding that "he is totally dedicated to his family and his career in public service."
>
> When asked if she knew her husband was gay, Ms. Schutz, who has not remarried, answered that she filed for divorce because "the public life was not for me."
>
> "I wanted to return to British Columbia," she said. "It is a different life here, and I was used to that."
>
> When asked if she knew that Mr. McGreevey was gay before their divorce, she said: "I'll leave it at that."

What more did I need? Jim hadn't been some young man who had been confused about his sexuality, who had tried marriage with a woman only to come to terms with the fact that he was gay. Jim was forty-three when we married, and he had been married before. By all accounts, he had known of his preference for men for many years before our relationship. And despite his lofty stance about his desire to live an authentic life as a "gay American," Jim's coming out had been prompted not by soul-searching or by a desire to live his truth but by blackmail. His decision to look deeply into the mirror of his soul had come about only because somebody had already shattered that mirror. And now our lives were shattered.

Nothing was comfortable. Staying in Drumthwacket felt like imprisonment, being out and recognizable felt too exposed, and being out but in disguise left me with an edge of anxiety all the time. So all I could do was cry. One day when I needed to go to the bank, I told the trooper to take me to the drive-through. Jacqueline also needed diapers, so after the bank, we headed to Babies "R" Us, but once we pulled into the parking lot, I realized I couldn't possibly go in, because I was sure to be recognized. Here I was, a mother who couldn't even buy her daughter diapers!

I often went to Lori Kennedy's to cry. But even there I found no peace, because reporters frequently waited outside her home hoping for a possible sighting of me and/or Jim. One of the days I went there, the trooper who was driving me told me that he would park and wait for me a block away to avoid being spotted. I thought it was an overreaction, but as it turned out, it wasn't. Just an hour or so earlier, reporters had been there. Were they ever going to leave me alone?

I was still having telephone sessions with the therapist, and during one of them she asked me if I could think of anyone else who'd been in deeply personal marital turmoil while also being stalked by the media.

"The only person who comes to mind is Hillary Clinton," I said. The former First Lady was now in her fourth year as a senator from New York.

"Well, then, why don't you call her?" she suggested. "See what advice she might have for you about dealing with the media."

It seemed like a good idea, so I asked Nina to get in touch with Hillary Clinton's office. She did, and she was able to set up a time for me to talk to Hillary the following day. Nina and Freddie were spending the days (and Freddie the nights) at Drumthwacket, and I was grateful for that, because they could distract Jacqueline whenever I broke down.

On August 18, not even a week after Jim's announcement, I left Drumthwacket for the day to visit several friends who had homes at the Jersey shore. My first stop was at the home of my good friends Jerry Casciano, our wedding photographer who became the governor's photographer, and his wife, Lori. These days, Jerry lives an enviable life—in a comfortable home with his wife and child and work that matters to him. That weekend, though, he told me a story about his life that he'd never before shared with me. Several years back, his mother had died, a friend had wrecked his car, and he'd broken up with his girlfriend after investing all his money in her farm. "Within a two-week period," he told me, "I was motherless, homeless, carless, penniless, and loveless." He said he was sharing a story this personal to give me hope. "I want you to know that I recovered," he told me, "and you will too."

After visiting with Jerry and Lori, I headed to visit my friend Mona. I'd known Mona for years. In fact, it was Mona who had come to the hospital to be with me and watch the returns on Election Night 2001, the night Jim had been elected. While I was at Mona's, Hillary Clinton called me on my cell phone. Right from the beginning, she was very compassionate. She asked how I was doing and warned me not to let Jim's advisers make decisions for me, because they would have Jim's best interests in mind rather than mine. She told me I should remember what was real and important, which was taking care of myself and Jacqueline. As for the media, she reminded me that they were just an intrusion and a distraction and not the point.

"You can't do this on your own," she said. "You have to get some support here." She told me she would have someone call my office back with the name of a crisis manager. "Call me to talk or for advice," she said.

I thanked Hillary for her counsel and her time. Her story was similar to mine in how publicly her husband had humiliated her with his adultery. But our circumstances were also different. Her marriage had not been based on a lie, and mine was. Nonetheless, I was grateful for the conversation. And for a moment, I thought that maybe this was an ordeal I could survive.

20 · STEALING HOME

THE WEEK FOLLOWING JIM'S announcement, I continued to feel a blinding pain, an emotional pain so intense that at moments it felt worse than any physical pain I'd ever endured. I could think of Jacqueline, and that was about it, and I couldn't even do that in a steady way.

After the disaster came the aftershocks: the rubble, the dust, the search for signs of life. Toward the end of that second week, I was convinced—finally—that someone *was* alive, and quite possibly that someone was me. The awareness that I had not died gave way to the thought that maybe there was hope. Slowly I began to think of recovery and what I had to do to restore order. Jim and I had not discussed what would happen after he left office on November 15. If he was no longer governor, we could no longer live in the governor's mansion. What then? Once I asked the question, of course, I knew the answer. Jim and I were not going to be looking for a home to live in together. That much was clear. And so, as I thought of the future, I was terrified. I knew I could engage a crowd of a thousand at a campaign rally, or raise a few hundred thousand dollars for charity in a day, or have a mansion renovated in a few weeks, but change a fuse? Turn on a furnace? Fix a leak? Forget it. I'd gone from my parents' house to Jim's house to the governor's mansion. I was thirty-seven, almost thirty-eight, but I'd never lived on my own, much less had to buy my own home.

There was much that had happened to me that I'd had no control over, and much that would happen, but I could at least begin to find a home for myself. Taking action itself provided a kind of relief and distraction. So, one morning in late August, I asked Elvie to bring Meagan and Nicole down to Drumthwacket to spend the day with Jacqueline so I could go house hunting.

Lori Kennedy had been wonderful, and would continue to be wonderful, throughout this ordeal. Now she had arranged for a Realtor—Marty, her cousin's husband—to look through the listings for homes in Union County, New Jersey, the county where my parents lived. Jim and I did agree that Jacqueline had to have access to a decent school system, and according to the Department of Education rankings, one of the towns on my short list had one of the better school systems.

I wanted to keep my house hunting private to avoid being followed by reporters. So, at my request, Lori asked Marty to find suitable houses and to arrange for me—and on occasion Jim and me—to visit them only when the owners were not present. We saw a few homes with potential, but after I'd viewed half a dozen or so over a week's time, I was discouraged. They all required so much work—new plumbing, new wiring, a new roof—but Jacqueline and I needed a place to live, and I knew that I would have to make a decision quickly.

At the end of the first week's search, still in my disguise, I ventured out to have dinner with Lori and Jimmy at a restaurant near Rahway. While we sat at our table waiting for our dinner, that infamous image of Jim standing at the podium and me standing beside him in my blue suit flashed on the television screen, prompting a waiter not ten feet away to begin a discussion of Jim's announcement with the people at another table.

"Do you believe that McGreevey bombshell?"

"Yeah, wasn't that something?"

"I think he's trying to mask all the corruption."

"Well, something isn't right. Can you imagine being his wife?"

At the word "wife," I slunk down as low as I possibly could, while Lori and Jimmy watched me sympathetically, not knowing what in the world to say. This was exactly the kind of public exchange I had been imagining and dreading. I was sure that I'd be recognized, especially since I'd been accompanied by a state trooper, who was now sitting at the bar. Every cell in my body was yanking me toward the door, but we'd already ordered, so I forced myself to sit, chew, and swallow. Then we got out of there as quickly as possible.

During this period, I was spending too much time away from Jacqueline, and it was making me uncomfortable. But what else could I do? It was impossible to go house hunting incognito with a two-year-old, so I would leave her either with my sister-in-law or with Freddie. As a result, my anger at Jim reached a new intensity—not only had he wrecked the stability of our lives, but he was taking only an intermittent role, and no active responsibility, in the rebuilding process. If there was going to be a home for Jacqueline in three months, it was on me to make it happen.

While I was still house hunting, Jim's sister Caroline called me to ask how I was doing. She was angry at Jim for what he'd done to me and to his family, and she told me so in no uncertain terms. It was nice to have such a close ally, especially since Caroline shared my outrage at the disruption Jim had caused in Jacqueline's life. From the moment she learned about his affair with Golan, Caroline hadn't been on speaking terms with Jim. Since Jim didn't want her at the house either, Caroline asked that we visit her at her home in Delaware.

On one of these August weekends, Jim, Jacqueline, and I planned to be with the Kennedys at the beach house. So on the Saturday morning of that weekend, I packed up to go to the shore. It was rainy, though, and Jim offered it as an excuse not to go. He said he had talked to Jimmy, and he and Lori weren't sure they could make it. But I needed to get out of Drumthwacket, and spending a weekend indoors locked up with Jim was untenable, so I told him that Jacqueline and I would be going down anyhow. In the end, Jim changed his mind, maybe because it turned out Jimmy and Lori were able to go, after all, and their presence would make him more comfortable.

Later on Saturday evening, they met us there. After dinner, Lori told me she wanted to have a talk with Jim, so the two of them went off on their own while Jimmy helped me entertain Jacqueline. I don't know the specifics of their conversation, but when they were finished and after Jim went to bed, Lori told me that one of the things they had spoken about was what Jim would do to earn money after November 15.

A number of jobs had been suggested to him, but Lori told me he wasn't going to take any of them and had given her all sorts of excuses as to what was wrong with each one. He also told her that he had no money. But, as I'd told her, that was incredible to me. Jim had sold his Woodbridge home within the last year, and he had to have sold it for at least $200,000. He hadn't answered my questions about that sale when I'd first raised them months earlier, and he hadn't answered them since. Where had all that money gone? Odd as it may sound to everybody and anybody, I just didn't know. We had never merged our finances, and Jim, as governor, never managed his own money anyhow. Even with months of legal maneuvering, it would be difficult for me to find out.

The last week of August, I took a deep breath and returned to work. I had to prepare myself for it in advance. People meant well, but the awkward greetings, one after another after another, were intolerable.

First there was the security guard who tried his best to greet me casually as I came in. "I like your hair in a ponytail!" he said. "It makes you look a lot younger." He appeared uncomfortable as he extracted foot from mouth. Then there was the physician who stuck his head in my office. "How're you doing?" he said, smiling a little too broadly and then disappearing before I could answer. A director whose office was just down the hall from mine popped in on the way to her office and said, "I always have trouble finding a parking space. There's never a place to park in that lot." Then she looked ill at ease, recognizing that she had now informed me of one more problem I'd have to face for the first time.

On the whole, though, I was relieved to be in my office, where I could more or less bunker myself. I had hoped that being back at work would be a distraction, but I was too distracted myself. I tried to focus on my job, and for a few hours that first day I was actually able to catch up a little and get some work done, but overall it was very difficult.

Meanwhile visions of homelessness continued to haunt me, and I continued to be shocked that Jim seemed to have no urgent concern about where Jacqueline and I would wind up. Sometime during September, when I couldn't stand his apparent indifference anymore, I posted a sign on my office door saying 67 DAYS TO HOMELESSNESS. Everyone who came in or out of the residence at Drumthwacket had to pass through my office, so everyone saw it. I updated it every day for about two weeks, until Jim ripped it down. It was an expression of rebellion. And fear.

ULTIMATELY I DECIDED ON a house that I'd seen on my first day of house hunting. It was on a road without much traffic in a pleasant suburb not too far away from either my parents or my job. After mulling things over for a few days, I called Marty to tell him I was ready to make an offer. In the meantime, I began the process of securing a mortgage, already assured in writing that I would in fact qualify. Still, I was nervous. The real estate market was so hot that a seller could generally choose from among multiple offers, and I knew that there were others who were interested. My salary was more than decently middle class, but I was hardly wealthy. Because I'd been single until my early thirties, I was comfortable managing my own finances, but I didn't know what would be required for a down payment, nor did I know when it would be required or, frankly, exactly where it would come from.

To get away from the tension, at least for the day, I took Jacqueline to visit Jim's sister Caroline and her family in Delaware. Caroline and I had a good conversation while her husband, Mark, prepared dinner and Jacqueline played with her two older cousins. I thought about how lucky she was to have such a wonderful husband, and I wished I had been as fortunate.

When I returned home, Jim was already there.

I fiddled in the kitchen as he began to talk. The elation of freeing himself had dissipated and was now replaced by anxiety as he began to try to figure out his own life after November 15.

"I have to figure out what to do about a job," he said. "It was never something I had to worry about. I always knew what I wanted to do. Now I have to figure out a new direction."

I nodded, not saying much.

"I've lost everything I've ever worked for, and now I don't even know where I'll be living. What do you think about Rahway? Do you think Rahway is a good place for me to live?"

"Good as anyplace. I have to figure that out for myself and Jacqueline also."

"Yeah, I know what you mean." But amazingly, even though I had mentioned Jacqueline, he didn't offer any suggestions or further comment. Here was this man who'd had the confidence to think he should be the one chosen to take care of every person in the whole state of New Jersey, yet he had not made a single effort to ensure that his wife and child had even a roof over their heads.

In the end, after talking at length about his concerns for his own future, Jim did ask outright if I'd found a place to live. I told him that I didn't know. In fact, my offer hadn't been accepted yet, so I didn't really know for sure, but my answer wasn't candid, and I knew it. The truth was, I didn't want to be candid. I had been pushed so far, pulled in so many directions, that I simply didn't feel like it.

I was scared of this new life I was going into as a soon-to-be-single parent, and a part of me longed to open up and feel the relief of confiding in him, despite the fact that he'd caused this end. I'd always felt better when Jim had soothed me by telling me not to worry, that we would find a way to deal together with whatever the problem at hand was. All too often, it was just rhetoric, I know, but it made me feel close to him, and it made me feel better. But now I didn't want to feel close to him. I wanted to feel distant, and I wanted to feel angry. As much as I could and as soon as I could. But there was more to it. If I had opened up to Jim and allowed myself to feel the full force of my fear, I couldn't have acted at all.

MARRIAGES DON'T DIE GRACEFULLY, of course, and at any given moment one or the other of us might lurch in an instant from chilly distance to molten rage. So it was a relief to spend time away from Jim. If we spent time together, it was easiest to spend it with the Kennedys. We didn't have to pretend with them, nor did we have to engage with each other.

Labor Day was now behind us, and though I was still in pain, I was also involved with trying to manage a transition I was now accepting as inevitable. Two days after I made my offer on the house, the owners accepted it, and I began looking at furnishings. Most of the furnishings at Drumthwacket belonged to the state, and a few others belonged to Jim. When I moved in with Jim after our marriage, I'd brought only my bedroom set, and when we moved from there to Drumthwacket, I'd given that away to a friend. So Jacqueline and I would be moving with almost nothing except her bedroom furniture.

Everything was so expensive. I would need to renovate, and I didn't know how I would be able to afford that plus pay the mortgage, let alone put food on the table. But just as I'd found a way to renovate Drum-thwacket, I was determined to find a way to give my daughter a decent home.

Drumthwacket represented destruction, devastation, and betrayal to me now, and I spent as little time there as possible. On the week-ends, I went to the beach house. The irony was that I spent more time at the beach after Jim's announcement than I had during the two and a half years that preceded it. I love the beach and had always dreamed of having a home on the Jersey shore—a coast every bit as beautiful as Cape Cod, the Hamptons, or any other beach on the Atlantic Ocean. In my opinion, the beach house was the best perk of being First Lady. It was a spectacularly lovely spot on a pristine beach—nothing but dunes, beach grass, and the lulling sound of the waves. Because Jim never made time to share it with us, I often stayed home on the weekends or went with him to whatever function he had to attend. Had I known that our time would be cut short, I would have taken advantage of that tranquil spot more often. I was determined to take pleasure in it in the time that remained.

My family—including Paul, Elvie, and my nieces, as well as my friends Freddie and Mario, who would later serve as my unofficial construction manager, spent as many August and September weekends as they could at the shore with me. But it wasn't always the reprieve I hoped for. One weekend in particular, when I was at the shore and Jim was at Drumthwacket, we had a phone conversation in which we were able to broach the subject of the new chapter each of us would be facing in our lives. Aided, perhaps, by the benefit of physical distance, we were able to discuss the future—Jacqueline, getting a house, and even the possibility that we could once again be friends. In spite of my reservations, and perhaps because of my fears, I opened up, confiding in Jim how nervous I was about being able to afford a decent house. I was immensely relieved to hear the kindness in his voice when he said that we'd figure it out together. Maybe *together* we could work out something amicable, and even have something of a friendship. Jim told me that he'd come down the next day—Sunday—and maybe take Jacqueline and her cousins to the zoo.

I went to bed that night feeling better than I had any night since the announcement. But when Jim arrived midafternoon on Sunday, something seemed to have soured in him. He had turned moody and, unaccountably, went straight to the bedroom without any explanation, without even greeting anyone. Jacqueline's crib was in our bedroom, and she was in there taking a nap. For the next hour, while she slept, he remained in the room with her.

"What's with him?" Paul asked.

I shrugged. "It would've been better if he hadn't come." Undoubtedly, he was uncomfortable being there because he felt—correctly—that my family did not feel welcoming toward him. Still, I felt I'd been foolish to let my guard down, however briefly.

Once Jacqueline had awakened from her nap, Jim spent some time, still in the bedroom, playing with her. After about twenty minutes, though, he came out holding her by the hand. "Here's Mommy," he said. "Daddy has to go now." No mention of the zoo. Then he was gone.

Jim and I were getting a divorce, but too often he acted like it was Jacqueline he was divorcing and had to create distance from.

Presumably, the only reason Jim was coming to the shore in the first place was to see Jacqueline, and yet on the rare occasions when he did show up he would usually go to the sunroom by himself and wouldn't interact with anyone. He often had breakfast or lunch in that room, where he'd read or spend time on the phone. Invariably he'd say that he was tired and just wanted quiet time. I thought he was careless of Jacqueline and rude, especially if my family was visiting. I never treated his family in this manner. Whenever we got together, I always spent the entire visit with them. It hurt me when he treated my family so badly, especially since they had already sacrificed so much to help raise Jacqueline while I helped him advance his political career.

By late summer, I still was uncertain about where I'd live after Drumthwacket. I didn't know how I'd come up with the funds for a down payment, so one Saturday (or Sunday) I followed Jim into the bedroom to have a conversation about it. "I have no money," Jim said, as he said so many times, wearily now, as if I should have known better than to ask by this point.

"How can that be?!" I said, as I had so many times before, this time impatiently. "What happened to the money from the sale of the house in Woodbridge?" By now I had done the math. In addition to the house in Woodbridge, which would have sold for about $200,000, there was Jim's salary. His gross income was about $156,000, which would have left him with a net of just under $100,000 annually, or close to $300,000 by the time he left the governorship. Since he had free residential housing, free recreational housing, free transportation, free household help, and an expense fund of $70,000, there should have been quite a bit left over.

"Where did it all go?" I asked.

"I don't have to explain anything to you," Jim said angrily as he headed for the bedroom door.

"I deserve an explanation," I told him. "You would have wanted one from me."

At that, Jim seemed to calm down. "Look, I don't have any money," he said, "but we can work things out." He suggested that we meet with a financial planner, and I agreed. My mother must have heard us arguing, because just as he entered the kitchen on his way toward the door, she went toward the refrigerator, in effect turning her back on him.

"I'll see you," he said.

I spent the rest of the afternoon watching *Stealing Home,* a movie that, ironically, had been filmed at both the beach house and Drumthwacket. After that, we all sat around telling family stories and, as it got dark, a ghost story or two.

I was happy to have my family there. They never asked me questions or tried to probe but instead treated me as they always had, maybe with even more indulgence than usual. Paul continued to be my personal techie, patiently making house calls to address the many disasters involving my computer, my cell phone, or the cable TV. Elvie was, at a moment's notice, available to take care of Jacqueline, along with her own girls, as was my dad. Rick, who is the quietest member of my family but also one of the most sensitive, showed up more at the beach house than he had in the past, and I knew it was to see me. My mom, who had always fretted over me—"You're too thin, you're too thin!"—as if I were in the midst of a hunger strike, continued to bake for me and make soup for me and send care packages home with me. I felt so alone in the world during this dark, lonely transition that having them physically near offered a comfort I couldn't have found anywhere else.

At the end of that day, close to midnight, I went to my bedroom to check on Jacqueline, who was sleeping. I straightened her sheets, covered her, and removed her empty milk bottle from her crib, and as I did so, I heard my cell phone beep on my dresser, indicating that I had missed a call. I checked to see who'd called and saw that it was Jim's number.

Sitting down on the bed, and bracing myself, I speed-dialed his number. Jim answered on the first ring, and as I sat there in the dark, we talked for a while.

"How are you?" he asked, with more concern in his voice than I'd heard in a while.

"OK," I said warily.

"I've been thinking about our conversation, and I felt so bad that after I left the beach house I almost turned around and went back to talk to you," he said.

I just listened, thawing, however reluctantly.

"So have you figured out where you and Jacqueline will be living?" he asked.

"Not yet."

"Is there anything I can do to help?"

I cried. Although the intimacy between us was gone, I hadn't yet gotten to the point where crying in his presence was out of the question. So I cried. It was all I could do whenever I had to think of the future.

After that weekend, I went back to Drumthwacket, determined to finalize the purchase of my house. I signed the mortgage papers and asked Mario and a friend of his who was a contractor to look at the house I'd chosen in order to assess its condition. The contractor told me that it was structurally sound but needed a lot of cosmetic work.

Marty, the Realtor, told me that if I now wanted the house, I'd have to give him a down payment the next day. Despite Jim's protestations of poverty, he'd finally told me a few days earlier that he would be willing to give me a check for the down payment. But when Marty asked for the check, I had to think quickly, since I didn't yet have the funds and obviously didn't want to share that particular piece of information with him. My attorney and the seller's attorney were in the midst of the review, but they hadn't yet dotted every *i* or crossed every *t*. So I told Marty that I wanted the review to be completed before making the down payment, and luckily he agreed.

That evening, Jim and I sat in the kitchen to touch base. Now there was a new complication. We had never actually used the word "divorce," though as we each talked about finding our own homes, it had been understood between us that we would be divorcing. However, as of this

evening, Jim wanted the down payment to be contingent on my immediate agreement in principle that we would be working out the terms of a
divorce settlement between us. I was not opposed to proceeding toward a
settlement, but the wrinkle was that Jim wanted us to come to this agreement without any lawyers (never mind, of course, that he was a lawyer
and that he was being advised at every step by Ray Lesniak, another
lawyer). He continued to assert his poverty, saying that he had three savings accounts—including one for Jacqueline and one for Morag—which
in total amounted to roughly $75,000. Besides that, he had an IRA that he
said he did not *have* to share with me since it preceded our marriage, but
that he *would* share it.

There was another piece of news. Jim had already been talking to people about doing a book, and one of the people he'd spoken with had suggested that a book coauthored by both of us would be worth a hefty
advance; apparently because of its novelty, it would be worth more than a
book by him alone. A novelty indeed! With me cast as the accepting, for-
giving, understanding cuckolded wife in this modern-day Saint's Life. "I
can get an advance of five hundred thousand," he told me. "After agents'
fees and taxes, we'd net two hundred fifty thousand, which would be one
hundred twenty-five thousand each."

He had to be kidding. My days as his partner were over. "No," I said.
"Not on your life."

Jim again demanded that we reach divorce settlement terms within a
week, or I could forget his "generosity."

The conversation ended without any agreement, but now as I walked
out of the kitchen to check on Jacqueline, I realized Jim was treating me
as his adversary and would fight me with whatever it took. Jim's resistance wasn't about money anyhow, not at its cramped little heart. It was,
once again, about secrets and betrayals. He had hidden from me what he
did with his time and he had hidden from me what he did with his body.
And now he was hiding from me what he'd done with money that, in
actuality, was ours. If he could get me to agree to a backroom settlement, then maybe he could keep his secrets.

How could Jim possibly be so impoverished? How could the proceeds from the sale of a house that was legally conjoint property suddenly disappear? How could another few hundred thousand dollars of income from Jim's job as governor also disappear? Had it gone to underwrite Golan's home purchase when they were lovers? Had it gone to Kari as a reward for being a compliant ex-wife? Unlike me, she'd been willing to let Jim arrange the terms of their divorce settlement without legal representation.

Seeing that Jim was now willing to regard me as an enemy, all at once something began to happen to me that had never happened before—I felt as if I couldn't breathe. My heart was pounding, my body turned rubbery, and I felt myself on the verge of blacking out. *Am I dying?* I wondered. *Am I having a stroke? A heart attack?* I was terrified, and the terror made it worse. I was in Jacqueline's room by then, and suddenly, and without warning, I collapsed.

Jim, who had followed me, was alarmed at the sight of me like that as well. He tried to help me get back to my feet, but I was too weak. My legs wouldn't support me, and I was so drained that I couldn't even speak, which frightened me further.

"Do you want to go to the hospital?" he asked.

I shook my head no. Jim picked me up without disturbing Jacqueline and helped me down the hall to bed, where I fell asleep almost instantly.

The following morning, however, Jim was back to badgering me, pressing me to agree in principle on a book and possibly a film deal. I was afraid that the conversation would become charged, leading me right back to the scary place I'd been the night before. This time I didn't say no, only that I wouldn't commit to it.

Put me in any really dire medical emergency and I will invariably, if irrationally, want to prove immediately that I'm perfectly fine. Therefore the morning after I'd collapsed, I was determined to go to work. And so I did. Later in the day, Jim called to ask how I was and to tell me that he had asked John McCormac, the state treasurer, to meet with us in the evening to discuss a financial plan. I felt sick all day—right on the verge of a recurrence of what had happened to me the night before—and even had chest pains. I considered going to my hospital's emergency room or to see a cardiologist I knew who was associated with the hospital, but I put the idea aside and somehow made it through the day.

When I got back to Drumthwacket, Nina had left a packet of mail for me. Included was an envelope sent by Cathy. Perhaps I'd scared Jim or made him feel guilty, but at any rate he had made good on his promise, and in the envelope Cathy sent, there was a check made out to the realty company, as I'd asked. It was what I needed for the down payment on the house.

Later I thanked Jim for the check, and he and I sat down at our kitchen table with John McCormac, who was also Jim's friend. Looking back, I suspect that Jim had already coached McCormac—known as Mac—as to what line to take with me. John said that, based on my income and Jim's, all I could afford was a house for less than $200,000. As he said this, I could feel my heart begin to pound and my face flush. With the real estate market as inflated as it had ever been, how was I going to find a house for $200,000 in New Jersey? You couldn't even get a refrigerator box for that amount. Besides, I had already found a decent home in a nice neighborhood where I could raise my daughter, and I was settling into the idea that that was where we would be living. Just knowing that this would be my home had brought me a little peace of mind.

But the house I had chosen was well over double what he was telling me I could afford. When Mac was finished, Jim followed up. "You're going to have to find something for less than two hundred thousand dollars." I knew there was nothing like that on the market. Jim and I had agreed that my housing search would be limited to towns with high-ranking school districts. But none of these towns had homes in that range.

I walked away from the kitchen table where we'd been meeting and went into the sitting room. A few minutes later, Mac left. Again, my memory of the event is fragmented, but I recall feeling weak and wanting to sit down on the floor. I began to cry, and soon I was lying curled up on the rug, terrified and unable to move. This time, I was sure I was dying.

When Jim came into the room, I asked him to call Lori Kennedy to come and take care of Jacqueline. He helped me to bed, but all I could think about was that I was going to die, and who would raise my daughter? Next Jim called Clifton Lacy, the commissioner of the Department of Health, who was a cardiologist. Cliff asked me in detail about my symptoms and told me that it didn't sound like a cardiac problem. He knew or could make apt inferences about our lives at this point, so he told me that it was more likely that I was suffering from anxiety. What I was describing, he said, were the symptoms of a panic attack. Cliff then called a psychiatrist, who spoke with me on the phone and concluded, as Cliff had, that it was indeed a panic attack. Jim also called a doctor friend of his who worked at Princeton University to come and check me out. She arrived shortly after Lori and Jimmy Kennedy, who had come at my request. By then, I was feeling a little better. The doctor and I talked for a while, and she gave me prescriptions for Xanax and Valium, which one of the troopers went to have filled at the pharmacy. Everyone left. I took both pills and went to bed. It was probably the first time since the beginning of August that I'd had a good night's sleep, but who wouldn't with a double dose of Xanax and Valium?

Unbelievably, the following morning Jim went right back to hounding me about the house.

"You just can't afford a house," he told me. "Look, I'll help you find an apartment, though." And, he added, if I couldn't afford to buy a condominium or co-op, I could always find a really nice rental apartment. "You could live in Union County or Hudson County, because they're both affordable." He said he had a developer friend who owned a number of apartments in Hudson County, and I could speak with him. I had no interest in looking for an apartment, and the locations he was suggesting weren't known to have good school systems, but apparently making sure Jacqueline lived in a good school district was no longer a major priority. I had already found a house where I'd hoped to give Jacqueline a happy childhood in a town where she would receive a good education. Plus, the house I wanted to buy was on a circle, not a road with lots of through traffic—and potentially lots of gawkers.

"I've found a house I can live in and want to live in," I said. As I spoke, I could feel my heart beginning to race. "I can't continue this conversation right now." I got up and walked out of the room. I had practiced meditation a little bit, so I immediately tried to apply what I knew to calm myself down. Once my breathing had returned to normal, I got dressed and went off to work.

Jim continued to push his agenda relentlessly. When I arrived home in the evening, he told me he had now talked to his developer friend, who could help me with an apartment. When I dismissed his suggestion, Jim went on to the next one he had ready.

"If you're really determined to have a house," he said, "I can have Mac McCormac find you one for two hundred thousand dollars."

That was an insult. If there were a decent house available for that price, I would have found it myself. Besides, by now I knew that in this housing battle Jim was not only relentless—he had become devious. My Realtor, Marty, was, as I've said, related by marriage to Lori Kennedy, and earlier in the day I'd learned from the Kennedys that Jim had called Marty to tell him I didn't want the house because I'd realized I couldn't afford it.

I didn't want to upset myself, so I didn't let on that I knew what he'd done. Instead I again got up and walked into another room. But Jim followed me, haranguing me and telling me that he wanted his check back. I didn't answer. If he wanted it back, he was going to have to put a stop payment on it.

The next morning, Jim changed tactics, sending in his "good cop" to replace his "bad cop" of the night before. Politicians make political appointments all the time as a way of rewarding their friends, a practice that is completely legal. Such appointments can pay stipends, some large and some small, and Jim had taken care of many of his friends in this way. In fact, he had already appointed Cathy to the Dental Board. Now

Jim was raising the possibility of appointing me to a board. But then "bad cop" horned in, making the appointment contingent on my willingness to live in an apartment.

"I'm not having this conversation," I told Jim. Really, he just didn't stop. When he'd left the house, I called Marty, who seemed surprised to hear from me. I pretended not to have any knowledge of what had transpired with Jim and told him that I definitely wanted the house. Next I called the attorney who was reviewing the documents needed for the purchase of the house to check on the status of the review and to discuss details regarding my down payment.

But there was a glitch. The attorney told me he wanted the check made out to his trust account, not to the realty company. I disregarded Jim's comment about wanting the check back and e-mailed Cathy, asking her to void the check payable to the realty company and to write another check payable to the attorney's trust account. I reminded her again to send me copies of the tax returns I'd requested five days earlier. Among other details, the returns would show the sale of the house in Woodbridge. I asked Nina to pick up the package from Cathy. First she was told to wait, and then, after twenty minutes, she was told that Cathy had had to leave suddenly to attend a funeral in Florida.

When Nina told me what happened, I was both furious and devastated. Whatever was going on wasn't right. I knew that. Was Jim having the tax returns amended now to conceal the sale of the Woodbridge house, his salary, or his savings? I never would have thought him capable of this, but I hadn't seen the man I thought I'd married in months. I'd been wrong about so much. Why not about his basic decency?

With Jim so resistant to doing the right thing in regard to housing for Jacqueline and me, I began to ask around for recommendations for a divorce attorney. Clearly, I was going to have to resort to legal help to get Jim to behave appropriately.

The next day, Jim called to tell me that he wanted to talk to me openly.

There was a novel idea. I suspect that Ray Lesniak or Jimmy Kennedy had sat Jim down and told him that he was behaving badly. On my way home from work, I stopped in at the Kennedys', and Jimmy told me that he'd spoken to Jim, who claimed *he* hadn't called the Realtor to say I was no longer interested in the house—*I* had called him myself.

At home that night, Jim was calm, I was distant, and we didn't talk at all.

The following morning Jim was gone very early. Later in the day I would be making my first attempt at simply going out to have a pleasant time. Lori Kennedy and I were meeting a friend for lunch, and then I would return home to change and head to Manhattan where Jimmy, Lori, and I would have dinner with my friend Nene and her boss, Gordon Bethune, the CEO of Continental Airlines, whom we both knew. Not bad, I thought, amazed that I was even able to consider a night out on the town.

After lunch, I went back home to change for the evening. As it happened, Jim had returned and was on the phone on the first floor of Drumthwacket (his preferred site for calls to Kari). He signaled for me to wait, but after a few seconds, when I saw he was not about to put the call on hold or hang up, I left. I hadn't known he was in, so I'd left a note for him upstairs in our kitchen telling him my plans. After dinner, I would be heading to the shore, where my parents and Jacqueline were spending the weekend.

On my way to New York, Ray Lesniak called. Did I have a divorce attorney? Ray wanted to know. I said I hadn't retained anyone yet. He told me that he'd been advising Jim about divorce terms, and offered me another version of Jim's "Settlement Without Lawyers" plan. Ray said that if I agreed to an uncontested divorce, Jim would give me $250,000. He was not forthcoming about exactly how my hard-up husband would scrape together this money, and I didn't ask. Ray's law partner, Paul Weiner, would take care of the details. All I'd need was for my attorney to sign off on the agreement, a requirement of state law mandating that in a divorce each spouse must have separate representation.

Well, that was something. When I got together with my dinner companions, I felt less burdened than I had in months, and ready to have a good time. And I did, thanks to the fact that Gordon Bethune is one of the funniest men I've ever met. For the first time since August 12, I actually laughed. Still, I had moments of sadness that I was there without Jim, who had learned of the gathering and called Jimmy to ask why he hadn't been invited.

I surmised that Nene hadn't invited Jim because she simply didn't think he'd accept. I felt bad, sort of, since Jim had invited me to attend some events with him. I had declined. My days of public appearances with him were over.

I arrived at the beach house late that night and went to church with Jacqueline on Sunday. It had been a pleasant weekend, but I knew I still had the housing headache ahead of me. On Monday, despite my e-mails and Nina's visit to Cathy's office, Cathy had no check and no tax returns to give Nina. Undoubtedly, Cathy was acting on Jim's orders. I wasn't going to ask again, but I needed the down payment for the house by that very day at 5:00 P.M. My anxieties were in some ways the anxieties that any and every newly separated woman will immediately recognize, but I also knew that I had options and resources available—or at least friends and family with resources—that are not available to most women. I needed to borrow money for the down payment in a hurry, and luckily Mario offered to help.

I wasn't home free, not by a long shot. By this point, Jim and I were very distant with one another. Civil and chilly. He left early and came back late, and the space we lived in was so large that even when we were both there, we didn't encounter each other much. Although neither of us had moved out of the bedroom so as not to further alert Jacqueline to a problem, we slept as if the mattress were the entire United States, each of us at the edge on our own side of the Continental Divide, me on the Atlantic Coast, him on the Pacific.

Thanks to my medications and my scrupulous efforts to keep myself from engaging in upsetting conversations with Jim, my panic attacks were now under control. I pretty much had my putting-one-foot-in-front-of-another plan for equilibrium. But now and then, despite my vigilance, things happened that could push me right back into my most devastated state. The worst of these happened on a Saturday in October.

I had meandered into the kitchen one morning, as I always do, with nothing more on my mind than a coffee junkie's need for her morning fix. I was in that still-rested post-sleep state—in my bathrobe, not my armor. On the kitchen table, I noticed a pile of papers—plain old Arial Bold typescript on white 8-by-11—indistinguishable from a routine memo or rough draft of a policy paper. I glanced at it idly. It began, "As you probably know, two months ago, my entire world blew up in an instant. . . ."

Altogether there were nine single-spaced pages, and they seemed to be the beginning of a book, probably the book he'd decided he would write once he accepted the fact that I would not co-author one with him. What can I say? I kept reading.

On page six was the following passage:

While my first marriage was a real attempt to try to live a normal life, my second was for political benefit. I married a woman for political gain. It was the lowest point of my moral life and I'm deeply ashamed of it.

And then, a little farther down:

Dina was still in the hospital with complications after the pregnancy. Golan came over to my simple condominium to talk. Eventually we went upstairs into my bedroom where we touched and explored each other.

It was an exhilarating night—yet forbidden.

I just stood there, feeling as if someone was putting a knife to my heart. I thought it couldn't get any worse, and it just had. The Kennedys, both of them, were my confessors, sounding boards, nurses, and therapists during those early months, and after I read these passages, I didn't know what else to do except head for their house with Jacqueline.

When I got there, I handed Lori the nine stapled pages and watched as she read. Throughout, there were murmurs of horror and disbelief, some of it unprintable. She was aghast, speechless, didn't know what to say. Who would?

I left Lori's house and went back to Drumthwacket. Jim arrived after me. I was completely walled off for my own protection. I certainly didn't mention the manuscript he'd left in the kitchen.

If he saw that anything was odd in my demeanor, he didn't mention it. He told me that he'd talked to the president at the University of Medicine and Dentistry in New Jersey regarding a job for me, and showed me a job description. I didn't say much in response.

In a little more than a month, I would be leaving Drumthwacket. Although the lawyers seemed to be moving toward a closing, I still didn't have a home I could call my own. During this time, I had not heard much from Jim's parents. I imagine they were just as uncomfortable with me as my parents were with Jim, though for different reasons. But now Ronnie, my mother-in-law, was in the hospital, and I went to visit her. Jack was there, and so were Caroline and Sharon. It was an excruciating hour and a half. We struggled to make small talk, all of us. They didn't ask me a single real question, and I didn't offer them a single real feeling. I was relieved when I could finally leave. Besides, I had other problems on my mind.

My move toward housing had now stalled. Not only was there termite damage, but there was a chance the sale would fall through. My insomnia returned, and I spent the darkest hours before dawn on the Internet looking for other possible houses. There weren't any.

The weekend came, and Jim asked me if I wanted to go with him to a dinner in New York City at which Ray Lesniak was being honored. I didn't get it. How could Jim not talk to us all week, not worry about whether Jacqueline and I even had a place to live, and then ask me to go to a dinner?

As First Lady, I hadn't added anything to my schedule in over two months. But I did think it was important to honor commitments I'd already made, especially when it was in service of organizations I cared about. That month, I attended the Women's Heart Foundation Gala, held at Drumthwacket. After an hour, though, I had to leave, because I kept breaking into tears whenever anyone asked me how I was. I did much better at a Bruce Springsteen concert in Philadelphia, where I could hide in the dark. I wasn't exactly in the mood for a concert, but the noise of the crowd overshadowed the noises in my head, and for that I was thankful.

I got back to Drumthwacket from Philadelphia very late, and Jim didn't come back at all. We no longer kept each other informed about our comings and goings. In the morning, I took Jacqueline shopping with Maria and Lori and had lunch with them. When I went back home, I found Jim in bed in the middle of the afternoon. I was heading out for dinner with the Kennedys. Jim had declined their invitation, but before I left, he asked me what I planned to do with Jacqueline with respect to school. I told him that I had to have a place to live before I could think about where she'd be going to school. I reminded him that I'd be homeless in forty-three days.

"Do you want some help in finding a place?" he asked.

It depended on whether a "place" was a house or an apartment, but I didn't say that. In fact, I didn't say anything.

The following day, I went to church with Jacqueline at St. Paul's in Princeton. It wasn't where we had regularly gone to church, but after Jim's announcement I never again went back to the Aquinas Institute, the small chapel a few blocks from Drumthwacket where we'd attended mass every Sunday and where Jacqueline had been baptized. I had come to know a lot of the parishioners and I just couldn't stand to face any of them.

Meanwhile, though I was in the throes of hiring an attorney, catching up at work, and organizing a major fund-raiser, Jim was continuing to hound me about housing. "You should make arrangements to move before the fifteenth of November," he told me.

"I'd move if I had someplace to move to," I told him.

"If you leave on the fifteenth," he said, "you will look like white trash."

"I'm leaving on the fifteenth," I said. "I don't have a place to live."

He looked at me contemptuously. "Don't you have any dignity or self-respect?" he said. "Jackie Kennedy wouldn't do that."

Her again.

"Jackie Kennedy's husband wouldn't resign without making sure that his wife and daughter had a place to live," I said angrily. *How dare he?* I thought. He had cheated, lied, and betrayed me, and he was calling *me* trash?

Perhaps to preserve what he thought of as my imperiled social standing, Jim had taken it upon himself to schedule an appointment with a real estate agent who was going to show me apartments for rent. Having nothing better to do and no house that was as yet mine, I went along for the ride. It was October 7, the day we might otherwise have been celebrating our fourth anniversary. But instead we were looking at apartments where Jacqueline and I might start living our lives apart from Jim. Jimmy Kennedy had suggested we go to dinner that evening. So, after looking at a number of apartments, we met them for dinner. It was so awkward. There was no mention of our anniversary, because we were hardly talking to each other. In bed that evening, I cried.

The next day, I had my first meeting with my divorce attorney. After interviewing several lawyers a few days earlier, I'd decided that I wanted to be represented by John Post, a decent man and a competent man. I was ready to take the first step toward divorce, but I just couldn't make myself take it on October 7, the anniversary of my wedding. Meanwhile, November 15 was only five and a half weeks away, and I still didn't have a place to live.

It was the night of the first debate between John Kerry and George Bush. Presidential debates were always engrossing to me, and this one was no exception. But it was also especially painful, steeped in so many feelings and memories. Less than three months earlier, Jim, Jacqueline, and I had been in Boston at the Democratic National Convention, where Jacqueline had charmed and amused delegates in our midst with her announcement that she was going to be voting for Kerry. Tonight I didn't even know where Jim was, and I knew that we would never watch an election debate together again.

I had tentatively planned to watch the debates with the Kennedys and another friend, but when Lori called me, I was looking at furniture for a home I didn't have, after having come from a lawyer who would help me end a marriage I didn't have and maybe had never had. I was having such a bad day that I said to Lori, jokingly, "I want to be put out of my misery. Now!"

"Who's with you?" she asked. "Which trooper?"

"Kevin, why?"

"Well, just tell him to shoot you. That should take care of it."

I turned to Kevin. "Why don't you just give me your gun so I can shoot myself?"

Kevin, who had obviously not been following the conversation, was momentarily startled and turned around to look at me. When he saw I was kidding, he relaxed. "Sorry, I can't do that," he said, smiling.

Not only were my days with Jim numbered, but so were my days with the troopers who had accompanied me everywhere for the past two and a half years. In a month's time, I would once again be grumbling about gas prices, bad drivers, and traffic jams—and would no longer be able to make a fast getaway by turning on the flashing lights and sirens. My brother Paul, who had always taken care of me in a way Jim never had, was facilitating my reentry by bringing home with him a car for me to test-drive.

The car was parked in front of his home when I arrived. I drove it around the block twice. It was fine, but I couldn't bring myself to make a decision that was such a big acknowledgment of the new life that lay ahead. I'd be in the driver's seat in ways I didn't think I was ready for. Besides, I didn't even have a driveway to park it in.

Later, watching the first Kerry-Bush debate with friends, I invited Kevin to come in and watch with us. I always felt bad keeping the troopers waiting for hours, sometimes sitting outside in a car, so I often invited them to join me, especially if I was spending time with my family and friends. He accepted the invitation, and we watched the debate.

The following day, I was inducted as a Lady of the Order of Santiago, an ancient and now-ceremonial Roman Catholic military order, the Spanish equivalent of the Ladies of the Knights of Malta. It should have been a very joyful and proud day, but it was a very sad one. I wasn't in the mood to celebrate, so I didn't invite anyone to the induction. Only Nina and Tom, my trooper-driver for the day, accompanied me. It was a long but beautiful mass, and as I watched the other inductees with their spouses or significant others, I grew even sadder.

THE NEXT DAY, IT was announced that Jim would join Ray Lesniak's law firm. I'd known it would happen, because Ray had told me himself. But the only reason I knew it *had* happened was that I read about it in the papers.

After that, the days remaining at Drumthwacket sped by. Right after I retained my divorce lawyer, I finally closed on my house and hired contractors, who quickly began to work on it. I had hoped to pull off a miracle that would enable me to move in on November 15, but I knew it wouldn't happen. Instead I was going to have to move back into my parents' house temporarily.

My last hurrah went on for almost two weeks. It began with a Halloween party at the beach house, with all the guests in costumes. I'd like to say that I came dressed as First Lady, since that was soon going to be little more than a costume, but I didn't really. I came dressed as a flapper—or, as my daughter proudly told everyone, "a showgirl." My thirty-eighth birthday was a few days later, on November 5, and I planned a big party for myself to take place on the twelfth, three days before moving day. When I told Jim about the party, he suggested that I turn it into a sort of thank-you party for everyone I'd worked with as First Lady. "My First Lady days are over," I said. "This party is about my family and friends." And on that day, dozens of friends and relatives came to celebrate with me at Drumthwacket.

For many it was a first visit, and for all it was the last. Ring out the old, ring in the new. It was as sad and as celebratory as the closing shots of a

Fellini movie. Everyone who mattered to me was there, except for my mother. She said life at Drumthwacket with Jim had made me too sad, and so it made her sad too. She said she just couldn't bring herself to come to Drumthwacket or be under the same roof as my husband. I told her I understood. In the meantime, the husband in question took it upon himself to make a birthday speech on my behalf, thanking everyone for coming.

During my final three days, I tried to ready myself to move on without Jim, my mind crowded with one image after another of every scary and overwhelming moment that might lie ahead. Most of all, I feared that I would be hounded and surrounded by the press, unable to protect myself or Jacqueline. Beyond the walls of Fortress Drumthwacket, there would be no place to run, no place to hide. Already, they knew where to find us. One day soon after my birthday, my mom had called to tell me she'd stopped by my new house and found three television crews parked outside my home, close enough to leave tire tracks on my front lawn. "How can you move into that house alone with the baby with those people out there?" she'd asked. A few days later I went by the house myself. While I was inside, a reporter posing as an advertising salesperson walked in, perhaps to get a glimpse of me. I hid in another room, signaling the trooper with me to get rid of her.

Three days from now, there wouldn't be a trooper. Jim would have a transition budget, as all departing governors do, but I would not, and therefore I couldn't think about hiring bodyguards, not even temporarily. To see what options I had, I set up a meeting with Rick Fuentes, the state police superintendent in charge of all state troopers, to talk about my fears. A compassionate man, he vowed to do whatever he could to help keep me and Jacqueline safe, including speaking to the chief of police in the town I was moving to and giving me all his own contact information, so I could get in touch with him twenty-four hours a day. I felt better knowing that in an emergency I could reach him.

Most devastating for me was thinking how this cataclysm would affect Jacqueline. She had already registered the stresses around her, hard as we'd tried to muffle them in order to protect her. Enormous changes lay ahead, and yet there was no way I could prepare her. Even with the few weeks' semi-reprieve while we waited at my parents' house for our new home to be ready, the shock to her system would be enormous. Her father would no longer be part of her daily life, and neither would the troopers and household staff whom she thought of as extended family. They would of course remain at Drumthwacket, as would almost all the furnishings she'd known her whole life. All that was coming with us to our new home was Jacqueline's bed and dresser, and our dishes, utensils, and two couches.

About a week before we left Drumthwacket, I had enacted a rite of passage that I knew would be the most difficult of all. When Jim moved out of Drumthwacket, he still wore his wedding band. I had put it on his finger myself four years earlier to seal my promise to love and honor him for the rest of my life. I had kept my vow to him, and so the ring on his finger still reflected the truth of my vows.

I remembered back to just over four years earlier when Jim slipped a ring onto my finger as I looked into his eyes, while he made a commitment to love and honor me for the rest of our days. He hadn't. And so the ring on my hand did not reflect the truth, only his mouthing of a vow that he knew, even as he said the words, to be a hoax. Amid trembling and tears, and with a tinge of panic, I slid the ring off my finger.

21 · MOVING ON

❧

EVEN THAT LAST NIGHT, Jim and I shared a bed, although by then my body was as blind to his as to a stranger's on an elevator. Since August, we had become increasingly estranged—never fighting but barely speaking. Some marriages die in fire, some in ice. Ours died in ice.

It was November 15, 2004: a Monday, and my mother's birthday. By the time I woke up that day—our last at Drumthwacket—Jim was out of bed and getting dressed. I had determined that I was going to try to make this day as normal as possible for myself, though nothing at all about it was normal, so I switched on *Good Morning America* for a few minutes. Then I got up and headed for the kitchen. The movers had already arrived. I could hear them a few rooms away. The electric drip coffeemaker I'd used every morning for the past two years was still on the counter (it would be staying), so I started to make myself a strong cup of coffee.

Waiting for the coffee to brew, I absentmindedly began to clean out my junk drawer, scooping up a few handfuls of pens, batteries, and rubber bands and dumping them into a Ziploc bag. I lingered for a moment over a small silver-plated picture frame, an extra left from those we'd given to our wedding guests. Meanwhile Jim breezed by, getting ready to go as if this were just another morning. I'm sure the magnitude of the day was obvious to him as well, but his easy demeanor, however forced, was nevertheless quite a feat.

"I'm going now," Jim said offhandedly, and barely pausing. "I'll talk to you later."

He didn't tell me where he was going, though I knew it wasn't to the statehouse, since I'd read that Richard Codey, Democratic leader of the state senate, had been sworn in the night before and was eager to get going. Later I read that Jim spent the day in Manhattan conferring with an editor, even though he'd told me he wasn't going to write a book. I watched him go through the door, and then he was gone.

I thought I was beyond being shocked by Jim, but I was shocked all the same. That was it? No farewell acknowledgment of the day, no I'm-sorry-it's-come-to-this? *Never mind*, I told myself as I poured myself a mug of coffee. *Concentrate on today. Your job is to get through today. You are not going to break down. Not an option.*

Jim had made his farewell speech to the people of New Jersey the previous week, giving them more of a farewell than he'd given me, actually. I only knew about it because among the newspaper clippings that were still coming through on my office fax every morning there was one about this speech. A few weeks earlier, Jim had alluded to the speech he would be making and said, vaguely, maybe I should be there, maybe I should say something. He didn't bring it up again. The night before Jim left office, his cabinet members had come to Drumthwacket for a farewell dinner in the official dining room downstairs. I could hear the merriment below, but Jim didn't ask me to come down, and I didn't offer to.

My role as First Lady would end that night at midnight, and I needed to say my own good-byes. Two weeks earlier, I'd sat down at the computer and begun jotting some notes. Originally the *New York Times* had wanted an exclusive, but after they read it, they declined to run it at all. I guess it wasn't juicy enough. Instead I gave it to the *Star-Ledger*. It was my only public statement following Jim's resignation, and I'd said nothing publicly since.

"Tomorrow is my last day as New Jersey's First Lady," I'd written for the article to be published November 14. "It is a bittersweet moment in my life—one that I greet with sadness, but also a sense of fulfillment. It has been a great honor and a great joy to serve my fellow New Jerseyans, and, simply stated, I will miss all of you." I went on to mention the issues, mostly affecting women and children, that I had championed and said I would continue to champion—prematurity; literacy; children's health care, including obesity; and women's health care, especially cancer and heart disease. My charity work had helped me through the last months and would, I assumed, helped me through the months ahead. Like many wounded helpers the world over, my work on behalf of people in pain would help me soothe my own.

Jim was gone, and the moving van was outside waiting to move everything I owned. So, coffee in hand, I walked through the rooms of our residence, trying to muster my energy for the day. It didn't look like a home anymore, and in fact it had been shedding everything that had made it our home for quite a while. Jim had moved his personal furniture a week or two earlier, even the two pink porcelain lamps from his grandmother I'd noticed that first time at his town house.

Jacqueline was now at my parents', where I would join her later in the day. I was glad that she wasn't here to see the further stripping-away of her life. The first day the movers went to work on our home, she had been terribly upset when they removed from the walls every milestone moment in our lives—me in my wedding gown, the three of us at Jacqueline's baptism, a portrait of the three of us hanging in the hallway that separated Jacqueline's bedroom from ours.

"The photographs are only coming down for a little while, pumpkin," I told her. "We're going to put them up again in our new house."

But it was no use. She wouldn't be consoled.

This morning, the movers continued to pack. Who knew that lives could be chopped up and stowed in two hundred boxes? In a few hours, the trucks would drive to my house and the movers would put all my belongings in my garage, the only option since the house was still full of behind-schedule painters, plumbers, and carpenters. Other boxes had already gone to my parents' house and to the homes of three or four of my friends. The plan was that for the next two weeks, until my house was ready, Jacqueline and I would be staying with my parents. My grandmother lived there too, and so we would be four generations under one roof, my poor father the only male. I didn't envy him.

Some items I'd be taking with me by hand—Jacqueline's Tiffany place setting, her Dora the Explorer spoon and fork, and her battery-operated Elmo. Also not to be packed away was Jacqueline's doll Caitlin. Because Jacqueline was so attached to Caitlin and got so upset if ever Caitlin was left behind or misplaced, we actually had five of them—one invariably under her arm and four body doubles. I wondered if it would make sense for Jim to keep one of the dolls at his apartment from now on. It made me sad even to think of separating the Caitlins.

I took a deep breath. I packed everything of importance in my two green floral rollie suitcases. Then I showered and dressed and looked around one last time. And then I went out the door.

Dawn, my trooper for the day, was downstairs waiting for me. Good, I was glad it was Dawn. After August 12, I'd asked that the troopers assigned to me be drawn from a list of six or seven I submitted. The troopers would be driving me to lawyers, to showrooms for kitchen cabinets or refrigerators, to real estate brokers who'd be waiting to show me houses for sale. I was making arrangements for my future without Jim, and I needed to know that the troopers could be relied upon to keep my private life private. There were half a dozen I was most comfortable with, and Dawn, who happened to be the only woman on my list, was among them. I trusted her and was glad that I was spending my last day with her.

As I walked toward Dawn, she got out of the car and greeted me somewhat awkwardly. "How are you, ma'am?"

"I'm OK. How are you?" I said, sliding into the backseat. Right after Jim's resignation, I had asked all the troopers to call me "Dina" rather than "ma'am," or "Mrs. McGreevey." Most did, when they remembered. But today, Dawn didn't remember. Understandable, I guess. This must have been uncomfortable for her, too.

"OK, Dawn. We've got a full day. First stop, Staten Island."

Starting tomorrow, Dawn and the state-owned Durango she was driving would be gone, and I would be in the driver's seat. The only problem was, I didn't have a driver's seat because I didn't have a car. So today I was going to see Paul at the Ford showroom where he worked at the time. After my previous test drive, he had arranged for me to come to the showroom, lease a car, and drive it away.

I found a gray Ford Freestyle I liked, and Dawn came with me for the test drive. I had always enjoyed driving and actually felt good zipping around in that car with her. Not quite Thelma and Louise, but inch by inch I was taking control of my own life.

"I'll take it," I told the salesman when I returned.

"What would you like for your mileage allowance? Twelve thousand? Fifteen thousand?" the salesman asked.

I had no idea. "Do you know how many miles I drive?" I asked Dawn.

"Some weeks when you've had a lot on your calendar, you've put fifteen hundred, two thousand a week."

"A week?"

"Yes, ma'am."

I couldn't have put more miles on if I'd been moonlighting as a cabbie. But even knowing that figure didn't help much, since I wasn't going to be the First Lady making appearances up and down the state anymore.

"So what'll it be?" asked the salesman.

"Let's say fifteen thousand miles annually." I could see there was going to be a steep learning curve.

I wasn't quite like George H. W. Bush, who'd never seen a cash register up close because he didn't carry cash, but I knew that I had to make some adjustments as I returned to civilian life. Not only would I have to take my car in for an oil change myself, but I'd have to pay for it too. I knew that it took half an hour to get from my parents' house, where I dropped Jacqueline off on weekdays, to my job in Newark. But that was with troopers who could cut through gridlock with lights and sirens.

How long would it take me in real traffic? I had no idea. Traveling with troopers, I never had to worry about parallel parking or even finding a parking place. I didn't even have to know where a parking lot was. That was going to change. It also occurred to me that when the troopers were driving both Jacqueline and me anywhere, we always sat in the back together, she buckled into her car seat and I next to her. She was not going to be happy about sitting by herself in the back while I was in the driver's seat.

By dinnertime, I had finished every errand on my list, with me in my new car and Dawn following behind. Now I had invited her to join us for my mother's birthday dinner. When we arrived, Jacqueline greeted me as if I'd been gone for weeks. My whole family was there—my parents, Paul, Elvie, my nieces, my brother Rick, and my grandmother. We all sat around the dining room table and ate barbecued chicken my father had ordered in, and for dessert we ate the birthday cake that Elvie had picked up from the bakery.

My family tried not to make a big deal of my presence, acting as if it were just another family birthday dinner, but we all knew better. At 10:00 P.M., Dawn left. We said our good-byes, and I made a point of not watching through the window as she, the Durango, and a major phase of my life headed down the street and out of sight.

Then I turned to Jacqueline. "C'mon, honey. Time for us to go to bed." I reminded her that we would be staying here for a while, with Vóvó and Vôvô, her grandma and grandpa, and that it would be an adventure.

"No," she said stubbornly. "I don't want to stay here. I want to go home. I want Daddy." She wasn't quite three, but she was nobody's fool.

Later that night, after Jacqueline was finally asleep, I crawled into bed beside her and one of the Caitlins. I was grateful to be here. What would I have done otherwise? But I had just turned thirty-eight, and returning to sleep under my parents' roof in a room that had become mine when I was a teenager—that felt like a defeat. The last time I'd slept in this room had been a wet October night a little more than four years ago, the night I'd come home from Father Counselman's office in the pouring rain, newly and secretly married to Jim. But here, curled up beside me, breathing evenly, with Caitlin's bow tickling her nose, was my daughter, Jacqueline. Whatever else, Jim was right about one thing: Our years together had not been worthless, and the proof was this child, lying here beside me.

Sleep was elusive that night, and I tossed and turned in the dark, trying not to wake Jacqueline, imagining what the future might hold. I couldn't bear to think about what life might be like. How could I explain to Jacqueline why her father wasn't there, why he wasn't coming home? The only silver lining was that she was too young to understand what was happening, too young to have friends who might cruelly taunt her because her father was gay. There would be time enough to prepare her for that.

This child had led a happy life amid a throng of people, all of whom doted on her—her family and our friends, but also the staff and the troopers. Wherever she looked, there was someone who was perfectly happy to swing her, play with her, carry her, spoil her. She wouldn't realize the change immediately. My parents had helped care for her since her birth, so their home was very familiar to her. But close as she was to my parents, she adored her father, and now she would not be living with him, or even seeing him every day.

I remained desperately worried about money. Even though I was working—had always worked—I wondered how I would be able to pay my bills. My parents had helped pay for renovations on the house, and my friends had bought me a secure alarm system. Now I was pretty much on my own. I had a steep mortgage, a down-payment loan to repay, and the usual cycle of bills. Would I be able to put food on my table? I didn't even have a table.

I was tense about how Jim would conduct himself in relation to Jacqueline and to me now that we were entering a new phase. Would he be a regular part of Jacqueline's life? Would he provide support? So far he hadn't contributed anything. Not a single cent. I had done everything I was supposed to do, but there'd been no response from him. Now that we were no longer going to be at Drumthwacket, expenses were going to mount. What would Jim do? He said he had no money, but was he crying poverty and withholding all support as his way of getting leverage? For months, he'd been badgering me to sit down with him and come up with a settlement on our own.

"We need to work out a separation agreement," he'd said to me, not for the first time, a few weeks ago.

"We have lawyers. Let the lawyers do it."

"I don't think we need attorneys complicating matters," he said. "Let's just sit down, the two of us, without attorneys. That's what Kari and I did, and it worked out smoothly."

That was in Canada. He'd married in Canada and gotten divorced in Canada. And whatever separation agreement he and Kari had worked out, he'd seen to it that it was sealed.

"Don't worry," he continued, his tone a little too thick with reassurance. "It'll be fair. We'll each have our attorneys look it over at the end and sign off on it."

Did he think I was an idiot?

That conversation, like all our others on the subject, ended without any resolution.

Here I was, an independent woman who had never even given up her job, and I was still in the hole. If I'd learned anything, it was that I should have saved more. If I'd known how short-lived Jim's governorship—and my marriage—was going to be, I would have. During my marriage to Jim, and especially during my days as First Lady, I spent what I earned on Jacqueline, food for our family, and other household necessities. But I'd also spent a huge amount on my second job as First Lady. As much as I put forth every effort to be the best First Lady I could, it was important that I also look the part. And that was very expensive.

Meanwhile, in my new house, the renovations crawled along, and December 1—the date by which the renovations were supposed to be completed—came and went with Jacqueline and me still at my parents' house. Amazing, I thought. As First Lady, I'd been able to get nine large rooms, one hallway, and five bathrooms renovated in three weeks. Now it was almost five weeks after the purchase of my home, and the contractors had not yet completed a much smaller renovation. I guess it was to be expected. Then the contractors had been working for the First Lady, wife of the governor. Now I was just a woman, and a single woman to boot. Apparently, I had left my clout at Drumthwacket, along with the coffeemaker.

Eventually, though, the job was done, and on December 18, 2004, I had a home of my own, ready for us to move into. I repacked our green floral rollies, got Jacqueline settled in her car seat, and off we went to our new home in the suburbs—twenty minutes away from my parents' home and half an hour away from my job in Newark. As Jacqueline and I walked in that first day, the house smelled of fresh paint, the bathrooms had running water, and the sun was shining. The house wasn't finished—there wasn't even a stove to cook on—but it was home. Our home.

Our furniture had arrived the day before, after which Jacqueline and I had walked in together to make sure everything was in order. No sooner had we reached the end of the entry hall than she surveyed the living room and gave a yelp of pleasure. In front of her was the only furniture I'd taken from our family room in Drumthwacket—two overstuffed couches that had been wrapped in plastic and standing on their sides in the garage for the previous month. They were still wrapped in plastic and masking tape, but at least they were where they belonged, in our living room, and standing on their own four feet. Jacqueline rushed to help me unwrap them as if she were unwrapping a birthday present.

When the plastic was off, she hugged and kissed them, calling them her couches. I'd never seen a child kiss a couch, much less do so with such fervor. I didn't know whether to laugh or cry, and I think I did a little of each. To her, the couches were two long-lost friends. Jacqueline's reunion with the couches was an apt beginning to her day. She had actually turned three just a week and a half earlier.

Crazy as it may have been, I planned her birthday party for our move-in day, with the half dozen women in my rat pack coming early to help me clean. I had presented it to her and to everyone else as a birthday/tree-trimming party, and Jacqueline was thrilled at other reunions the day held, including those with a few of her favorite troopers, who arrived to celebrate the day with her.

The house was full that day. Along with the troopers, Jim and his family came too and mingled happily with everyone. It was hard having him in the house that he tried so hard to prevent me from buying, but my focus was on Jacqueline, and making it a memorable day for her. If I thought about Jim at all—and I tried hard not to—it was with sadness, that this lovely day was the exception, and not the norm. Jacqueline was delighted to see Jim and rushed to hug him when he came in. Looking around the room, I saw my friends and my family, everyone who had done so much for me. *These are people who know me,* I thought gratefully, watching them enjoy themselves. They know who I am and where I've been. Two friends had been my wedding attendants, another one had gotten me to the hospital right before the election and been there to decorate the tree with me right after Jacqueline's birth, and still another had sat with me the night of the election. All of them had known me ten or fifteen years, longer than Jim and his family had known me.

The only person to trim the tree was me, but . . . oh, well, I'd always loved holidays, so trimming my tree in my own house meant something to me. The lights on the tree twinkled, and the ornaments glittered, and when it started to get dark, I turned on the living room lamp in my brightly lit home.

Jacqueline was a happy three-year-old that day, but it was a respite for both of us, not really an arrival, a moment of light in a dark and difficult winter.

THIS WAS INDEED A period of adjustment—for Jacqueline and for me. And Jim didn't make it any easier for us. He continued to plead poverty, despite the fact that he managed to afford a leisurely stay at the Meadows, a high-priced celebrity rehab center in Arizona, whose previous clientele included supermodels Kate Moss and Amber Valletta. Meanwhile he was often as absent emotionally as he was financially.

Though he would regularly call Jacqueline on the phone, weeks would go by when he didn't see her at all. When he did, usually at my parents' house while I was at work, he'd be in and out in minutes.

I found out about Jim's retreat to rehab in the desert in a roundabout way, when he dropped Jacqueline off after a visit early in the new year. "Listen," he said, when she was out of earshot for a moment, "I'm going to be going away for a few weeks to figure things out."

He didn't tell me where he was going. A vacation to the Caribbean? A soup kitchen in Chicago? I didn't learn anything more until one day I came home to find a FedEx envelope in my mailbox containing a questionnaire asking me what I thought Jim's "issues" were, how I would characterize his interactions with his family of origin, and what I thought had brought him into treatment.

Didn't these people read the papers?

Also enclosed was a letter from his counselor at the Meadows asking me to fly out to Arizona and participate in "Family Week." A third sheet listed "desert lodging fees," visitation rules, and the cost of meals and airfare. How I was supposed to pay for all this was beyond me. Had a similar envelope been sent to Jim's parents? If so, were they going? I had no idea. I filled out the questionnaire, because I wanted to help him come to terms with his demons. Subsequently the counselor called, asking if I'd be attending. I said no. I didn't offer any explanation. Jim would have to continue his personal path to healing without me.

After his return from the center, Jim never mentioned the invitation or my absence, nor did he discuss what had happened there, but he said he felt better about himself. I've since learned from mutual friends that Jim's major "problem," as he saw it, was his need for approval, his need to be loved above all else; and since securing the love and approval of others was at odds with his authenticity, then it was his authenticity he abandoned. Change is a slow process, but when Jim returned, he still seemed lost to me. Sad and lost.

As for me, I wish I could have had some more therapy myself. I'd spoken to a therapist a few times, not only on the day of Jim's resignation but a few times subsequently, seeing her in her office in Manhattan. When I could barely put one syllable after another, it was such a relief to spill it all out to someone who was willing just to listen. I couldn't talk this way with my family, because I knew it would upset them too much. Still, for reasons of time and money, I had to stop.

SINCE WE'VE MOVED TO our home in the New Jersey suburbs, we've continued to make our adjustments. Jim himself remains the most difficult element in my life. Nevertheless, we share a love for our beautiful daughter, and that will keep him in my life forever. Still, I don't know if I can ever fully trust him, or if I will ever really know who he is. His deep-seated need for approval unfortunately does not extend to me, and his grasp on truth seems to be tenuous—as I thought when I saw, on the jacket of his book, his claim that Jacqueline lived with him and his partner.

Not true then and not true now.

Jim remains a man of secrets, keeping from me information I need to know, especially with regard to Jacqueline. All too often, she becomes the source of information he should tell me but doesn't. One Friday, he picked her up from home. I called his cell phone later that evening, just to see how she was doing, but there was no answer. Since I know that Jim often doesn't answer the phone when his caller ID tells him it's me, I let it go. The following morning, at nine thirty or so, when I thought Jacqueline would be awake, I called again. Again there was no answer. Jim didn't return either call, but later that morning when I called for a third time, he answered, and after we greeted one another, not warmly but at least civilly—he handed the phone to Jacqueline.

Yes, she was fine, and yes, she'd had breakfast. We had a little chat, and I asked her all the usual questions: Had she brushed her teeth? Was she having fun? What were she and Daddy going to do today? Jacqueline sounded a little excited and very happy, but when she told me that not only was she going on a tour (she didn't know what kind) but that she'd stayed the night at a hotel (she didn't know where), I panicked. My heart was pounding, but I tried to stay calm—as calm as possible.

"Jacqueline, honey . . . um, where are you?"

A murmur of voices, and then something about Washington.

As soon as I could without its seeming too sudden, I asked Jacqueline to put Daddy back on the phone.

"Hi," said Jim when he came back on the phone.

"You took her to Washington, and you didn't tell me?"

"What's the problem?"

"What do you mean, 'What's the problem?' If you're taking her out of state, you have to tell me."

"You don't tell me where you take her all the time."

"Well, I don't take her out of the state!"

"It's not a big deal. Why are you getting so upset? Besides, we're coming back today."

"That's not the point."

"Look, she's having a good time. I took her to the Washington Monument and to the Capitol."

I cut the conversation short so that Jacqueline wouldn't hear any more of the dissension between us. The following day, when I read the *Star-Ledger*, I learned why Jim was in Washington. It was the weekend of BookExpo, and since Jim's book was scheduled to come out three months hence, he'd gone there with his partner and his editor to hawk an excerpt and sign autographs.

Jacqueline's precocity is such that much of what I know about Jim and his life, I learned from her. When Jim started spending weekends with his partner, Mark, the news came my way from Jacqueline. First I heard about Daddy's "friend." Then it was Daddy's "partner." When he gave up his apartment in Rahway and moved with his partner to Manhattan, Jacqueline was my original source as well. The first weekend Jacqueline spent in Manhattan, I didn't quite get the picture, so I asked Jim why he and Jacqueline had spent the weekend there. All he said was,

"I'm there now." He has never mentioned his new home, just as he's never mentioned his new partner or his book.

Like any child in her position, Jacqueline has lobbied ingeniously to restore a marriage whose end she still cannot easily bear and certainly doesn't understand. "Mommy, will you marry Daddy again?" she's asked me more than once.

"I can't marry Daddy again," I tell her.

"But why?" she always asks.

I give her the stock answers divorced parents always give. Just yesterday, we were talking, and I said, "You know you're the most important person in the world to me."

"Yeah, I know I'm number one, and Daddy's number two, and Meagan and Nicky are number three, and Vóvó and Vôvô are number four."

I should have let it go, but instead I said, "No, Meagan and Nicky are number two."

"No, Daddy is," she said.

I changed the subject—or tried to. But it took me a while, as Jacqueline continued to lobby on behalf of her father.

Some days, she is at once so old and so young that I could cry. One day, she came back from an outing with her cousins.

"Mommy," she said, "we went on a ride and we passed the beach house. But you know what?"

"What?"

"There's a gate in front of it now." She started to cry.

"A gate?" I had heard that Jon Corzine was renovating the beach house now that he was New Jersey's governor. Maybe he'd installed a gate?

"OK," I said. "But why is the gate making you cry?"

She looked at me as if I were unspeakably obtuse. "With the gate there, how will we ever get in?"

JUST AS JACQUELINE IS trying to make her way with the help of those who love her, I am trying to make my way too, not only with the help of those who love me but with the help of God. As a Roman Catholic, I have always practiced my faith with prayer and attendance at weekly mass, but over the last two years my faith has grown and my spiritual practices have deepened. Otherwise I could not have survived. Faith, or at least my faith, is not passive. Americans believe in self-help, and it informs everything we do, from faith to therapy to fitness. In my hours—and months and years—of need, I have found that a group of contemporary spiritual writers speak to me, among them Wayne Dyer and Rick Warren. Dyer especially has helped me with his conviction that when you change the way you look at things, the things you look at change.

When my life fell to pieces two years ago, the shock to my system was so profound that my body couldn't even manage it, which is how I now understand the panic attacks that made me fear I was dying. But now I am training myself through my spiritual practices not only in the way I look at my experience but even in what I look at. I try every day to remember and make real that what I focus on is my choice. I know that a higher power exists and that if I can tap into that power, God's power, God will help me get through my struggles.

Thankfully, I am now able to shift not just how I'm thinking, but what I'm thinking. One afternoon, I cleared my calendar, and Jacqueline and I went into Manhattan with Samantha, her American Girl doll, to the American Girl Café on Fifth Avenue. We met a friend of mine there and had tea. Afterward we got matching pink robes for Jacqueline and Samantha. At the end of the afternoon, nothing new had developed in relation to my problems, but somehow, amid all that pink and all those hopeful little girls, my concerns seemed more manageable, less overwhelming to me. I know that I'm a stronger person now than I've ever been or thought I could ever be.

What remains is to speak of work and love. As of today, I'm still employed at the same Newark hospital I worked at when I was First Lady, in part because its familiarity has been soothing and stabilizing. Had I lost my home, my husband, and my job, I'm not sure I could have

survived. When I was First Lady, people would ask me why I was working in a hospital in Newark—not a major medical center, but a small
community hospital that is the primary health-care provider for a large
percentage of the Newark-area population. Those who rely on our hospital, routinely using its ER for non-emergency health issues, are generally the neediest members of the community.

My answer, then and now, is that everyone—and especially uninsured
families in urban areas—is entitled to quality health care. As a fund-
raiser for the hospital, I'm doing my part to make sure everyone gets that
care. My volunteer work remains important to me as well, especially for
the March of Dimes, because prematurity is still a problem, and for the
Cancer Institute of New Jersey—not only because my father is a patient
there but also because New Jersey ranks at the top in the nation in the
incidence of cancer. Whenever I attend an event or talk to people who
are served by either of these two organizations, I realize that there are
many people whose circumstances are much more dire than mine. I
know that there are others who have to bear more than I did, and if I can
help them or someone in their same circumstances in any way, I feel a
sense of satisfaction and forget my problems, at least momentarily.

As Jacqueline gets older, I will be able to consider other job offers, but
I know that whatever I choose to do, it will involve helping people. If
there is a Guinness World Record, or at least a Guinness New Jersey
Record, for the longest time needed to obtain a divorce, Jim and I should
surely be under consideration. As of the beginning of 2007, our divorce
is in sight but not in hand. I'll just leave it at that. I am not yet unencum-
bered emotionally. I am still dealing with my anger and pain. Recently a
friend mused that it would be great if I could end this account of my life
on a note of forgiveness. "It would be great," I told her. "And I want to be
able to forgive, but I'm just not there yet."

As to love? I'm not there yet either. Despite an amusing tabloid head-
line in a New Jersey newspaper announcing that I was seen "nuzzling"
John Whitmire, a Texas legislator whom I'm allegedly dating, there is,
as usual, no truth to the rumor. In the last two and a half years, I've had

a few dates, but nothing sustained or serious. I'm not sure if I haven't yet met the right person, or if I'm not yet prepared to meet the right person. And then there may be those who are reluctant to approach me because they're not sure that I'm ready. The question is not am I capable of loving again, but am I capable of trusting again, enough to allow myself to love?

And perhaps what I most need to reckon with is not whether someone else is trustworthy but whether my own judgment is trustworthy. My confidence in my own judgment is what Jim has most seriously damaged, and it's occurred to me that there may be a need for some more therapy in my future to repair that confidence.

I am forty now, and curious as to what this decade will bring, in work and love and spirit. The absence of pain is still so novel as to be an almost-palpable pleasure, like the silence after the vibrating furor of a jackhammer stops. I have yet to unpack the last box, the heat in my house is sometimes balky, and I still have a bare bulb over my dining room table, but my house has now become my home, as I furnish it and warm it with memories of good times with family and friends seated under that bulb around the table. For a while, I thought my sense of humor was still packed away, maybe even missing, but it's returned—with a vengeance, you might say. Out in the world, I can now reasonably estimate a mileage allowance for my car lease, and Jacqueline has made her adjustments to sitting in her car seat in the back without me. In my travels here and there, I've met a man or two worthy of a mild crush, a practice crush, a bit of flirtation. And I once again see small things I'd previously been too numb to notice or take pleasure in. Last summer, I saw the cautious approach and quick retreat of a tiny wave on the beach, a little shell in the sand waiting to be found, and, back at home, as I looked out my kitchen window, I noticed a trio of doves making their way up my front walkway, heading in the direction of my front door. They don't know that they're said to be harbingers of peace and of love. But I do.

INDEX